AF505989

Haunting and Spectrality in Neo-Victorian Fiction

Also by Rosario Arias

MOTHERS AND DAUGHTERS IN THE FICTIONAL
WORK OF LESSING, ATWOOD AND MANTEL

MOTHERS AND DAUGHTERS IN PSYCHOANALYTIC
FEMINIST THEORY

Also by Patricia Pulham

ART AND THE TRANSITIONAL OBJECT IN
VERNON LEE'S SUPERNATURAL TALES

HAUNTINGS AND OTHER FANTASTIC TALES
(edited with Catherine Maxwell)

VERNON LEE: DECADENCE, ETHICS, AESTHETICS
(edited with Catherine Maxwell)

Haunting and Spectrality in Neo-Victorian Fiction

Possessing the Past

Edited by

Rosario Arias
Senior Lecturer in English
(University of Málaga)

and

Patricia Pulham
Senior Lecturer in English Literature
(University of Portsmouth)

First published 2010 by
PALGRAVE MACMILLAN

Palgrave Macmillan in the UK is an imprint of Macmillan Publishers Limited,
registered in England, company number 785998, of Houndmills, Basingstoke,
Hampshire RG21 6XS.

Palgrave Macmillan in the US is a division of St Martin's Press LLC,
175 Fifth Avenue, New York, NY 10010.

Palgrave Macmillan is the global academic imprint of the above companies
and has companies and representatives throughout the world.

Palgrave® and Macmillan® are registered trademarks in the United States,
the United Kingdom, Europe and other countries.

ISBN-13: 978-0-230-20557-4   hardback

This book is printed on paper suitable for recycling and made from fully
managed and sustained forest sources. Logging, pulping and manufacturing
processes are expected to conform to the environmental regulations of the
country of origin.

A catalogue record for this book is available from the British Library.

A catalog record for this book is available from the Library of Congress.

10   9   8   7   6   5   4   3   2   1
19   18   17   16   15   14   13   12   11   10

Printed and bound in Great Britain by
CPI Antony Rowe, Chippenham and Eastbourne

Contents

Notes on Contributors

Rosario Arias is Senior Lecturer in English at the University of Málaga (Spain). She has published a number of articles and book chapters on contemporary women's fiction and psychoanalysis. Among them are an entry on the 'Mother/Daughter Relationship' in *An Autobiography of Women's Autobiography*, edited by Victoria Boynton and Jo Malin (Greenwood, 2005), and an article on Doris Lessing's vision of London in the *Journal of Gender Studies* (2005). Her current research is focused on the occult, spectrality, and haunting in neo-Victorian fiction. Her recent publications include several articles in refereed journals such as *LIT: Literature, Interpretation, Theory* (2009), *Variations: Literaturzeitschrift der Universität Zürich* (2006), *Estudios Ingleses de la Universidad Complutense* and *Revista Canaria de Estudios Ingleses* (2005). In addition, she has contributed a chapter, 'Female Confinement in Sarah Waters's Neo-Victorian Fiction' to Frank Lauterbach and Jan Alber's *Stones of Law – Bricks of Shame: Narrating Imprisonment in the Victorian Age* (University of Toronto Press, 2009).

Silvana Colella is Associate Professor of English at the University of Macerata (Italy). She is the author of *Economia e letteratura. Intersezioni discorsive nella cultura inglese di primo Ottocento* (1999) and *Romanzo e disciplina. La narrativa di Charlotte Brontë* (1996). In addition she has published articles on a range of Victorian topics including 'Sweet Money: Cultural and Economic Value in Trollope's *Autobiography*', *Nineteenth-Century Contexts* (2006) and 'Gifts and Interests: *John Halifax*, Gentleman and The Purity of Business', *Victorian Literature and Culture* (2007), and has contributed a chapter, 'In the Interest of Feminism: *The Freewoman* and Economic Discourse', to *Networking Women: Subjects, Places, Links, Europe-America, towards a Rewriting of Cultural History, 1890–1939*, edited by Marina Camboni (Roma, 2004).

Agnieszka Gołda-Derejczyk is Lecturer in Contemporary British Literature at the Institute of English Cultures and Literatures, University of Silesia (Poland). She has published a number of works on twentieth-century British fiction and film including 'How to Travel in Time? Retro-Victorian Cinema' in *Multicultural Dilemmas: Identity, Difference, Otherness*, edited by M. Kubisz and W. Kalaga (Peter Lang Verlag, 2006), 'Meta(form)osis: Theft and Gift in the Postmodern Revision of Victorian Historical Space' in *The (Trans)Human: Bodies, Spaces, Virtualities*, edited by W. Kalaga (Publishing House 'Śląsk', 2005) and 'Postmodern Post-Mortem on a Victorian Corpse or How Postmodern Fiction Re-writes the Nineteenth Century' in: *We, the 'Other Victorians'*, edited by Silvia Caporale Bizzini (Publicaciones de la Universidad de Alicante, 2003). Her forthcoming book entitled *'Through the Looking-Glass': Postmodern Revision of Nineteenth-Century British Culture*, to be published by University of Silesia Press, is due out in 2009.

Ann Heilmann is Professor of English at the University of Hull (UK). Her research interests include neo-Victorianism, Victorian and Edwardian literature, and nineteenth-century to contemporary women's writing and gender discourses, especially the *fin-de-siècle* New Woman, the Anglo-Irish writer George Moore, and women's historical fiction writing. She is the author of *New Woman Fiction* (Palgrave Macmillan, 2000) and *New Woman Strategies: Sarah Grand, Olive Schreiner and Mona Caird* (Manchester University Press, 2004) and has edited a number of collections, including *Metafiction and Metahistory in Contemporary Women's Writing* (co-edited with Mark Llewellyn) (Palgrave Macmillan, 2007) and *New Woman Hybridities: Femininity, Feminism and Consumer Culture 1880–1930* (Routledge, 2004). She is now completing a book on *Neo-Victorianism: The Victorians in the Twenty-First Century* with Mark Llewellyn. She is the general editor of Pickering and Chatto's Gender and Genre and Routledge's History of Feminism series.

Mark Llewellyn is Lecturer in English at the University of Liverpool (UK). A specialist in late-Victorian and contemporary literature, he has published widely on the turn-of-the-century writer George Moore, including two volumes in the recent edition of *The Collected Short Stories of George Moore* (Pickering and Chatto, 2007). His work on contemporary literature has included articles and chapters on Sarah Waters and, more recently, theorizations of the neo-Victorian including 'What is Neo-Victorian Studies?' (*Neo-Victorian Studies*, 2008) and 'Neo-Victorianism: On the Ethics and Aesthetics of Appropriation' (*LIT: Literature Interpretation Theory*, 2009). Editor of the *Journal of Gender Studies* and Consultant Editor to *Neo-Victorian Studies*, Mark is currently working on a book entitled *Incest in English Culture, 1835–1908*, and completing writing towards a co-authored book (with Ann Heilmann) entitled *Neo-Victorianism: The Victorians in the Twenty-First Century*.

Francis O'Gorman is Professor of Victorian Literature at the University of Leeds (UK). His most recent publications are an edition of Conan Doyle's *The Hound of the Baskervilles* (Broadview Press, 2006), an edited collection of essays entitled *Victorian Literature and Finance* (Oxford University Press, 2007), and essays on Coleridge, Wordsworth, Swinburne, and Tennyson. He edited *The Cambridge Companion to Victorian Culture*, now in press, and is writing a book, *Victorian Literature and the Dead*, for Manchester University Press. He continues a long-standing interest in Ruskin. He is presently Head of the School of English at Leeds.

Patricia Pulham is Senior Lecturer in English Literature at the University of Portsmouth (UK) and author of *Art and the Transitional Object in Vernon Lee's Supernatural Tales* (Ashgate, 2008). She is co-editor (with Catherine Maxwell) of the first annotated edition of selected short stories by Vernon Lee, *Hauntings and Other Fantastic Tales* (Broadview Press, 2006); and of *Vernon Lee: Decadence, Ethics, Aesthetics*, the first collection of critical essays on Lee's work (Palgrave Macmillan, 2006). Her most recent articles include: 'The Eroticism of Artificial Flesh in Villiers de L'Isle Adam's *L'Eve Future*', published in the online journal *19: Interdisciplinary Studies in the Long Nineteenth Century* (2008); 'From Pygmalion to Persephone: Love, Art and Myth in Thomas Hardy's *The Well-Beloved*', *Victorian Review* (2008); and 'Tinted and Tainted Love in Olive Custance's Sculptural Bodies', *Yearbook of English Studies* (From Decadent to Modernist issue) (2007). She is currently writing a book, *Perversions of Pygmalion: The Sculptural Body in Victorian Literature*, and co-editing a collection of essays, *Crime Cultures: Figuring Criminality in Fiction and Film*, to be published by Continuum in 2010.

Esther Saxey has published on the intersection of sexuality and narrative in literature, fanfiction, film, and comics. She is the author of *Homoplot: The Coming-Out Story and Gay, Lesbian and Bisexual Identity* (Peter Lang, 2008) and her articles include 'Lesbian Bastard Heroes: The

Uses of Illegitimacy for Modern Lesbian Fiction', *Women: A Cultural Review* (2005), and 'Desire Without Closure in Jaime Hernandez's *Love and Rockets*', *ImageText* (2006). She has annotated and introduced the Wordsworth editions of *The Well of Loneliness* (2006) and *Lady Audley's Secret* (2007).

Introduction

Rosario Arias and Patricia Pulham

The spectral presence of the Victorian past is all around us: it exists in the municipal buildings of our major cities; it is visible in our education system; it informs the legacy of immigration; it underpins cultural tourism; it is ever-present in popular culture in fashion, film and television adaptations, and is evident in the 'Classics' section of every bookshop in the country where major novels by Dickens, the Brontës, George Eliot, and Thomas Hardy are always to be found. In her recent book, *Victoriana: Histories, Fictions, Criticisms* (2007), Cora Kaplan offers 'Victoriana' as a collective noun that 'might usefully embrace the whole phenomenon, the astonishing range of representations and reproductions for which the Victorian – whether as the origin of late twentieth century modernity, its antithesis, or both at once – is the common referent' (2007, p. 3). She suggests that any examination might benefit 'by asking whether the proliferation of Victoriana is more than nostalgia – a longing for a past that never was – and more too than a symptom of the now familiar, if much debated, view that the passage from modernity to postmodernity has been marked by the profound loss of a sense of history' (Kaplan, 2007, p. 3). This collection of essays, the first to focus on the neo-Victorian novel against the backdrop of the master trope of spectrality and haunting, participates in such debates and offers an alternative way in which to view this fascinating subgenre of historiographic metafiction, a term which is itself ripe for reconsideration.[1] Since Linda Hutcheon coined the term in her seminal work, *A Poetics of Postmodernism: History, Theory, Fiction* (1988), historiographic metafiction has become increasingly the subject of serious critical scrutiny. Used to describe 'well-known and popular novels which are both intensely self-reflexive and yet paradoxically also lay claim to historical events and personages' (Hutcheon, 1988, p. 5), the genre contributes to a postmodern engagement with history which, according to Fredric Jameson, results in 'a new depthlessness' and 'a consequent weakening of historicity' (1991, p. 6). In naming such interactions with the past a form of 'nostalgia', Jameson introduces a question which is considered in Dana Shiller's essay 'The Redemptive Past in the Neo-Victorian Novel' (1997), and discussed at length in Christian Gutleben's *Nostalgic Postmodernism: The Victorian Tradition and the Contemporary British Novel* (2001).[2] The difficulties inherent in the debate are already implicit in the terms applied to literature that specifically appropriate a Victorian past. In her 1997 essay, Shiller calls such works 'neo-Victorian' while Sally Shuttleworth (1998) refers to such novels as 'retro-Victorian'; Shiller's term implies reinvention, while Shuttleworth's suggests a return to and/or retrieval of the past. Jameson's own comments on nostalgia highlight its inadequacy to explain our postmodern engagement with history. Referring to postmodern architecture's cannibalization of past styles to create new 'overstimulating ensembles', he writes: '[n]ostalgia does not strike one as an altogether satisfactory word for such fascination' (Jameson, 1991, p. 19). He is similarly unhappy in applying the term to '[n]ostalgia films' which are not concerned with 'some old-fashioned "representation" of historical content', but approach the past 'through stylistic connotation, conveying "pastness" by the glossy qualities of the image, and "1930s-ness" or "1950s-ness" by the attributes of fashion', making 'postmodernist "nostalgia" art language' incompatible with 'genuine historicity' (Jameson, 1991, p. 19). As Dana Shiller observes:

> What appears to disturb Jameson most about postmodern representations of the past, be they fictional, filmic, or architectural, is that they strip away its specific political content to focus on its aesthetics. Instead of respecting the radical difference of bygone eras, postmodernism projects onto them contemporary culture, fabricating a "privatized", or subjective, history denuded of its specific cultural resonance.
>
> (1997, p. 539)

While she acknowledges the validity of Jameson's unease from his own Marxist perspective, Shiller suggests that 'neo-Victorian fiction addresses many of Jameson's concerns by presenting a historicity that is indeed concerned with recuperating the substance of bygone eras, and not merely their styles' (1997, p. 540). She argues that such historical novels 'take a revisionist approach to the past, borrowing from postmodern historiography to explore how present circumstances shape historical narrative' and shows how they 'are also indebted to earlier cultural attitudes toward history' (Shiller, 1997, pp. 539–40). In order to do so, she turns to a Victorian historical novel, George Eliot's *Middlemarch* (1871–2), to demonstrate how Eliot's own concept of history – that 'there is no "universal" past, but a past that continually changes shape based on individual perspective' (Shiller, 1997, p. 542) – informs the neo-Victorian novel, and how it is possible 'to recapture the past in ways that evoke its spirit and do honor to the dead and silenced' (Shiller, 1997, p. 546).

We suggest that the Victorians' own engagements with the past, or perhaps more accurately critical evaluations of such interactions, inform contemporary debates on postmodern modes of nostalgia. As Raymond Chapman points out, '[n]ostalgia is a recurrent feature of Victorian literature [itself], ranging from a general assertion that things are not as they used to be in the old days, to attempts to enter deeply into a lost world and recover its treasures' (1986, p. 4). John Rosenberg argues that '[t]he Victorians who speak to us most urgently today thought of themselves as living not in an age of peace or progress but, in John Stuart Mill's phrase, in "an age of transition," caught between a vanishing past and an uncertain future' (2005, p. 1). In their introduction to *The Imagined Past: History and Nostalgia* (1989), Malcolm Chase and Christopher Shaw identify three key conditions for the emergence of nostalgia: 'a secular and linear sense of time; an apprehension of the failings of the present; and the availability of evidences of the past' (1989, p. 4), all of which seemingly existed – if not unproblematically – in the Victorian period, contributing to their 'nostalgic yearning' for 'a simple and stable past as a refuge from the turbulent and chaotic present' (Lowenthal, 1989, p. 21). The return to classical, medieval, and renaissance pasts is evident in the works of nineteenth-century writers and poets ranging from Sir Walter Scott to Oscar Wilde. However, the deployment of the past in such writings is not always simply nostalgic. Chapman argues that the Victorians' own awareness of the past was accompanied by a consciousness of the future: '[o]ne concern of the Victorians was how their own time would appear in years to come. Looking back to the past, either in nostalgia or complacency, they knew they too would eventually be available for inspection' (Chapman, 1986, p. 7). In this context, the Victorians become not merely spirits of the past, but agents of the future. This is perhaps evidenced most clearly in our critical deciphering of encoded political, sexual, and racial messages in Victorian literature.

In his conclusion to *Nostalgic Postmodernism*, Gutleben argues that 'retro-Victorian fiction displays signs of nostalgia in its very principle, namely the revival of a bygone tradition, in the conservatism of certain Victorian aesthetic precepts and the imitation of a language of the past' (2001, p. 193), and that '[i]f retro-Victorian fiction reverts to the past, it is then, at least partially because the present is deemed inadequate, wanting, deficient' (2001, p. 195). In doing so, Gutleben posits a more simplistic – 'Victorian' if you will – sense of 'nostalgia'. But, as David Lowenthal observes, our contemporary interpretation of the nostalgia is complicated by its perceived association with 'commercialisation' and 'inauthenticity'; by its 'pervasion of the media, with its attendant sense of unreality'; and by its 'reactionary slant' which glosses over 'the past's iniquities and indignities' (1989, pp. 21–2). The key conditions for the emergence of a 'traditional' form of nostalgia, discussed by Gutleben, and Chase and Shaw have, as Lowenthal points out, been replaced by a mistrust of nostalgia. In critical terms, we no longer subscribe to 'a secular and linear sense of time', we are conscious of theories that posit a multiplicity of 'times', and undermine a singular linear, authoritative history. We no longer seek in the past a refuge from the present; instead we excavate the past to expose its 'iniquities and indignities' (Lowenthal, 1989, p. 22). Our own twenty-first century sense of nostalgia is therefore far more complex than Gutleben's thesis suggests and, arguably, the root of that complexity lies in the word's etymology. If we set aside the conventional definition of nostalgia as a 'wistful yearning for a past or earlier time' (Chase and Shaw, 1989, p. 1), and consider its original meaning: that is, homesickness (often manifested in physical symptoms) formed from the Greek words *nostos* meaning 'homecoming' and *algos*, meaning pain, grief or distress (Banhart, 2006, p. 710), we disclose the significance of the 'home' or the return 'home' in the neo-Victorian engagement with the past.

In his discussion of E. L. Doctorow's *Ragtime* (1975), Fredric Jameson argues that the book, in which well-known historical figures interact with 'a fictive family, simply designated as Father, Mother, Older Brother, and so forth [...] operates powerfully and systematically to reify all these characters' and makes it impossible 'to receive their representation without the prior interception of already acquired knowledge or doxa' (1991, p. 31). He suggests that this 'lends the text an extraordinary sense of déjà vu and a peculiar familiarity one is tempted to associate with Freud's "return of the repressed" in "The Uncanny" rather than with any solid historiographic formation on the reader's part' (Jameson, 1991, pp. 23–4). In the case of neo-Victorian fiction, it is even more common to experience a 'sense of déjà vu' and the desire to examine the phenomenon as an example of Freud's 'return of the repressed' is decidedly more tempting.

In his 1919 essay, Freud refers to what he describes as the 'joking saying' that 'Love is a home-sickness', which suggests that 'whenever a man dreams of a place or country and says to himself, while he is still dreaming: "this place is familiar to me, I've been here before", we may interpret the place as being his mother's [...] body' (1955, p. 245). If we recall the feminized description of the Victorian age in Barrett Browning's *Aurora Leigh* (1857) as a 'full-veined' and 'double-breasted Age' (1993, p. 201, V. l. 216), the nostalgic return to the Victorian 'maternal' body implied by neo-Victorian fiction underlines a simultaneous longing and anxiety that manifests itself in a series of recognizable features which Freud describes as uncanny. Freud's list of psychological triggers for uncanny sensations include the double; repetition; the animation of the seemingly dead or, conversely, the death-like nature of the seemingly animate; ghosts or spirits; and the familiar made strange. If we consider these in relation to the neo-Victorian novel, its uncanny nature proves clear: it often represents a 'double' of the Victorian text mimicking its language, style and plot; it plays with the conscious repetition of tropes, characters, and historical events; it reanimates Victorian genres, for example, the realist text, sensation fiction, the Victorian ghost story and, in doing so, seemingly calls the contemporary novel's 'life' into question; it defamiliarizes our preconceptions of Victorian society; and it functions as a form of revenant, a ghostly visitor from the past that infiltrates our present.

It is precisely this last version of the uncanny – Victorianism understood as a revenant or a ghostly visitor from the past – that is explored in this collection. Utilizing the trope of haunting and spectrality, the essays in this volume demonstrate the validity of this approach in contemporary engagements with the Victorian past, and lay bare the pervasive presence of the Victorians through their textual/spectral traces in popular culture. Acknowledged as showing full potential for the analysis of the dialogue between the historical past and the present (Morrison, 2003, pp. 24–5), this trope has come to occupy a central position in contemporary criticism. Colin Davis (2007), who has undertaken a full-length study on the 'return of the dead' from a deconstructive and psychoanalytic point of view, identifies two closely connected critical sources of haunting and spectrality: on the one hand, Jacques Derrida's *Specters of Marx: The State of the Debt, the Work of Mourning, and the New International* (1994), and on the other, Nicolas Abraham and Maria Torok's works, *The Wolf's Magic Word: A Cryptonymy* (1976) and *The Shell and the Kernel* (1987), which condense the main tenets of their theories.

For Derrida, 'hauntology' (Derrida, 1994, pp. 10, 51, 161) consists of 'the logic of haunting' (1994, p. 10) that characterizes the ghost of Marxism in Europe which, in an acknowledgement of the 'haunted' nature of literature itself, is discussed alongside one of Shakespeare's most famous ghosts, that of Hamlet's father. Derrida notes that, significantly, the *Manifesto of the Communist Party* (1848) opens with a reference to spectrality: '"[a] spectre is haunting Europe – the spectre of communism"' (quoted in Derrida, 1994, p. 4). This spectre is, in fact, a revenant, an apparition which returns and disrupts temporal linearity. As Peter Buse and Andrew Stott affirm: '[t]he question of the *revenant* neatly encapsulates deconstructive concerns about the impossibility of conceptually solidifying the past' (1999, p. 11; original emphasis). Derrida favours this notion of the spectre as revenant to deconstruct 'all historicisms that are grounded in a rigid sense of chronology' (Buse and Stott, 1999, p. 11). In this sense, '[h]aunting would mark the very existence of Europe' (Derrida, 1994, p. 4), and hegemony, despite its efforts, cannot dispel the spectral presence of Marxism in the Western world, an idea which Derrida develops later in his essay (1994, p. 37). The link between Derrida's hauntology and Sigmund Freud's uncanny is made explicit in the concluding passages of his study where Derrida claims that he could have replaced the title *Specters of Marx* with '"Marx – *das Unheimliche*"' (1994, p. 174), thus associating Freud's ideas about the 'unhomely' (Freud, 1955, p. 219, n. 1) with his own concept of the ghost. Derrida's ghost is a liminal presence, out of time, dislocated, and characterized by 'temporal disjoining' (1994, p. 19). Therefore, his ghost is neither present nor absent; instead it is 'a deconstructive figure hovering between life and death, presence and absence, and making established certainties vacillate' (Davis, 2007, p. 11).

If Derrida's spectre or ghost, that encourages us to speak with the dead, opens up possibilities or alternatives for meanings in a still-unrealized future (Derrida, 1994, p. 176), Nicolas Abraham and Maria Torok's phantom is founded on the wounded past of individuals or communities, and shows no interest in the future. Published prior to Derrida's theorization, Abraham and Torok's work is now receiving renewed critical interest. There are few common aspects in these two theories of haunting and spectrality. Although Derrida himself knew their work well (he wrote a foreword to *The Wolf's Magic Word*, 'Fors: The Anglish Words of Nicolas Abraham and Maria Torok' (1977)), and Abraham shared with Derrida a fascination with *Hamlet*'s ghost (Davis, 2007, p. 76), Abraham and Torok's phantom has little to do with Derrida's spectre. The concept of the phantom stems directly from their reassessment of Freud's case 'The Wolf Man',[3] and might be defined as an unspeakable secret which is lodged inside the subject, who is haunted by the gaps and silences of others; those silences and secrets that are unconsciously transmitted to later generations in, what they call, 'transgenerational haunting': '*[t]he phantom which returns to haunt bears witness to the existence of the dead buried within the other*' (Abraham and Torok, 1994, p. 175; original emphasis). It remains clear that the only shared characteristics between the Derridean spectre and the phantom are their capacity to return and their permeable boundaries, since there is no distinction between past and present, inside and outside in a haunted subject, or in a haunted text.

There are also crucial differences in how both concepts are developed and explored. For Derrida, 'what is vital is to remain open to an encounter with the unstable, unassimilated spectre because it is through such an encounter that something previously unheard of might occur'; for Abraham and Torok, the main objective is 'to exorcise the ghost by putting its unspeakable secrets into words, and thereby to bring the ghost back to the order of knowledge' (Davis, 2007, pp. 84, 87). To put it simply, Derrida underscores what the spectre has to reveal, thus inducing us to listen to what it may say in the future, while Abraham and Torok's phantom is concerned with a traumatized past, which has to be disclosed, exorcized and, finally, dispelled. Similarly relevant to Abraham and Torok's notion of the phantom is their concept of the crypt, which gives its name to their interpretive method for reading the encrypted symptoms that are hidden in that concealed psychic space: 'cryptonymy'. The crypt, a locked topographical space, 'is neither the dynamic unconscious nor the ego of introjections. Rather, it is an enclave between the two, a kind of artificial unconscious' (Abraham and Torok, 1994, p. 159). Their theories provide ample space to interpret how outside influences, transmitted from one generation or community to the next, have important bearings not only on one's subjectivity, but also, more generally, on culture itself; they are not simply 'descriptive of individual neurosis, as in the Wolf Man's pathology, but interpretive of cultural encryptment, of the magic words a culture does *not* say to itself' (Lloyd Smith, 1992, p. 306; original emphasis).

Although differently structured and defined, these two distinct sources of the trope of haunting and spectrality have spawned a substantial number of critical studies which have contributed to the dissemination of ideas about the spectral, the uncanny, the double and the ghostly in literary contexts. That the figure of the ghost remains of considerable importance in late twentieth- and early twenty-first-century contemporary criticism is exemplified by the publication of two special issues of *Mosaic* on reappraisals of 'the uncanny' and 'haunting' in 2001 and 2002, followed by Nicholas Royle's *The Uncanny*, a one-volume study solely devoted to this concept, published in 2003.[4] More recently, the Spring 2006 issue of the *University of Toronto Quarterly* has specifically considered whether the trope of haunting and spectrality might be especially useful in the analysis of Canadian cultural artefacts given that 'contemporary Canadian authors, artists, and filmmakers are obsessed with ghosts and haunting' (Goldman and Saul, 2006, p. 645). Although several critics have approached literary and non-literary texts from this point of view, it is Julian Wolfreys's in-depth studies on the spectral traces of the past that have been most influential in neo-Victorianism. Not only has his *Victorian Hauntings: Spectrality, Gothic, the Uncanny and Literature* (2002) decisively contributed to the propagation and dissemination of Derrida's theorization, but also it has demonstrated the value of the trope of haunting and spectrality as a powerful metaphor for a 'transgenerational' return of the dead and the repressed in literary texts. As he affirms: '[t]here can be no narrative [...] which is not always already disturbed and yet made possible from within its form or structure by a ghostly movement' (Wolfreys, 2002, p. 3).

In other words, literature is permanently haunted by ghosts, revenants and spirits which travel across time and make an appearance in the form of textual/spectral traces. Wolfreys takes up the notion that the gothic, although defunct as genre, is spectralized and invoked as a series of apparitional traces in several writings of the nineteenth and twentieth centuries. He goes on to suggest that the spectralization of the gothic 'manifests itself as both a subversive force and a spectral mechanism through which social and political critique may become available and articulable, as we come to apprehend material realities, political discourses and epistemological frameworks from other invisible places' (Wolfreys, 2002, p. 11).[5] Similarly, one might argue that the Victorian age is spectralized and appears as a ghostly apparition in contemporary literature; in returning as a revenant, it opens up multiple possibilities for re-enactment, reimagining, and reinterpretation.

The spectral motif is also significant in the context of the Victorian supernatural and the occult, which has attracted considerable attention in cultural histories of the Victorian period, as well as emerging as a key theme in neo-Victorianism. Important work in this field has been performed by cultural historians and feminist critics such as Alex Owen, Janet Oppenheim, Judith Walkowitz, Alison Winter, Diana Barsham, and Marlene Tromp, who have undertaken the archaeological project of resurrecting the Victorian dead, thus disclosing the gaps and silences left by the encrypted stories of women who did not comply with Victorian constructions of femininity, namely, the criminal, the hysteric and the spiritualist medium.[6] In particular, they have focused on the relevance of women in the Spiritualist movement, and in doing so they have resurrected the Victorian passion for Spiritualism. However, the Victorians' belief in the other world cannot be divorced from their ambivalent responses to nineteenth-century technological advances experienced from the 1840s onwards, beginning with the inception of photography and other related technologies, or from the rise of Darwinism and the subsequent crisis in conventional religious faith.

In *The Victorian Supernatural* (2004), Nicola Bown, Carolyn Burdett, and Pamela Thurschwell examine the pivotal role played by the supernatural in the Victorian age, in relation not only to cultural productions such as the ghost story, but also associated with scientific and medical discourses of the period. Neo-Victorian literature recurrently engages with the haunting presence of Spiritualism and the occult: 'mediums, spirit guides, séances, possessions, and dark circles abound, together with the paraphernalia of accompanying trickery and possible misrepresentation' (Kohlke, 2008, p. 9). Neo-Victorian writers resurrect and talk with the Victorian dead, a process which has been defined as 'ghostwriting' (Schor, 2000, p. 247), both in regard to the channelling of Spiritualist beliefs and the reanimation of Victorian genres. What is at stake here is the way in which the Victorian past and the contemporary age establish a dialogue, a two-way process, a dual relationship by means of which the Victorians come to life in neo-Victorianism, and contemporary revisions of the Victorian past offer productive and nuanced ways of unlocking occluded secrets, silences and mysteries which return and reappear in a series of spectral/textual traces. Bearing in mind the transformative potential of the disembodied figure of the ghost, the essays in this volume explore how haunting and spectrality, as a unifying principle, offer a model via which to examine the interplay between the following binaries: absence/presence, incorporeal/corporeal, spiritual/material, the Victorian past and the present.

The first essay in the collection, by Francis O'Gorman, analyses the presence of the Victorians in contemporary fiction through an examination of Salley Vickers's *Miss Garnet's Angel* (2000). This novel is not, properly speaking, neo-Victorian as it is entirely set in the contemporary period, but the Victorians' ideas are felt in the enduring presence of John Ruskin's reading of Venice in Vickers's novel. In addition, it is the image and Apocryphal story of the angel Raphael (a redemptive pattern) which comes to signify the Victorian past's disruption of the present. Vickers's novel actively engages with the nineteenth century and shows the ways in which the intervention of the Victorian past in the present can be full of life-affirming possibilities in the Biblical pattern of redemption and the metaphor of restoration. O'Gorman's essay ponders on the serviceability of the Victorians and that of Ruskin's vision of a redeeming city in contemporary culture. He concludes by alluding to the nature of fiction itself which permits the reader to have access to (or, rather, to feel and sense) the nineteenth century and the links between the Victorian age and the present: 'narrative fiction sometimes also offers a persuasive, perhaps dangerously, but also enthralling convincing sense, a belief in, the continuing vibrancy, the living ambiance, of the past'.

In Mark Llewellyn's essay, the metaphor of restoration is also at play, not only in terms of the reconstruction of the past, but also in a religious sense. The neo-Victorian novels under study, Sarah Waters's *Affinity* (1999), Charles Palliser's *The Unburied* (1999), Jem Poster's *Courting Shadows* (2002), and John Harwood's *The Ghost Writer* (2004) and *The Séance* (2008), address key issues concerning our contemporary attitude to Victorian crises of faith and belief. The glass motif provides him with an apt metaphor to explore how spectrality in these novels reflects and refracts nineteenth-century crises and the question of secularity. In doing so, Llewellyn under-lines the inherent tensions found in 'the relationship between the spectral, the scriptural (in both religious and authorial senses) and the spiritual' in neo-Victorian novels featuring ghosts, spectres and the return of the dead. Another common feature between these two essays is their shared conviction that the reading of the (neo-Victorian) novel is based on sensed experience, and on the desire to make a connection with the past through the narrative text, so much so that 'the sense of being haunted is frequently re-enacted at a textual level'. Llewellyn compellingly argues that there is a metafictional element in the overwhelming invocation of spiritual-ists, spectral presences and séances in the neo-Victorian novel, and that this provides a commentary on our own contradictory response to nineteenth-century spectrality and s(p)ecularity.

The next chapter in the collection addresses a contemporary revision of the story of the spiritualist medium Florence Cook, and her supposed liaison with William Crookes, well-known nineteenth-century scientist and discoverer of the thallium ele-ment, as deployed in Michèle Roberts's *In the Red Kitchen* (1990). Agnieszka Golda-Derejczk sheds light on Roberts's novel by focusing on nineteenth-century spiritualism and haunting as 'useful tool[s] to problematize the question of women as subjects *in* and *of* history' (original emphasis). Past and present in this novel fuse together in the mingling of different female voices which speak across temporal and geographical boundaries (Ancient Egypt, Victorian London, and the twentieth century), but it is the Victorian voice, of Flora Milk, that brings together all the women's experiences of sexual abuse, incest, discrimination, and, also, self-inscription. Golda-Derejczk considers Julia Kristeva's 1979 essay 'Women's Time' and observes that eternity and repetition, 'the cyclical and monumental modalities of time', can be discussed in juxtaposition with the history of women in Roberts's novel. Spiritualism, mediumship and self-writing in the novel suggest a textual/spectral/historical continuity, where women are presented as sharing experiences across time and space. Victorian Spiritualism, according to Golda-Derejczk, serves two related purposes: first, it provides a spiritual dimension to the connections between writing, repetition, communication (often defective), and eternity; second, it illustrates the challenges posed by the female spiritualist to Victorian normalcy, a subject already examined by feminist historians such as Alex Owen.

Like Golda Derejczk's, Esther Saxey's chapter foregrounds the question of female sexuality and self-representation in the context of Victorian sexual mores and examines the following novels: Margaret Atwood's *Alias Grace* (1996) and Valerie Martin's *Mary Reilly* (1990). The unifying element is the supernatural, which allows the female protagonists to release their own repressed and/or displaced desires. Both novels are representative of what Saxey calls the 'plot of repression and liberation [that] derives its pleasure from surprize and contrast'. In this context, she examines the supernatural as a means to transgress class distinctions in the novels under consideration, since both protagonists are Victorian maids. Hannah Cullwick (1833–1909), whose uncanny figure haunts both *Alias Grace* and *Mary Reilly*, is also discussed in terms of social and sexual transgression. Saxey comments on this uncanny double, which informs both novels, as a starting point to examine further instances of duplication and repetition. She concludes with a discussion of the 'speaking maid', and problematizes questions of self-representation and self-inscription in the protagonists' use of the first person to record their experiences. The supernatural, lastly, intervenes to destabilize the notion that self-representation equates with liberation, as 'Atwood and Martin employ the ghost and the monster to toy with the idea of liberation, but then to undermine it'.

A somewhat different approach to the uncanny, haunting presences, and spectrality is taken by Silvana Colella in her chapter on Michel Faber's *The Crimson Petal and the White* (2002). She addresses the spectral pervasiveness of (neo-) Victorian odours in an essay which juxtaposes the cultural history of smell with recent critical theory about the hauntedness of the Victorian past to persuasively argue that 'olfactory hauntings create a sense of the unfamiliar within the familiar conventions of narrative realism'. As in O'Gorman's and Llewellyn's essays, Colella's analysis of Faber's novel underlines how the reader is invited to access the past via sensorial experience – this is particularly true in a novel where the reader is urged to 'sense' the past through the quality and quantity of smells. Colella brings together the trope of haunting and olfactory experience through the ghostly characteristics of odours which 'have an intangible and spectral quality that defies the power of language to represent reality'. Paradoxically enough, this sense contributes to a more 'material' apprehension of reality, according to Colella, who argues that smells are liminal entities, 'both material and immaterial'. Colella's essay further investigates the duality implicit in smells and considers it an apt tool to analyse neo-Victorianism since olfactory experience functions as a mediator between past and present. Finally, Colella affirms that Faber's novel 'neither mourns nor derides the legacy of Victorian fiction', thus inhabiting a liminal position akin to that of the ghost.

Ann Heilmann's essay returns to a more traditional example of haunting – the Victorian ghost story. Heilmann explores the spectral presence of Henry James's novella *The Turn of the Screw* (1898) in several revisions and re-imaginings: Joyce Carol Oates's 'Accursed Inhabitants of the House of Bly' (1994), A. N. Wilson's *A Jealous Ghost* (2005), Sarah Waters's *Affinity* (1999) and Alejandro Amenábar's 2001 film *The Others*. Heilmann considers how these texts prove imagination's enabling capacity to create veritable simulacra, following Jean Baudrillard's concept of the 'hyperreal'. Moreover, the texts under analysis 'are all structured around six categories in crisis or transformation at the turn of the century: social architecture, the family, the question of (narrative) authority, femininity, sexuality, and identity'. While Oates, Wilson, and Waters, to a greater or lesser degree, shift the narrative focus and give predominance in their retellings to the ghosts of the novella, the disturbed mind of the protagonist, and Peter Quint's 'deviant libidinality' respectively, it is Amenábar's *The Others* which is particularly concerned with blurring the boundaries of reality and fantasy, point of view and identity; this is accomplished using the cinematic medium, which further reinforces the dissolution of frontiers between reality and imagination. Heilmann ultimately identifies the spectral motif in James's novella, not only in the portrayal of the governess and the representation of doubles, echoes, and unreliable narrative perspectives, but also in the rewritings and revisions, which prove the cultural endurance of James's text in the contemporary imagination.

The final two chapters in the collection focus on the spectral traces of the Victorian past in neo-Victorian novels that are set in London. Rosario Arias examines the haunted nature of Victorian London in neo-Victorianism through the reappearance of the River Thames and the mid-nineteenth-century sanitation movement in Matthew Kneale's *Sweet Thames* (1992) and Clare Clark's *The Great Stink* (2005). The master trope of haunting and spectrality, more specifically Derrida's 'hauntology' and his concept of the 'specter', as well as Abraham and Torok's notions of the 'phantom', the 'secret' and the 'crypt', provide models for the analysis of three interconnected aspects in these novels: first, the Great Stink and the subsequent reform undertaken by Joseph Bazalgette, a Victorian civil engineer; second, the sewer as a haunted/haunting space; and last, the leaky body in relation to the sanitary mapping of the period. This notion of fluidity resonates with the image of the river Thames and the flowing nature of Victorian London, a city permanently in flux whose spatial boundaries are dissolved in the interdependence of street and underground levels, the surface, and the verticalized space of the sewer. In addition, mid-Victorian London appears to be haunted by encrypted traces of cultural and individual pasts. Therefore, the fluidity of the river further contributes to the dissolution of temporal boundaries, thus creating the image of a 'spectralized' city/body/ self. Arias's essay finally affirms that '[i]n rereading and reimagining the topography of the mid-Victorian city, and in unearthing the encrypted traces of a spectral past, these neo-Victorian writers attempt to add a new layer to our own interpretation of Victorian London, thus rebuilding [...] the Victorian urban landscape'.

While Patricia Pulham shares with Arias an interest in the encryption of the past in London's cultural heritage, her essay considers the importance of detection and Jewish history in Iain Sinclair's *White Chappell, Scarlet Tracings* (1987) and Peter Ackroyd's

Dan Leno and the Limehouse Golem (1994), and examines the spectral motif through the subtext of the Golem myth which features in both texts. Pulham argues that despite the novels' ostensible concern with two key events in nineteenth-century history – the Ratcliffe Highway murders of 1811, and the Jack the Ripper killings of 1888 – Ackroyd and Sinclair's works encrypt spectral traces of Jewish history in the mythical figure of the Golem, which also functions as a form of unpresentable 'truth'. Activated by language, moulded from the history-laden strata of London clay, and embodying a disruptive potential, the Golems in these works bring together temporal, spatial, and narrative concerns that inform and problematize the neo-Victorian novel's engagement with, and recreation of, the past.

In conclusion, the essays in this volume demonstrate that the impact of the Victorian age on contemporary culture can be interpreted as a form of haunting and spectrality. The ghost's liminal existence, neither present nor absent, functions as a powerful metaphor for the dynamic relationship maintained between Victorianism and neo-Victorianism. As Judith Johnston and Catherine Waters acknowledge in their introduction to *Victorian Turns, NeoVictorian Returns*, duality and doubling are significant aspects of neo-Victorian fiction (2008, p. 10). The essays in this collection significantly underscore the relevance of such doublings, which consist of looking backwards to the Victorian period while simultaneously exploring uncharted territories in contemporary fiction, providing nuanced readings and interpretations of the Victorian age and our own contemporary period. This volume represents our own attempt to open a channel of communication between the spirits of the past and the critical field of neo-Victorian studies which, we are certain, will continue to listen to what the Victorian ghost has to say.

Notes

1. In identifying the neo-Victorian novel and the metahistorical romance as subgenres of historiographic metafiction, Dana Shiller (1997) and Amy Elias (2001) respectively demonstrate the need for a reconsideration of Hutcheon's umbrella term in the light of recent developments in the historical novel genre.
2. The significance of 'nostalgia' as an adequate term for postmodern culture's engagement with the Victorian past also dominated discussions of neo-Victorianism at the first major conference on the topic,

'Neo-Victorianism: The Politics and Aesthetics of Appropriation' held at the University of Exeter, September 2007.

3. The 'Wolf Man' was a Russian patient of Freud, Sergei Pankejeff, who suffered from depression and was unable to complete a bowel movement without the help of an enema. Pankejeff told Freud of a childhood dream of white wolves which bore foxes' tails. Freud interpreted this as a primal scene witnessed by Pankejeff and, through analysis, reputedly cured him. He wrote of the case in 'From the History of Infantile Neurosis' (1918) where he used the name 'Wolf Man' to protect Pankejeff's identity.

4. For critical studies which are informed by Derrida's hauntology, see Peter Buse and Andrew Stott's 'Introduction: a Future for Haunting' (Buse and Stott, 1999, pp. 1–20), and Slavoj Žižek's 'Introduction: the Spectre of Ideology' (Žižek, 1994, pp. 1–33). Derrida himself has contributed an essay, 'Marx and Sons' (1999, pp. 213–69) to a volume dedicated to the relevance of his *Specters of Marx* in contemporary criticism. Esther Raskin is, in turn, concerned with Abraham and Torok's ideas about the phantom, the secret, and the crypt in *Family Secrets and the Psychoanalysis of Narrative* (1992).

5. Terry Castle makes a similar case for lesbian identity in her *The Apparitional Lesbian: Female Homosexuality and Modern Culture* (1993). Most interestingly, Wolfreys 'returns' to the haunting presence of the past in the topography of the city of London in *Writing London: Volume Two: Materiality, Memory, Spectrality* (2004) and in *Writing London: Volume Three: Inventions of the City* (2007). The trope of spectrality is also significant in relation to postcolonial theory (Goldman and Saul, 2006, p. 649), and trauma theory (Kohlke, 2008, p. 7).

6. Alex Owen's groundbreaking *The Darkened Room: Women and Spiritualism* (1989) is an oft-quoted critical text in any account of Victorian Spiritualism and women's cultural position in the Victorian period. Similarly, Janet Oppenheim's *The Other World* (1988) also deals with the Spiritualist movement in connection with women. Diana Barsham (1992) explicitly connects the occult to the emergence of the Women's Rights' Movement, and Alison Winter (1998) pays particular attention to mesmerism and hypnotism in relation to women. Marlene Tromp has recently discussed the stories of several mediums, and has interpreted the séance as a potential in-between space, a site of transgression and subversion (2006, pp. 21–46). Interestingly, she considers how questions of race, class and sexual dynamics interplay in the dark room (2006, pp. 75–96). In turn, Judith Walkowitz is tangentially concerned with Spiritualism in a chapter of *City of Dreadful Delight* (1992), where she addresses the story of unconventional women who were wrongfully confined in asylums (2000, pp. 171–83).

Part I Histories and Hauntings

1
Salley Vickers, Venice, and the Victorians

Francis O'Gorman

> But no writer would be without writers on [Venice] itself. The greatest is Ruskin.
>
> — Salley Vickers[1]

Are 'haunting' and 'spectrality' the best figures for describing the contemporary novel's sense of the Victorian? Are 'haunting' and 'spectrality' the best figures, indeed, for describing the presence of the past of any sort? They are useful tropes – but they come at a cost. To go straight to their problems: ghosts are, for the most part, passive. They appear, but who knows by what mechanism? Bernardo's uncertainty in *Hamlet*, 'Is not this something more than fantasy?' (Shakespeare, 1974, 1.1.54), is unanswerable. Phantoms may speak of the accidental, unwilled lingering of history into different periods, as if history always appears unbidden. Ghosts do not suggest literature's deliberate imaginative engagements with the past or its will to encounter it. Ghosts do not speak, either, of history's vibrant presences, its powerful and vital reassertions, because ghosts are traces of the dead not their living return. They suggest the loss of the living past and history's persistence only in faint shadows. History's capacity to reappear, startlingly, to shape human lives decisively in the present is not what they imply.

This is an essay, at least at the beginning, about firmer, more consequential assertions of the past in the present. It is also about plots which cut the past away, yes, but which also affirm history's living possibilities, its liberating potentiality. Loving angels instead, this is not for the most part an essay about ghosts. Tintoretto was absorbed by the violent interventions of the divine into the ordinary: the *Annunziata* in the Scuola di San Rocco in Venice proposes an astounding scene of the arrival of God's messenger in the ordinary with nothing of, say, Fra' Angelico's scintillating calm. The agent of such dynamic intervention was angelic. And this essay, in thinking at the beginning about a claim for history's active presences, takes another angel as part of its subject. Tintoretto's heavenly messenger marked the new dispensation, the beginning of the Christian era, and the luminous fulfilment of what the past had promised. The angel of my essay breaks from the past with a new order, too, and it also endeavours to confirm the promise of other pasts. The angel is the vehicle not the message. But it is, all the same, a suggestive figure for articulating a notion, against the ghost, of urgent and vital disruptions of the present. Salley Vickers's *Miss Garnet's Angel* (2000) is not a volume without challenges for its reader. Its caricatures of politics, unanalytical conception of religion, unsophisticated Christian apologetics, and its psychologically undeveloped characterization are not easy to overlook. Yet it is, in other ways and for other reasons, enchanting and moving. And it usefully enables a readerly meditation on how the past can return redemptively, like Tintoretto's burst of the angelic into the 'old' Judaic order. Vickers's text sets history beside the present to find continuations of life and, while her central interest is in the enduring vitality of the Apocrypha, her novel is informed by conceptions of and from the Victorian. Her novel delicately, but consequentially, engages with the livingness of the nineteenth century. In examining this, my essay looks in particular at Ruskin's presence in the novel, measures the problems of invoking Victorian discourses of seriousness, and assesses the significance of Vickers's non-realism as a way of writing about the Victorians. I conclude with a claim about contemporary fiction in general as a mode of 'knowing' the nineteenth century.

Thinking about the presence of the past in any sense could not happen in a more susceptible European city than Venice. There, the past takes exceptionally seductive form. It is a location bound up, in cultural imagining, with the visibility of history. It also, as part of that, has a habit of ghosts. Ruskin, Venice's most influential Victorian commentator, named it the 'ghost upon the sands of the sea' (Ruskin, 1903–12, ix., p. 17); Villanelle, the heroine of Jeanette Winterson's *The Passion* (1987), still in the same mood, calls it a 'city [...] littered with ghosts' (Winterson, 1987, p. 61). Sometimes Venice's pastness irritates. 'Venise fait l'effet d'une carcase, d'un fossile vidé' (Debray, 1995, p. 42)[2] thinks Régis Debray in *Contre Venise* (1995), repudiating an affection for something as hollow as a mask. But he cannot do without that trope, however shifted in purpose. 'Tant que vous', he begins,

> n'aurez pas tué le fantôme de Venise en vous, decouragé tout rôle, penchant, pose, tentation ou songerie qui puisse mériter le qualificatif de «vénetien», vous ne serez pas quitte avec l'ennemi intime.
>
> (Debray, 1995, p. 11)[3]

The enemy is the love of Venice, and it is a ghost needing to be exorcized, a cultural pretension, or rather a pretension to culture, best overcome. Ghosts and Venice are hard to separate. But Vickers's novel, set in Venice, and thinking cautiously of Victorian versions of the city, still does not want the trope of haunting. Hugh, the hero of William Rivière's *By the Grand Canal* (2004), feels the presence of the departed in the city, the 'dead young soldiers' (Rivière, 2004, p. 123), from the Great War beside the *rii*. The presence and pastness of the past matter for Vickers too. But, to borrow Wilkie Collins's title, Venice is no haunted hotel.

There are other things to say first, though, about the Victorian in this fiction. To start with a deceptively simple question: What is Victorian in a 'neo-Victorian' novel? *Miss Garnet's Angel* is not neo-Victorian in the sense of, say, Matthew Kneale's *Sweet Thames* (1992), Sarah Waters's *Fingersmith* (2003), or Colm Tóibín's *The Master* (2005). It is set in the contemporary. Yet it conjures the Victorian throughout in a different and more contingent and demanding form of Victorianism, moving ultimately to a point where the Victorian in a specific sense is reasserted as an intriguingly modern and enabling presence. But Vickers's text, musing in other ways on the continuations of the Victorian, suggests provocatively first of all that recognizing the 'Victorian' depends in part on what the reader knows to be Victorian. What is apprehended to be history depends on what readers know to be historical. *Miss Garnet's Angel* deals with a particular version of this visibility/invisibility of history in its conjuring of versions of Venice. Venice is a city peculiarly engaged with the past. But they are nineteenth-century conceptions of the city that most clearly shape its high and popular cultural reception in the twenty-first. Romantic period and Victorian myths define Venice. The Byronic locale of seduction and political intrigue; the Ruskinian city of a lost paradise; Wilkie Collins's scene of murder, fraud, and decay; Henry James's site of plots and fragile beauties: each plays alchemically in the imagining of Venice still, sometimes overwhelmingly. The appeal of writing contemporary fiction about a pre-nineteenth century Venice – Christopher Whyte's *The Cloud Machinery* (2000), Michelle Lovric's *The Floating Book* (2004), Barbara Quick's *Vivaldi's Virgins* (2007) – is not only intrinsic but eases some of the pressure of the nineteenth-century's legacy. Yet what a reader recognizes of the past, whatever it is, in fictional representations of the city is dependent, partly, on what the reader brings to it. Recognizing what is an element of a nineteenth-century legacy is a teasing challenge of *Miss Garnet's Angel* and an episode in the larger matter of defining what is 'Victorian' in the present day.

How far is *Miss Garnet's Angel* conscious, for example, of John Ruskin (1819–1900)? How far is it a novel that negotiates its way through Venice with a consciousness of Victorian England's most significant Venetian critic? Vickers's epigraph to her novel (as well as mine) point in the direction of a sustained engagement. Ruskin's statement from *Modern Painters* V (1860), 'If some people really see angels, where others see empty space, let them paint the angels' (Ruskin, 1903–12, vi, p. 28), introduces *Miss Garnet's Angel*. The words neatly catch the centrality of the angelic, and the text's interest in painting. But Ruskin's statement is about things which some people see and others do not. The same might be said of ghosts. But the novel prefers to associate itself with the duality of a different incorporeal form. Whatever the case, and whichever trope is adopted, it is true that among those things that might be so ambiguous, so open to opposing perceptions, is Ruskin's presence itself. Through him the novel fashions a quiet pointer back to the ampler issue of how history's presence is, or is not, recognized.

The epigraph implies the novel's sense of Ruskin. And elsewhere, Ruskin explicitly figures in the plot. Vera, Julia's tiresome Marxist friend, visits Venice carrying Ruskin as if in possession of a key to the city. She reads from him intrusively and with the confidence of having found a reliable authority (she also becomes rather distracted with

Effie, Ruskin's wife, and their unconsummated marriage). Nothing of Vera's self, the reader is invited to see, is touched by Venice's charm; the city works no redemptive change on a desiccated personality. Carrying Ruskin, as E. M. Forster had mischievously suggested much earlier, is a sign of narrow-mindedness, a closed-up failure to be moved by Italy: Ruskin's cultural authority is an impediment. The novel wants, in this sense, to be rid of a Victorian. Julia, incidentally, is accompanied by what sounds like a (stereotype of a) Victorian text with her when she first arrives: *Venice for Historians*, by the Reverend Martin Crystal MA (Oxon). An unengaging and impersonal account, to be laid aside when Julia begins to feel the city her own, the volume is not, so far as I know, a real text. But, suggestively nineteenth-century in title, it adds a little to the text's desire to code Victorian writers on Venice as a gloomy obstacle.

More extensively, but also more privately, *Miss Garnet's Angel* seems to negotiate around a peculiarly non-Ruskinian city as if subterraneously confirming that the modern city is better without him. But these negotiations are less visible: the plot's contest with Ruskin, here, is open to debate. What is the past, what the Victorian, depends on what is recognized to be Victorian. Ruskin's Venice, for instance, was at its high point artistically in the period of the Bellini family, Carpaccio, Giorgione, Tintoretto, Titian, and Veronese. Eighteenth-century Venetian art was, to him, the exhalation of a city already dead. But Vickers's concentration on the suggestibility of Guardi's *La Storia di Tobia* (1749) on the organ loft panels of the Chiesa dell'Anzolo Raffaele can be read as a calculated insistence on the primacy of a city's art perceived without Ruskin, an instance of the spiritual and affective power of painting from an age Ruskin believed to be beyond Venice's death.[4] Celebrating Guardi was, in this sense, quietly to defy Ruskin, as the novel's setting chiefly in the western Dorsoduro kept largely away from Ruskin's preferred territories. Sarah and Toby are art restorers (the metaphor of restoration is important to the novel) and this, too, might be intended to rebuke or irritate Ruskin. Twins who befriend Julia, they are distinctively un-Ruskinian labourers. Preservation was necessary for Ruskin – but restoration, in the age of the neo-Gothic remodelling of English churches, was barbarism and fraud. Better allow something to fall down than falsify it. And nowhere did Ruskin feel that more than in Venice.[5]

Such implications are subtextual, up for debate, and, like Ruskin's angels, some may see them and others not. That issue is emblematized with literally visible clarity in the first-edition English paperback from HarperCollins. There the publisher reproduced on the cover a detail – the visiting angel – from Carpaccio's *Il Sogno di Orsola* (1495) from the Orsola cycle, now hanging in the Accademia in Venice. Of course, the relevance to the angelic theme and to Venice is plain. The first of those meanings, at any rate, is impossible to miss: no one can fail to see *this* angel. But what should a reader do if he or she knows that *Il Sogno di Orsola* was one of Ruskin's most precious pictures in the 1870s? Is this 'Victorian' presence in the novel intended for recognition or not? And if it is intended, here is a peculiarly submerged/visible instance of the more general matter: the cryptic and coded nature of how the 'Victorian' might be defined in the modern. Ruskin was entranced by Carpaccio's painting, the 'sweetest, *because* the truest [prophecy], of all that Venice was born to utter' (Ruskin, 1903–12, xxviii, p. 732; original emphasis); he copied it, particularly the head of the sleeping saint;[6] obtained special permission as an honorary member of the Accademia to move it into a private room; he came to think that Rose La Touche, his lost love, communicated through it; and in Christmas 1877 he felt that the picture was bound up with the supernatural revelations he believed he was experiencing.[7] He sensed that Ursula, combined with Rose, had become a tutelary spirit. Perhaps these associations spoke chiefly of Ruskin's fragile mental health (though I think they did a lot more than that).[8] But, whatever the case, there are obviously elements in Ruskin's Venetian narrative of partial redemption which fit Julia Garnet's. In their uncertainty about whether Ruskin's relationship with *Il Sogno di Orsola* is 'there' or not, readers are permitted to feel with a delicate but penetrating force, looking even at the design of the book, the strange contingencies which help define the contemporary sense of the 'Victorian'.

How the past shapes and lives in the present, as the uncertainty about Ruskin's presence suggests, is the provocative conception of Salley Vickers's novel in a variety of ways. The text asks the reader to perceive the potential force of history's presence in the contemporary even if it is not labelled as 'history'. Of the West's explanatory models for the return of the past, the most well used is Freud's (or that which is imagined to be Freud's). His whole conception of psychoanalysis of the patient, under the analyst's guidance, returning to scenes of past trauma in an effort to defuse their power offered a notion of history as that which was best escaped from. Yet the liberating return of the past, its freeing reassertion, its triumphant refusal to be cast out because it is what the present needs, are counter-Freudian apprehensions of what the past can do to cure when it maintains its vitality in the present instead of being banished by therapeutic care. Freud taught the West to mistrust the returns of history, to frame them as retrogressive iterations of the unhealed. But a recollection of history's reprises as regenerative, of the past as therapeutic in its returns, makes for the welcoming of history's reassertions, a celebration of history's capacity to live not die, to bring life rather than inhibit it. Vickers does not take on the Freudian tradition with anything like adequate symbolic or intellectual weight. But her novel permits the reader to begin to meditate on a challenge to Freud through its quiet proposition about the recurrence of redemptive patterns of history. *Miss Garnet's Angel* offers a plot of the reassertion of history as healing (as Raphael is the archangel of healing); it salutes moments of recuperation when instants in time are brought together enablingly.

In the symbolic language of the novel, such reassertions are associated with the intervention of an angel, seen only by some. The Tintoretto-like interruption of the day-to-day with a redeeming and other-worldly presence provides the symbolic vocabulary of the novel's contest with a notion of history as inhibiting. Yet angelic interruptions, posing a counter-narrative to Freud, also return to Freud. The novel offers nothing merely naïve or single-minded in its apprehension of history as that which is therapeutic. Vickers, if she is interested in the recuperative reprises of the past, is also conscious of history's more traditional role in psychoanalysis as that which needs to be set aside. Whether or not the reader notices the Victorian sub-themes of *Miss Garnet's Angel*, the novel's employment of the Apocryphal story of Tobias and the Angel makes its dual case about the seeming recurrence of history unmissable. It is worth pausing over this before returning explicitly to the question of the Victorians because the handling of the Apocryphal story proposes clearly what the nineteenth-century presence suggests more subtly. Interweaving a version of Tobias and the Angel – a story in which Tobias is accompanied on a journey to meet his future wife by the disguised Archangel Raphael – with the contemporary story of Julia Garnet, Vickers poses a succession of parallels which suggest the necessity of casting out one form of history and welcoming another.

Tobit (Tobias's father) spends part of his life in digging graves for the dead, fulfilling a rule of his religion that requires proper burial of the faithful. Yet his principle becomes an obsession, and it drags his family into misery. Julia Garnet, in the modern story, arrives in Venice with the baggage of an unfulfilled, dry past confined by apparently Marxist principles and sensitive neither to art nor to mystery. Both she and Tobit learn to give up their pasts, their 'moribund way of being' (Vickers, 2000, p. 310), and are brought to a new life. Tobias's marriage, thanks to the intervention of Raphael and the companionship of Kish, the dog, helps restore the family's fortunes. Writing the story down, Tobit manages to '[leave] the dead alone' (Vickers, 2000, p. 332). Julia moves beyond what she comes to think of as her 'old life' (Vickers, 2000, p. 63), touched by the allure of Venice, refreshed by a consciousness of the aesthetic and, as Vickers sees it, of holiness. If this is only another variant on the familiar fictional trope of an English or American man or woman being revived or changed for the better by Italy – Forster's *A Room with a View* (1908), Elizabeth von Arnim's *Enchanted April* (1922), *Italian Fever* (1999) by Valerie Martin – then it is made more complex than usual by its interleaving with the Biblical narrative which gently expands its scope.

Yet the notion of leaving the past, of breaking away from a stultifying history, can be confirmation of the past, too. History, *pace* Freud, can be redemptive. The idea of patterns in history as templates for the present is a notion embedded in Judaeo-Christian culture. With the Christian sense of typology, of Judaic history as that which prepares the patterns for the new dispensation, history can readily be seen as anticipatory, awaiting a fresh version of events already past. But the more neutral idea of recurrences in history as enabling, without the progressive, teleological direction provided by a Christian typological reading of history, is worth remembering. What lies behind Vickers's novel is a sense of patterns of human experience, not wholly unlike Jungian archetypes in narrative form, which repeat themselves, in fresh guises, through history and which are patterns of redemption. To be sure, such patterns belong with conventional Christian notions of human salvation as that which is enacted throughout human history. But they are suggestive beyond this: they are narrative archetypes which, outside theology, hint at valuable and challenging comprehensions of history's persistence in the present. Vickers's novel muses on this historical model most clearly in its use of Tobias's story against that of Julia's. As Tobias finds his wife, Sara, through the intervention of Raphael, so Julia finds a new and quasi-erotic fulfilment in her love for Venice which opens her eyes to new values and ampler forms of being. There is redemption of the eye and heart, signified in part by her greater sensitivity to angels, represented and 'real'. And there are other cases. Sarah and Toby, the restorers, re-enact, as their names make clear, the narrative of Tobias and Sara in another way. Sarah is troubled by fantasies (she lies about being abused as a child) and disturbed by the death of her father. Like Sara in the Apocrypha, she is possessed by a 'demon'. Marriage heals, or is part of the healing, for both. As the smoke of the burning fish bladder drives out Sara's malady through the guidance of Raphael, so Sarah seems to be saved by the presence of the angelic, too, the 'nameless, fathomless brilliances' (Vickers, 2000, p. 274) that attend momentarily on her distress in the (fictional) Chapel of the Plague.

History repeats its patterns, and, attended by the angelic, they are salvational. But does this patterning concern the Victorians or suggest anything useful about the nineteenth century in the contemporary? The force of Salley Vickers's reflection on history is to disinter redemptive plots from the ancient world and make them serviceable for the present. Is this in itself, regarded simply as a practice of writing, a glance back to any nineteenth-century habits? Certainly, the notion of comparing the present with the past obtained a powerful visibility in the Victorian period. Pugin's *Contrasts* (1836) and Carlyle's *Past and Present* (1843) were only two of the most obvious acts of cultural paralleling; Ruskin's *The Stones of Venice* another, in its urgent encouragement to England to measure itself against the history of Venice, to avoid a fall from 'prouder eminence to less pitied destruction' (Ruskin, 1903–12, ix, p. 17). But in fiction, the broad notion of the modern day repeating or living through narratives of the past was not commonplace in the Victorian period. Nineteenth-century fiction declined for the most part to test a contemporary plot against an ancient one. Rider Haggard's *She* narratives – including *She* (1887), *Ayesha: The Return of She* (1905), and *Wisdom's Daughter* (1923) – were among the exceptions. Joyce's *Ulysses* (1922) offered the twentieth century a sophisticated modern 're-enactment' of an ancient myth. Somerset Maugham's *Then and Now* (1946) ventured a starker form of contrast between one period (the Florentine Renaissance) and the present more in the manner of *The Stones*. But contemporary popular novels and films of the present repeating the past – Kate Mosse's *Labyrinth* (2006), Matthew Pearl's *The Dante Club* (2004), Stephen Sommers's 1998 film *The Mummy* and its sequels – owe more to Haggard than to the cultural ambition of Joyce or the cultural analysis of Carlyle and Ruskin. Vickers looks for her conception of history first to Christian typologies. But Haggard's alluring sense of modern men and women re-enacting the lives of their predecessors is not far from her. Yet, in the richer *interstices* of the novel, there is a closer connection with the Victorian, even as there is, it may be, the dimmest echo of *The Stones of Venice*'s intentions to juxtapose a historical narrative against a contemporary one. Vickers's novel, suggesting more amply through Ruskin a Victorian's view of things – restating a hard-won claim from the nineteenth century – makes its 'Victorianism' partly from its reassertion of a Ruskinian notion of the redemptive force of Venice and, through that, of the aptness or enduring service-ability of a Victorian's moral vision. Restating the Apocrypha, *Miss Garnet's Angel, pace* Vera and her travel book, finds also an anchor in acknowledging – sometimes explicitly, sometimes implicitly – the mythic terms of *The Stones of Venice*.

In coding Venice as a place possessed of salvational force, Vickers's novel is not merely drawing on the trope of Italy's reviving charms. It is tranquilly saluting *The Stones of Venice*'s influential argument, familiar in conceptions of Venice even to those who have never read Ruskin, that the city held a key to redemption. For Ruskin, this was not only for the human soul but for England. *The Stones of Venice*, and Ruskin's subsequent writing on the city into his last creative decade, posed the history of a culture which had once, in the Gothic period from the twelfth century to the early Renaissance, reached an apex of Christian virtue and aesthetic accomplishment. The history of Venice was the history of faithful human achievement and its fall to ruin and death consequent on a rejection of the principles of faith and vaunting of the human over the divine. To learn of that salutary history, to profit from the narrative of Venice's rise and fall, was, in the 1850s, to be reminded of the foundational virtues of a civilized society and encouraged to compare the England of the mid-nineteenth century with the fate of the once-civilized Venice, *quondam*, another imperial island power dependent, like England, on trade by sea. England's chances of avoiding Venice's decline into ruin, Ruskin's national sermon proposed, were best found in learning the history of the Sea City: redemption, of soul and state, was implicit in the history of Venice's decline. In staging a narrative of personal redemption, of the movement towards Julia's conviction that 'Venice has changed me' (Vickers, 2000, p. 169), Vickers implicitly transforms Ruskin's conviction of what Venice *could* do, if she was properly known (the pronoun is Ruskin's), and personalizes it as a modern story of human recovery.

No wonder that Julia Garnet in important moments of her 'conversion', the opening of her horizons, sounds a little like Ruskin or, directly, speaks his words or words believed to be Ruskin's. Julia's change is, in part, towards a greater sensitivity to art, Christian liturgy, and mystery. That in itself is not an un-Ruskinian change. Her words might faintly echo with the final celebrated paragraph of *Praeterita* (1885–9) when she says, of tea to Toby, 'We've drunk enough of it together!' (Vickers, 2000, p. 290).[9] And perhaps even the plot of Tobias was half-suggested by Ruskin, writing of the Palazzo Ducale in the central volume of *The Stones*. Speaking of the figure of Tobias on the Palazzo's capital carvings, lucid expressions of Gothic fidelity and Renaissance debasement, Ruskin noted:

> The peculiar office of the angel Raphael is, in general, according to tradition, the restraining the harmful influences of evil spirits. Sir Charles Eastlake told me, that sometimes in this office he is represented bearing the gall of the fish caught by Tobias; and reminded me of the peculiar superstitions of the Venetians respecting the raising of storms by fiends, as embodied in the well-known tale of the Fisherman and St. Mark's ring.
>
> (Ruskin, 1903–12, x, p. 364)

Julia will eventually find that Raphael is 'one of the holy angels who is over the spirits of men' (Vickers, 2000, p. 221) and who, she understands, purges 'evil spirits' (Vickers, 2000, p. 222). Toby will remind her early on that Raphael was, in Venice, 'popular with the sailors' and supposed 'to have visited this area' (Vickers, 2000, p. 106). These might all have been dim hints from *The Stones* remembered as, elsewhere, Julia recalls more clearly the sensational events of Effie Ruskin's life in Venice.[10]

Yet Julia is more surely Ruskinian when facing Andrea Palladio's neo-classical Basilica di San Giorgio Maggiore (completed 1610), a church of particular significance in Ruskin's plotting of the fall of Venice. 'Look at it, our finest piece of Palladio', Julia's patrician American friend Charles Cutforth tells her, with proprietorial confidence. But then Vickers's heroine pauses:

> Julia, about to agree, changed her mind. 'I don't like it. I'm probably being philistine but it feels unholy, somehow.' Once she had ventured inside the famous church's marmoreal interior and had crept out again, frozen to the bone.
>
> (Vickers, 2000, p. 169)

Associating the Renaissance manner of Palladio's church with the unholy, Julia seems inert to the orderly pleasures of the building, one of the few churches in Venice that largely preserve the design of a single architect. But she is, at the same time, at one with Ruskin's impatience with the man whom he regarded as a 'wholly virtueless' (Ruskin, 1903–12, v, p. 93) architect. In his conception, from the central chapter of the central volume of *The Stones of Venice*, 'The Nature of Gothic', the neo-classical implicitly stood in opposition to the authentic Christian architecture of the Gothic. Neo-classicism, reversing the principles of Gothic, privileged human achievement not God's; it reached for a cold perfection which was arrogant and benighted; it replaced a reverence for the natural world and its revelations with a colder preference for the non-natural; and, in its return to the form of 'pagan' buildings, it was, for the evangelical Ruskin in his early career, unholy. Where the Gothic celebrated God, the natural world as an expression of God, and the fallibility of human creativity, a Palladian design for a church was an abuse: it 'cast aside [...] religion' (Ruskin, 1903–12, ix, p. 45). So much for holiness. 'It is impossible', Ruskin added in the 'Venetian Index' at the end of *The Stones* specifically about San Giorgio, 'to conceive a design more gross, more barbarous, more childish in conception, more servile in plagiarism, more insipid in result, more contemptible under every point of rational regard' (Ruskin, 1903–12, xi, p. 381).

Where Julia is in unison with Ruskin's sense of where unholiness lay in the city, she is pulled back to what she believes are his literal words towards the end of her life, shortly after experiencing the 'remediate gaze' (Vickers, 2000, p. 312) of the angelic in the Chapel of the Plague. Looking at the figure of St Theodore standing on the back of a crocodile, one of the two statues on the columns of the Piazzetta, Julia thinks that it is Ruskin's phrase which comes back to her. 'A "splendour of miscellaneous spirits", Ruskin had called Venice', she says to herself (Vickers, 2000, p. 325). Now alert to Venice as a city with a spiritual heart – however impressionistically and sentimentally the novel defines this – Julia believes she is in sympathy with Ruskin in describing Venice's spiritual identity as bound up with multitudinous artefacts, overlapping histories, and composite guardian figures. Speaking words she understands to be Ruskin's at this instant, Julia, standing before St Theodore, suggests the novel's more consequential engagement with the city imagined in a more ample Ruskinian sense: a city proposing a chance of healing and deliverance, a return to art, seriousness, moral values, humility, and a sense of the divine. Vickers's novel allows the reader to feel the contingency of the 'Victorian' – what is and what is not Victorian. But it also admits, in its sub-themes, the 'living' continuance of a Victorian's conception of the city's meaning. To be sure, there are other ways to read that conception. Henry James had turned what would later be Vickers's interest in *The Stones of Venice* upside down in his Venetian tale not of redemption but of moral downfall in *The Wings of the Dove* (1902); Thomas Mann's *Der Tod in Venedig* (1912) took that trope of decline further.[11] But Julia Garnet refreshes a different Ruskinian vision, or, rather, a different vision of Ruskin, the 'greatest' of all writers on Venice, according to Salley Vickers. The novel's desire to 'bury the dead' (Vickers, 2000, p. 330), to escape from particular forms of constricting history, occurs only with a gentle restatement of the past, a hint of the livingness of the dead in the continuing life of Ruskin's apprehension of what Venice, a redeeming city, might eloquently impart to those able to understand.

Vickers's novel proposes that Ruskin's notion of Venice, as it has entered the fabric of modern-day imaginings of Venice, can 'live' again, possess meaning, pertinence, intellectual and emotional vitality. The angel that breaks into the life of Tobias and Sara continues to manifest its presence millennia later, and its redemptive force, in the life of Julia, Toby, and Sarah, is its ancient form. As a figure for the recurrence of redemptive patterns, that healing ideal adverts to the novel's sense that some verities are not extinguished but pertain to new generations. Ruskin's commentary on angels inaugurates

Vickers's novel and his conception of Venice as the site of a possible redemption lingers about it. History is not here to be brought back in phantasmal forms, glimpsed as the dead relics of a past culture. A conception from the past is, instead, deftly, discreetly, saluted as continuing to possess vital meaning. Venice, of course, has prompted other reflections on the 'livingness' as well as the 'deadness' of the past. Hugh, the diplomat hero of William Rivière's *By the Grand Canal*, faced with the loss of a friend and the dying of another, suddenly thinks that he has comprehended something new. His dying companion is the descendent of an ancient family, the Veniers. But, even with the prospect of that extinction, Hugh is possessed by a new idea: 'The past wasn't dead', he says to himself, 'the past was that which was already alive [...] time was never irrevocably lost.' 'Time', Hugh concludes, looking around him, was 'all about [...], only he'd never noticed – or rather, he hadn't understood before that this was time's way of being alive' (Rivière, 2004, p. 214) To that notion of the 'aliveness' of time, the reassertions of the past as vital, Vickers's novel allows another intriguing (and more rationally comprehensible) shape in the penumbra of its plot.

It would be a weak historicism to think modern imaginings of the Victorian were only suggestive of the preoccupations of the contemporary, that shaping the past in the present had little to reveal about the past itself. Cora Kaplan's *Victoriana: Histories, Fictions, Criticism* (2007) is marketed with the flat announcement that modern interest in the Victorian is primarily about the present. 'Victoriana, the book argues', according to the blurb, has 'developed a modern history of its own in which we can trace the shifting social and cultural concerns of the last few decades' (Kaplan, 2007, blurb). It would be hard to think of a period of modern history about which such a claim could not, with some plausibility, be made. But is there nothing useful about the period itself to be learned from contemporary writings about the Victorian? One of the problems with contemporary studies of cultural 'afterlives' is that, in privileging reception, the *after*life, they sometimes occlude what might usefully be learned from reception history about the *life* itself in its own historical moment. Do modern fictions about Henry James reveal nothing about Henry James? Does A. S. Byatt's *Possession* (1990) have no comment to make on the working of real Victorian poetry? Kaplan, more sensitive than her blurb, offers the intriguing idea that Byatt's '*Possession* performs imitation as if it were a better, and certainly higher, criticism' (Kaplan, 2007, p. 95). If it is unclear what the distinction between 'better' and 'higher' implies here, the notion of fictional writing on the Victorians as an act of criticism, an effort more adequately to comprehend the past, is valuable (though Kaplan leaves it undeveloped). It is not hard to see that some of the legacies of such literature have, however, not been quite as 'critical' as could be hoped. Some have affirmed truisms and stereotypes which, in scholarly discourse, are either now hedged with qualification or discredited.

Were the Victorians hypocrites? Scholars may sigh at the return of this unanalysed notion, which had proved so important for modernist period writers to divide themselves from their predecessors. Ivy Compton-Burnett had been ruthless on the topic – take the dissection of a Victorian family in *A House and its Head* (1935); or take Lytton Strachey, arch in his probing of alleged duplicity in *Eminent Victorians* (1918). But, in the twenty-first century, with the period no longer a parental presence in need of banishing, the 'hypocritical Victorians' still provide Sarah Waters with a useful idea for a plot. *Fingersmith* offers the veneer of respectability under which Christopher Lilly lives, collecting a vast collection of pornography, pursuing his will with cruelty and the charade of impartiality. As a novel about double-crossing, the hypocrisy trope is a particularly helpful one. But, read incautiously, *Fingersmith* affirms only a category in need of challenge.

Vickers's novel prompts more historicized thinking about why one might turn to the nineteenth century, and what limits that might involve. Recognizing a category which belongs with a peculiar closeness to the Victorian period, it poses the reader with the outlines of a Victorian dilemma, even as it imbricates that dilemma with a modern query. *Miss Garnet's Angel*, for all its confined literary and intellectual ambition, asks a serious question about – the language of seriousness. Its themes are of salvation, human recovery, and the wisdom of cautious judgement. And it finds, in a half-realized Ruskinian vision of Venice the environment in which best to play out, with undemanding accessibility, a biblically inflected story of the surprising presences of grace. Vickers, it seems, finds it hard to speak of significant moral themes, of human salvation, without invoking the mental condition, the lexis, the temper, of a selectively imagined Victorian. Are 'the Victorian' and 'seriousness' secret synonyms for her? Matthew Arnold thought that literature needed to be serious – but Vickers's definition of seriousness as being tied to Christianity raises a version of the same problem Arnold experienced. As the author of *Literature and Dogma* (1873) endeavoured to transform Christianity into a set of non-miraculous tenets for a moral life, he felt the consequential problem that would challenge the twentieth century about the apparent need for a moral discourse to be rooted in the non-human, in an absolute, in the theological. Matthew Arnold fashioned a language for speaking of ethical responsibilities and of the full development of human life without rejecting Christianity – understood as a discourse of moral guidance – but also without invoking its claims for supernatural authority, its dependence on miracle. Arnold's effort to negotiate between morality and Christianity did not find a safe home in the twentieth century.

The heart of his difficulty is played out in shadows in one possible reaction to Salley Vickers's gauche but revealing Christian apologetics. What is the relationship between the language of seriousness and the discourses of Christianity in the present 'post-Christian' culture? Vickers's novel looks back nostalgically to Victorian seriousness in its gentle gestures to the Protestant sermon of national admonishment in *The Stones of Venice*. But the text cannot invoke such gravity without rerouting its meditation back to the Christian certainties Arnold found unpalatable and on which even Ruskin, after *The Stones*, was to shift his emphasis.[12] Can a gesture back to the Victorian language of seriousness, Vickers's novel implicitly enquires, now only revive a foundation for ethical or spiritual language which Victorians themselves found to be in jeopardy?[13] Does the novel allow the modern (secular) reader to feel with unusual clarity the inaccessibility of one sort of 'Victorianism' by declaring itself a text unable to reinterpret the basis of the nineteenth century's most visible moral discourse in new terms for a contemporary world?

Vickers's gesture to the Victorian as an appreciated location of, to say the least, serious thought, thought on serious matters, reminds the reader of an obstacle in the legacy of the period. While it might be true of the present day that Victorian moral seriousness is understood more sympathetically in criticism than before (the interest in Victorian religion is a noticeable feature again of literary criticism, for instance), that seriousness remains for the most part caught in the historicist museum. Vickers's implicit acknowledgement, her turn to the Christian, speaks cautiously of her nostalgia for a nineteenth-century culture which had, at least mythically, a more shared understanding of Christian language. And, to the modern, secular cultural critic, it speaks of the pastness of the Victorian past.

What is there for the literary critic in this possible imagining of the Victorian and the envisaging of blockages between the present age and theirs? *Miss Garnet's Angel* flirts with an imagined Victorian. But it does so outside the terms of realism, the major literary bequest to fiction from the nineteenth century. It hints, at that plainest level, that approaches to the past necessitate non-realist strategies; that there is an interleaving of fantasy, self-conscious and overt acts of imagining, required in the representations of the Victorian, and perhaps of the historical. Matthew Kneale's *Sweet Thames* attempts a scientifically realist approach to the Victorian period but Neil Stephenson could only describe 'neo-Victorians' in futurist science fiction. A. S. Byatt's *Possession* is subtitled *A Romance* with something of the same view as Vickers's regard for history in mind: the nineteenth-century past seen from the present is coloured by fantasy, mapped by patterns created by the genres of representation. Angels in Vickers's novel are linked with historical convictions or narrative patterns which reassert themselves. But they suggest also the move into the non-realist as a valuable mode for figuring history as if there is always to be something not-quite-rational, not-quite-graspable in the ways in which the past can be apprehended in the present. Part of this not-quite-rational identity concerns what *feels* real about the past in a fictional account. And that feeling has a lot to do with – feeling.

Vickers's meditation on the changed life of Julia Garnet in Venice seeks in part to give fresh affective life to an ancient Apocryphal story, to round it out in flesh and blood as Arnold would say, even as it retells a story which is neither wholly earthly nor rationally explicable. Fiction, in this respect, reasserts itself as a useful way of communicating to a reader a myth of the still-continuing nature of the past, of the illusion of that continuation as something which can be felt more than it can be rationally known or explained. Robert Browning, convinced of the reanimating power of poetry over the voices of the dead, the ability of verse to transcend, in the reader's apprehension, the limits of the possible, defined a challenging poetics of vitality for the mid-Victorian period.[14] In its affective force, Vickers's novel, aiming to allow a reader to feel, to *sense* more than to analyse, links between the past and present in fictional narrative, underscores something not dissimilar in the capacity of the novel as a practice of writing to restore to an apprehension of the past – restoration is indeed one of Vickers's guiding motifs – *felt* vitality.

It is the force of written words to enable a sense of history's continuances that *Miss Garnet's Angel* finally, elusively, suggests. Literary texts, in the broadest definitions, are among the best and most intriguing ways in which the novel envisages how one might sense the enduring presences of the past. Lines from books, passages from earlier narrations, return as parallels or, to Julia herself, as sudden intuitive points of realization. Tennyson commemorated the curious effectiveness of once-read words from the past, returning in the memory, in capturing a distinctive feature of the present moment in his unbidden recollections of Catullus in 'Frater Ave Atque Vale' (1885). The idea of a presence in the mind, distantly, of things once read which can still return suggests, in Vickers's novel, one of the most subtle ways in which writers might retain vitality and in which history might seem in closest connection with the living present. A distinctive ability to hold on to, and renew, the historical is embedded in the heart of a reading experience – or in acts of remembering the reading experience – for it is there that renewal and continuation is most convincingly felt. The lost, unknown authors of the story of Tobias and the Angel still maintain, through Vickers's double narration, a presence in the present. And it is some of the once-read, still-remembered words believed to be from John Ruskin that Julia finds, like Tennyson recalling Catullus, adequate to express a little of her own redemptive change of heart in the City of the Sea.

What sometimes is thought history is sometimes fictional, a fantasy. But sometimes fiction can give a more 'living' sense of the past than anything else, a more engaging sense that the words of the dead are neither lost nor the ideas of those from previous generations paralysed in the aspic of antiquity. As a mode of 'knowing' history, fiction brings misapprehensions, sentimentality, illusion, and deception into the heart of a reader's experience. But narrative fiction sometimes also offers a persuasive, perhaps dangerously, but also enthrallingly convincing sense of, a belief in, the continuing vibrancy, the living ambiance of, the past.

Salley Vickers does not write 'neo-Victorian' fiction. But, within her more overt concentration on present-day continuations with the Apocrypha, the nearness of the Victorians is not irrelevant to her meditation on a 'living' underlay of nineteenth-century thought beneath a modern life. The extent of Ruskin's ideas within the novel's purposes is an open question, and her text, after all, uncomfortably searches mistaken perceptions, half-grasped facts, and deceptive appearances. But 'there' to some degree the Victorian is. Literature can make one 'believe' many things in the temporary entrancement of the reading experience. Vickers's novel, for luminous moments in the implications and layers of its plot, suggests that both a narrative from the ancient world and conceptions from the Victorian still have forms of aptness, cultural and moral energy, longevity, enduring meaning in the present. Complicated ruminations might not seem to characterize Vickers's first published novel. But *Miss Garnet's Angel* allows the reader to be intrigued by complicated matters all the same. When Julia ends her will with Petronius's statement '*Ut mihi contingat tuo beneficio post mortem vivere*' (Vickers, 2000, p. 335),[15] she imparts new sense to the words of the Roman satirist from the first century. And Vickers's novel, altogether, searches ways in which pasts might not die. With its layering of ancient and modern, her text suggests the 'living' continuation of the Apocrypha. But it suggests also, enigmatically, the tantalizing thought that a Victorian's ideas might be sensed, through the enchanting power of fiction, as strangely constitutive of present-day ways of living and being, too. Such continuations are, I think, among the past's most persuasive ways of being alive.

Notes

1. See http://www.salleyvickers.com/pages/missgarnetsangel/venice_feature.htm (accessed 4 December 2007). Vickers goes on, candidly: 'The greatest is Ruskin, but only a well-muscled fanatic would cart his *Stones of Venice* there. Better take Sarah Quill's *The Stones Revisited*, a digest of Ruskin's Venice with stunning photographs'. See Quill (2000).
2. 'Venice is like a carcass, an empty fossil.'
3. 'So long as you do not kill the ghost of Venice within you, discourage every posture, inclination, pose, temptation, or daydream that it is possible to describe as "Venetian", you will not be quit of the enemy within.'
4. Ruskin makes only two references to 'Guardi' in the *Library Edition* – see Ruskin (1903–12, vii, p. 255 and xiii, p. 109) – neither warm. The panels may be by Francesco or Giannantonio Guardi, or possibly both. Vickers

always calls the church 'Angelo Raffaele' but it is more widely known in its Venetian dialectal form.

5. Nowhere was Ruskin's impatience with restoration more visible than in his efforts, partly successful, to check the progress of the 'restorations' of the west front of San Marco, 1877–79. See, for instance, the letter to Count Zorzi, in Ruskin (1903–12, xxiv, pp. 405–11).

6. One now hangs in Somerville College, Oxford.

7. See Burd (1990).

8. See O'Gorman (2005).

9. Cf. 'We drank of it together', Ruskin (1903–12, xxxv, p. 562).

10. See Vickers (2000, pp. 185–6).

11. Vickers suggests on her website that *The Wings of the Dove* influenced her presentation of Venice as a scene of 'love, duplicity, and folly' (in the relationship of Julia and Carlo, presumably): see http://www.salleyvickers.com/pages/missgarnetsangel/venice_feature.htm (as accessed 4 December 2007).

12. See, for instance, the very different temper of Ruskin's *St Mark's Rest: The History of Venice, Written for the Help of the Few Travellers who Still Care for her Monuments* (1877–84).

13. I do not mean to suggest that Ruskin himself can be easily included among those who found Christianity in jeopardy. Ruskin abandoned his Evangelical faith and eventually returned to a more broad-based form of Christianity: it is not clear that he ever ceased, for a significant period of time, to believe in God.

14. On Browning's revivalist poetics, see Roberts (2004), Helfield (2006), and O'Gorman (2007).

15. 'that by your kindness I may find life after death' (Vickers's translation, 2000, p. 337).

2
Spectrality, S(p)ecularity, and Textuality: Or, Some Reflections in the Glass

Mark Llewellyn

> Out flew the web and floated wide;
> The mirror crack'd from side to side;
> 'The curse is come upon me', cried
> The Lady of Shalott.
> — Tennyson, 'The Lady of Shallot'
> (1883, p. 29 [1842])

> [T]he Past, the more or less remote Past, of which the prose is clean obliterated by distance – that is the place to get our ghosts from.
> — Vernon Lee, 'Preface', *Hauntings* (2006, p. 39 [1890])

> Those who are dead are not dead
> they're just living in my head
> And since I fell for that spell
> I am living there as well.
> — Coldplay, '42' (2008)

Alfred Lord Tennyson to Coldplay via Vernon Lee might normally make for a tenuous line of enquiry and yet all three quotations given above reflect, albeit in different ways, on the idea of spectrality, specularity, ghosts, the dead, and the living. The historical pull of the past, the configuration of the present through the timeworn lens, and the melancholic nostalgia which is always a foreboding of our own mortality are each (dis)embodied in our awareness of a sensory reality that is fragile, transient, and yet endures beyond ourselves. One might think here of Slavoj Žižek's Lacanian 'philosophy of the real as absent, non-existent' (Belsey, 2004, p. 5) and the impact this has on our rereading and re-visioning of the past through fiction, itself in some ways a non-real construct. The past is forever a reflection that our individual human future is not limitless, and in that sense ensures that our return to history and our belief in something beyond the here and now are indivisibly linked within the imagination. For the Victorians, such earthly limitations were accepted and acceptable while the persistence of the soul in an immortal condition held sway; after the religious crises of the mid-nineteenth century, such certainties were replaced or perhaps shadowed by faith in a spiritual world of ghosts, séances, and a different plane of existence. As Ronald Pearsall puts it, 'Spiritualism and the resurgence of the occult found fertile soil in Victorian England [because it] ... provided a respectable fulfilment of this desire' (Pearsall, 1972, p. 57).

In recent neo-Victorian fiction the figure of the Victorian ghost, or the sense of the ghostliness of the Victorian past, has increasingly come to the fore. As a motif, the idea of the nineteenth-century spectre serves as a useful corollary to the contemporary author's awareness of the 'haunting' presence of the Victorian period even into the twenty-first century. However, while critical work has explored this haunting and ghosting in terms of the refracted moment of historical fiction more generally, relatively little has been done to assert the more connective threads surrounding shadows and ghosts of the Victorian period in the present as a re-articulation of the Victorians' own fascination with séances, spectres and other spooky things. While other essays in this collection focus on the specific sites of spectrality, be it in the ghostly presence of the Victorian text, the summoning of the past through the séance in the work of Michèle Roberts, new 'histories' of Victorian class, or London as the enduring location of nineteenth-century imperialism even in the realms of the spectre, rather than seek an interpretation of the neo-Victorian spirit (in simultaneously ghostly, temperamental, and psychical senses) through contemporary novels' reworking of Victorian motifs, this essay instead seeks to provide a reflection on our sense of belatedness and the need to write out or exorcize our Victorian spirits in the contemporary sphere. My argument is that even as we are obsessed by knowing, summoning up and possessing/being possessed by the Victorians we are enacting a specifically nineteenth-century preoccupation with the spectral, s(p)ecular and reflective possibilities of the historical mirror, whether intact or 'crack'd'. While neo-Victorian novels may frequently debunk the Victorian belief in spirits and séances, their own narratives speak to the notions of spiritualism, mediumship, and the desire for a version of the Victorian afterlife; in this sense, the chapter also probes the issue of secularity then and now, and the problem of how contemporary fiction set in the nineteenth century can truly address the Victorian crisis of faith given our own post-Christian contexts. I begin with a brief discussion of the glass and spectral motifs in two recent pieces of Victorian criticism, which sets up the mirroring theories I want to use when turning my gaze to some reflections on the fictional neo-Victorian spectral text through the specific examples found in John Harwood's novels *The Ghost Writer* (2004) and *The Séance* (2008), Charles Palliser's *The Unburied* (1999), Jem Poster's *Courting Shadows* (2002) and Sarah Waters's *Affinity* (1999).

Glassworlds

Isobel Armstrong's most recent book, *Victorian Glassworlds* (2008), is a reflection on the cultural possibilities of reading the Victorians' fascination, even obsession, with glass as part of a wider metaphorical and metaphysical investigation of transparency as a political, social, and philosophical ideal. Armstrong's evocation of the nineteenth century's optical refraction through the idea of the 'Victorian glassworld' poses important questions about the nature of Victorian vision in multiple senses. As Armstrong writes, during this period:

> [a] scopic culture developed from the possibilities of just three vitreous elements combined and recombined, the glass panel, the mirror, and the lens. These had been available for centuries but they now took different forms. In the nineteenth century glass became a third or middle term: it interposed an almost invisible layer of matter between the seer and the seen – the sheen of a window, the silver glaze of the mirror, the convexity or concavity of the lens.
>
> (Armstrong, 2008, p. 3)

The 'middle term' of Armstrong's discussion, the intermediary state of window, mirror or lens, is, I would suggest, adaptable to the ways in which neo-Victorian literature sets up a mirror-like or reflective stance between our own period and that of the nineteenth century. The 'invisible layer of matter between the seer and the seen' could usefully be viewed as the textual layering of the contemporary novel and its Victorian narrative, the text becoming almost a glass permitting a double-viewed reflection. This double view and the visual sense of 'looking backwards' to the Victorians through contemporary lenses has been explored in several recent critical works, such as Simon Joyce's *The Victorians in the Rearview Mirror* (2007) and Cora Kaplan's *Victoriana: Histories, Fictions, Criticism* (2007). But while such analyses have explored the disconnected continuities and fragmentations of those reflections using a range of literary and cultural moments from recent years, very little has been written on the ways in which the neo-Victorian spectrality at work in several cases is in some respects a sinister reflection of our inability to recapture the Victorians, and the impossibility of see(k)ing to find the 'truth' of the period through either fiction or fact. Texts themselves become shadows, spectres and written ghosts which never quite materialize into substantive presences but instead remain masquerades or hoaxes of the 'real'.

Much of this impossibility or even inability to provide the 'proof' comes down to a sense of the antithetical nature of our religious or spiritual relationship with the Victorians. Patricia Duncker has recently spoken of the neo-Victorian novel's reticence concerning the discussion of the multiple crises of religious faith undergone in the nineteenth century.[1] Yet I would argue that both the failure to voice these crises and the dangers of overlooking them when they do occur in contemporary texts is to miss the 'small blemishes' in the glass which Armstrong writes about in a powerful discussion of the human presence of glass. Armstrong comments on this investment in the human nature of glass – not only in terms of its manufacture at a general level but through the way in which glass and its divinity, its magic, captured, in many respects, the 'ghostly' or spectral presence of its creator's breath – that:

[t]o look through glass in the mid-nineteenth century was most likely to look through and by means of the breath of an unknown artisan. The congealed residues of somebody else's breath remained in the window, decanter, and wineglass, traces of the workman's body in the common bottle, annealed in the

substance he worked. Held up to the light a piece of common nineteenth-century window glass will display small blemishes, blisters, almost invisible striae, spectral undulations that are the mark of bodily labour and a brief expectation of life.

(Armstrong, 2008, pp. 4–5)

Although Armstrong does not bring out the parallel explicitly here, there is a sense in which her description is related to the question of Victorian spiritualism and the desire to see the mist of the mirror both as human and spirit-like, divine and earthly. The mystical, even magical nature of the glass object is always a deception, just as the mirror is never a true reflection of reality. The textuality and materiality of the window, mirror, or lens is thus a filter through which imagination and difference might meet, as closely as possible, the true or authentic. In this respect, it is worth considering the ways in which the visuality of the spectral and textual is posited in contemporary fiction which has to deal with the contrary nature of Victorian experience and the potential contradictions of this to contemporary negotiations of the past. One way in which this happens is through the return to the Victorians' fascination with the potentialities of the spirit world and mediumship. Again, I think Armstrong's Victorian narrative is a useful lens here, particularly when she configures the nature of the duality of glass; as she writes, 'Glass is an antithetical material. It holds contrary states within itself as barrier and medium. The riddles it proposes arise from the logic of its material and sensuous nature' (Armstrong, 2008, p. 11). Such 'riddles', one might argue, are the core tensions of Victorian belief, drawn into the division between the stained glass window providing a pathway to God on the one hand, and the scientist's microscope exploring the evidence for human origins on the other.

This visuality is spectral and specular in the sense that it haunts by its very presence in and dislocation from the real. Although the mirror or glass sets up the difference between states – reality, mirage – and the spiritualism of the Victorians provides a similar binary – living, dead – these are nevertheless permeable barriers. 'Transparency', Armstrong comments, 'encourages a simple dualism, or, what is the opposite form of the same thing, the collapse of seer and seen into one another' (Armstrong, 2008, p. 11). Armstrong's suggestion here of the inherent ontological and epistemological tensions of glass bears relation to Julian Wolfreys's Derrida-influenced comments on the nature of spectrality itself. Wolfreys writes: '[t]he identification of spectrality appears in a gap between the limits of two ontological categories [...] by emerging between, and yet not as part of, two negations: *neither, nor*. A third term, the spectral, speaks of the limits of determination, while arriving beyond the terminal both in and of identification in either case (alive/dead)' (Wolfreys, 2002, p. x). Spectrality and glass, clarity and opacity, visibility and obscurity – all these terms are connected within the thread of the '(alive/dead)' parentheses of Wolfreys's statement and within those 'blemishes' of Armstrong's Victorian glassworlds. The danger of espousing a (neo-)Victorian liberal humanism is evident, but it appears in the following reading of neo-Victorian texts that it is precisely these elements, fragments, spectres, and dislocated visions of potential faith beyond the 'real world' that are at stake. Wolfreys's text demonstrates in different ways, but in some respects in a similar vein, the continuing hauntingness of the Victorian spectre at a textual level, ranging from Charles Dickens through to Virginia Woolf. As Wolfreys states in the series of questions at the beginning of his book, 'What does it mean to speak of spectrality and of textual haunting? What does it mean to address the text as haunted? How do the ideas of haunting and spectrality change our understanding of particular texts and the notion of the text in general?' (Wolfreys, 2002, p. ix) To these and in this specific context I would add 'What does it mean to write about Victorian spiritualism and/or faith in a neo-Victorian (con)text? What is it we want to see and in what do we desire to believe?'

Ghostwriting

A spectre is haunting the neo-Victorian novel. 'To speak of the spectral, the ghostly, of haunting in general', Wolfreys notes, 'is to come face to face with that which plays on the very question of interpretation and identification, which appears, as it were, at the very limit to which interpretation can go' (Wolfreys, 2002, pp. x–xi). In this context it is useful to think about how many neo-Victorian novels rely upon this sense of 'interpretation and identification'. Much neo-Victorianism winks knowingly at the reader who can recognize the allusion to other texts, and plays on the margins with a self-reflective and metafictional stance. Notable examples of this include Michael Cox's two novels *The Meaning of Night* (2005) and *The Glass of Time* (2008). The meta-authentic nature of the introductions and footnotes, provided by Cox's 'J. J. Antrobus, Professor of Post-Authentic Victorian Fiction' at the University of Cambridge, signal that just as the spectre is summoned through the text's mimicry so, too, is the suspicion of the investigation involved in the reading of the narrative. Jodey Castricano, in her discussion of Derrida's work, uses the term 'cryptomimesis' which 'draws attention to a writing predicated upon encryption: the play of revelation and concealment lodged within *parts* of individual works' (Castricano, 2001, p. 6). It is my contention in this chapter that much of the spectral nature of the play between ghostliness and writing in the novels I am discussing comes from this cryptomimetic method, that it constitutes a form of ghostwriting at multiple levels. One prominent figuring of this can be found in Sarah Waters's 1999 novel *Affinity* and it serves as a useful and brief way into the theme.

Waters's novel is set in and around Millbank prison in London in the 1870s and involves a dual narrative divided between the diary entries of two female protagonists. The novel is discussed in some detail in Ann Heilmann's essay in this book (see also Llewellyn, 2004), and so here I want only to draw attention to the scopic metaphor in Waters's text at two important moments. The first occurs when Margaret has just taken up her duties as a lady visitor at Millbank, and involves one of the female wardens telling her about the therapeutic nature of observing the prisoners. Margaret writes in her diary that: 'She said she had never had a visitor yet that didn't like to stand at that window and watch the women walk. It was as curative, she thought, as gazing at fish in a tank. After that, I moved from the glass' (Waters, 2000, p. 17). What is important at this moment is that we are watching Margaret through her own narrative as she is repulsed by the idea of watching and being watched. The move away from the glass cannot be enacted against the reader's observation of Margaret and, in the act of recording it in her diary, Margaret draws attention to her inability really to understand the nature of scopic power. This is fundamental to our perception of the nature of the trick which Waters plays on her readers later in the text, for the clue, the cryptomimetic line, is there for us to follow from the earliest point of the narrative. What we are faced with, however, is a desire to believe, to place our faith in the act of storytelling itself and our unbounded trust in the spectral narrator of the text.

While observation and looking is the key to *Affinity*, we don't really 'see' what is presented to us. Indeed, in terms of spectrality we are blind to the Marxist implications of the term. For what we see(k) in this version of neo-Victorian fiction is satisfaction for our interest in the Victorians and their hidden sexuality. We ignore the original 'spectres of Marx' declared in *The Communist Manifesto* ('A spectre is haunting the continent of Europe') when we fail to realize that the servant in the household carries the key to the narrative. This exploitation of our cultural weak spots (inherited from the Victorians, like so much else?) serves to play in a sophisticated way with the spectral presences we will permit ourselves to see and those we will not. We are prepared, potentially, to suspend our disbelief through the narrative of *Affinity* and believe that Selina is able to contact the spirit world and transplant herself to Margaret's bedroom rather than acknowledge the presence of the servant woman Ruth Vigers. In the scene where Margaret realizes that the locket she places on the dressing-table mirror every night has gone, we, like she, want to believe in the spectral otherness of the misted mirror: 'It [the water] was not quite chill, but it had misted the looking-glass; and as I wiped that I looked, for I always looked, for my locket. – *My locket was gone!* and I cannot say where' (Waters, 2000, p. 90; original emphasis). The desire to place faith in what that 'misted … looking-glass' might represent places both Margaret and the reader at a disadvantage. It serves to deflect our attention away from the figure in the background, the 'presence' inside the mirror and behind Margaret as she looks into the glass. The clarity with which Margaret does not see into the mirror reveals our own selectiveness when examining what lies in that 'rearview mirror' in cultural and social terms, too.

At both the margins and the core of Waters's novel is the figure of Margaret Prior's father, the professional historian George Prior. Invoked as muse to his daughter's journal ('I wish that Pa was with me now'; Waters, 1999, p. 7), Prior also features – as the surname indicates – as a haunting presence in the narrative at key moments, and may even be the character whose breath she also desires to have clouded that mirror (she is dreaming of him just before this moment). The second novel I want to look at also features professional historians, not in the sphere of the prison but in the equally cloistered and entrapping narrative of ghosts, faith, and spectrality in the cathedral close.

Charles Palliser's *The Unburied* is, like the 'so-called restoration work' (Palliser, 1999, p. 19) being undertaken on the cathedral at its heart, a text which attempts to reconstruct the possibilities of Victorian narrative technique through an able pastiche of the late-Victorian/Edwardian ghost story. The novel is centred round the Cambridge scholar Dr Courtine's Christmas visit to Thurchester to stay with an old friend from whom he has been estranged for two decades. His friend, Austin, tells him the story of murderous rivalry from the town's history during the English Revolution, although the historian Courtine is actually seeking to discover a manuscript in Thurchester's cathedral archives. This unseen manuscript is doubted to even exist by many of Courtine's fellow scholars, and his burning desire to unearth its narrative is driven not only by scholarship but personal rivalry with another academic. Academics, college politics, the world of the cloister history, superstition and folklore, facts and authentication of the evidence: all these elements are blurred in Palliser's narrative, which carries the spectre of the ghost stories of M. R. James and the unreliable narrative strategies of Henry James in *The Turn of the Screw* (1898). The narratives of both Jameses are of course 'spectral texts' in their own right; each looks back to an earlier period and dislocates a sense of textual time and historicity from the present moment of the act of story telling. In the case of Henry James this is via reminiscence, and in the work of M. R. James it is to be found in the fact that his stories are themselves haunted in their Edwardian looks backward to a late-Victorian past.

Like many neo-Victorian novels, Palliser's text often provides a metafictional commentary on the nature of historical fiction writing and the reasons behind our readerly (and writerly) desires to evoke the spectral text. As the Dean of Thurchester's wife, Mrs Locard, asks Courtine: 'Don't you think that we read our own desires into the figures from the past about whom we reflect because, as erring mortals, we cannot be dispassionate?' (Palliser, 1999, p. 135) Passion in the sense of intellectual craving, physical desire and Christian theology is a loaded term in this text, which contains many disquisitions on the nature of faith and religious belief. Earlier in the text, Courtine engages in a debate with his former friend Austin about precisely such matters. Austin, once a 'Tractarian of a very dandyish kind' (Palliser, 1999, p. 36), is placed into contrast with Courtine and his 'conviction that religion was a conspiracy of the powerful against the rest' (Palliser, 1999, p. 36). What most dispirits Courtine is Austin's articulation of religion as the placing of faith in narratives, in story. As Austin declares, 'without faith, all you have is superstition. Fear of the dark, of ghosts, of the realm of death which continues to frighten us, whatever we believe. We need stories to stop us being frightened. You've created your comforting myths and fictions from history ... You are creating your own stories to console you' (Palliser, 1999, p. 37). While Courtine admits that he respects the morality of Christianity, it is historical truth, the verifiable fact and documentary evidence that holds a higher power over his view of the world. In many ways what the text explores is Courtine's inability and even reluctance to look more closely into the glass and imagine something beyond the temporal; it is a narrative as much concerned with secularity as specularity. Austin, however, too willingly proposes the confidence in the act of faith:

> What I'm talking about is faith, belief, acceptance of the absolute reality of salvation and damnation. You – and others of our generation – lost your faith because you decided that science can explain everything. I believed that myself for a while but I came to understand that reason and faith are not in conflict. They are different orders of reality. Although I understand that now, when I was younger I shared your error. I know now that because there is darkness, there is light. That because there is death, there is life. Because there is evil, there is goodness. Because there is damnation, there is redemption.
>
> (Palliser, 1999, p. 37)

The restoration metaphor is at work here again, and in the religious sense. There is the dialectic of the mirror or shadow in evidence, too. The view of the contraries that prove the existence of the othered and yet corollary counter state demonstrates that sense of faith in a balanced, ordered, rational, and structured universe. One can believe, this argument follows, even if one cannot know, and one might think again of Armstrong here and the description of the 'antithetical material' nature of glass in the period, holding two contrary states in a unified object. Austin's thinking is glass-like in this respect, and posits a kind of spectral logic which Courtine finds uncomfortable. This unease is of course something which is also reflected in our own contemporary relationship to the spiritual and the secular, and it raises the important question of how we address those issues of faith and belief that so fundamentally informed the Victorians' approaches to the world.

One of the key moments of Palliser's novel occurs when the narrator undergoes a momentary vision which throws into question his dogmatic non-belief in the world of the spirit. Dreamlike but also nightmarish, the vision of Dr Courtine is itself centred around the idea of observation and the specularity of glass:

> When I glanced up at the organ-loft I suddenly became aware of where I was and had no idea how much time had passed or how I had got to where I found myself. Over the edge of the rail was a pale spot in the darkness and as I watched, it resolved itself into a face which seemed to be gazing straight at me. A cold, white, empty face with eyes that were two pieces of glass – empty and yet they seemed to peer into me. They looked through my soul – or rather my lack of a soul for they found or created an answering emptiness within me. It was the face of a creature not of our world. How long we stared at each other – or rather I stared at him for I cannot be sure that he was looking at me – I have no means of knowing. The face disappeared and I seemed to awake with a shudder and in a cold sweat, and it was at that moment that I reconstructed the sequence of events. I had an idea about who it was that I had seen, but I could not accept it. Everything I knew and believed would be thrown into confusion [...] I had seen William Burgoyne. I was sure of it. In that case, the world was not as I had imagined it. The dead could walk again, for a man who had died two hundred years ago had appeared before me. That meant that all that I believed – all the decent, rational, progressive ideas by which I lived – were childish games that could only be played in the daylight.
>
> (Palliser, 1999, pp. 151–2, 153)

The protagonist's desire to question, the scholarly pursuit of truth, and yet the anxiety about the nature of material reality, have always been representative of the mid-Victorian angst of the characters represented in the narrative. As Catherine Belsey comments, using Freud's theories of the uncanny and supernatural, such 'supernatural events [...] are not in themselves uncanny: magic, apparitions, spectres and secret powers do not disturb us when they appear in fairy tales [...]. But their occurrence in what seems like realism, when the Gothic invades the mimetic, produces a degree of unease' (Belsey, 2004, p. 9). The unease is shared here by both character and reader at the same level as such supernatural interventions work in the ghost stories of M. R. James, Sheridan LeFanu, Conan Doyle and numerous other Victorian writers of suspense. By interposing the spectral into the secular imagination of Courtine at this moment in the novel, Palliser reconfigures the doubt of the Victorians into not a questioning of the one true church but into a challenge to rationalism and secularity itself. For if seeing is believing, then the hallucinatory status or otherwise of Courtine's vision changes the status of the narrative perspective on the tale.

However, there is the possibility in this passage that Palliser's trickery is to dupe the unsuspecting reader at this point into questioning the narrator's reliability, perhaps even his sanity. For him to visualize such a thing as a ghost from several centuries before is in many ways a clichéd element of the narrative. The conviction of being unable to determine what is seen but to then leap to the most (ir)rational conclusion is symptomatic of the claustrophobic tales of M. R. James, with his scholars driven to distraction by an inability to read logically the evidence before them. What I would like to suggest, however, is that this moment of vision is ambiguous and plays with the identity of the author as much as the narrator or a character within the text in a kind of imitation of John Fowles's self-portrayal in sections of *The French Lieutenant's Woman* (1969). In an interview with Susana Onega published in 1993 after the appearance of his epic *The Quincunx* (1989), Palliser commented that 'although [Fowles's novel] is a very clever, witty book, [...] there is too much of Fowles coming and explaining and there are times when you really want him to leave the reader alone with the characters' (Onega, 1993, p. 281). Despite this criticism of Fowles's technique of interventionist narrative, Palliser's novel's knowingness, such as when one character says to another that 'we don't exist in and for ourselves but only in as much as we are re-created in the imagination of another person' (Palliser, 1999, p. 62), indicates a certain playfulness about the idea of this spectral presence in Courtine's dreamlike vision. The spectre is the figure of the neo-Victorian novelist, acting as the medium conjuring forth the spirits of the dead literature through pastiche, and also spectrally haunting those characters; the author is not entirely dead, but he is a representative of the living dead (in multiple senses) within the text itself.

This is not made clear to the reader, and part of the reason for this may be found in another statement made by Palliser in the same interview that fiction is 'not expository, it's actually experiential. You are not told things. You are actually made to feel them' (Onega, 1993, p. 282). This 'experiential' moment in the reading of the neo-Victorian text is evidently present in Courtine's description of the 'creature' he 'sees'. His unease within the environment is reflected back to the reader but is also received through that reader's awareness of a large range of previous ghost stories. It thus becomes not only a reflection but a refraction through the lens as contemporary readers speculate on the contemporary writer's attempt to capture the spectrality of the Victorian ghost tale. In the absence of the Victorians' omniscient God – who was of course replaced in many ways by the omniscient narrator of classic high realism – we might have instead the spectral presence of the neo-Victorian writer, ghosting an identity in both present and past.

There is also a continual play being enacted here on the idea of the spectral and reflection as imagination and thought as well as image and presence. Jem Poster's *Courting Shadows* (2002), another story about the idea of restoration and returning to the past at community and individual levels, provides a useful example of this in a scene where two characters argue over the 'reality' of the past even down to its very fabric. Having discovered a coffin while undertaking excavation and modernization work in a remote English village, the minister, Banks, declares, 'I want you to experience the active presence of the past, to know this object [a brass coffin-plate] as it really is, charged with the energies of other lives' (Poster, 2002, p. 58). There is an inevitable irony here – made clear very soon after as we read 'when you disturb the dead, you disturb the living too' (Poster, 2002, p. 60) – in the idea that one holds a coffin-plate to connect with the living. But alternatively, Poster's character is correct to see the coffin-plate and its inscription as a textual haunting and a moment of spectrality which can act as a pertinent and physical memento mori.

The connectiveness between past and present and the idea of the spectral as a virtual embodiment of that coercion between living and dead is fundamental to the way in which we look through that distorting glass back to the Victorians. Indeed, what we might be seeking in the spectral summoning-up of the Victorian narrative in contemporary fiction is precisely distortion, both of our own period and the nineteenth century. I want to move on now to two recent novels by the novelist John Harwood which for me underline the tensions I am trying to articulate concerning the relationship between the spectral, the scriptural (in both religious and authorial senses), and the spiritual. *The Ghost Writer* (2004) and *The Séance* (2008) are both novels which explore the ways in which individuals seek to make a connection with the past through narrative, and how the desire to acknowledge and even embrace the sense of being haunted is frequently re-enacted at a textual level. They are also novels about faith at different levels.

The Ghost Writer is the story of Gerard Freeman, a teenager in Mawson, Australia. Gerard lives with his mother in a kind of hermetic sphere, socially and culturally obscured from the world around them. While rummaging in his mother's room one day, Gerard discovers a manuscript, 'just a thick bundle of pages with typewriting on them, tied together with rusty black ribbon. As I drew out the bundle, a photograph slid into my lap' (Harwood, 2005, p. 4). This photograph proves just as important as the manuscript because of the way it stimulates Gerard's interest in his maternal history. As such, it represents the visual and textual as a spectral combination which releases an uncanny sense of the real captured in the imagined. Gerard's narrative voice comments that 'the woman in the photograph was calm and beautiful and *alive*, more alive than anyone I had ever seen in a picture' (Harwood, 2005, p. 5; original emphasis), and we are reminded of the Victorian attraction to photography as a means of containing and not just representing an aspect of the spirit.

Such echoes of the nineteenth century in a text partly set in contemporary Australia and London and partly figured through the 1890s and mid-twentieth century, are layered at a textual as well as visual level. The text plays with the invocation of symbolic acts of naming, so that Gerard's female pen pal in the UK (and around whom much of the mystery will later centre) is called Alice Jessell. In terms of spectrality and looking glasses, of course, Harwood is able to bring into the frame of reference Carroll's Alice and James's deviant governess. Like the reader, Gerard, himself a bookish child, is haunted by the presence of these earlier women, especially the governess: as he puts it, 'I wouldn't be able to look at her without thinking of Miss Jessell [...] with her dead white face and long black dress' (Harwood, 2005, p. 75). Blurring in the imagination both his real friend and the fictional character, Gerard presents us with a mirror to our own annotative awareness of the past signalled in such acts of homage. Alice will later write to Gerard that she does not 'want to be <u>fixed</u> by a picture' (Harwood 2005, p. 25; original emphasis), so that the surrogacies of the imagination have to stand in for reality.

Gerard's account of his delvings into his family history, the releasing death of his mother, and his burgeoning relationship with Alice through letters (again, textuality will prove fundamental to the unlocking of the inherited mystery in a cryptomimetic manner) is interleaved with a series of Vernon Lee-esque short stories written by his great-grandmother, Viola Hatherley, also the author of the manuscript first discovered by Gerard at the novel's start. The stories are always signed off as by 'V. H.' and have plots which conjure up late-Victorian gothic with titles such as 'Seraphina', 'The Gift of Flight', 'The Revenant', and 'The Pavillion'. What transpires is the realization when Gerard comes to London and finds the Hatherley house that the tales are not fictions but histories, ghost stories in the sense that they provide him with the investigative and interpretative clues (to use both Wolfreys and the idea of the 'cyptomimetic' text). The narrative – and it is difficult not to write about its conclusion without giving away a stunning denouement – reveals that it is not the supernatural but the scientific, not the past of the late-Victorian period but the more modern techniques of the early twentieth century, that are at the root of the Hatherley family story. As such, Harwood's text enacts a kind of double-cross on the reader: see(k)ing the horrors of the pastiche Victorian ghost story we are instead confronted with a spectral fabrication, a slippage between the narrative desires in which we place so much faith and suspended disbelief and the more terrifying technological realities of the modern world.

In this sense one might draw a comparison between what the neo-Victorian novelist seeks to do in narrative returns to the fractured faith of the Victorians and the recent work of the critic George Levine. Levine, at the outset of his 2006 book *Darwin Loves You*, which is about Darwin and contemporary society, states that 'Evolution by natural selection seems to have removed both meaning and consolation from the world; those who discovered it and who now argue for it often engage in a kind of triumphal rationalism that treads all affective and extramaterial explanation underfoot. It is one thing to believe that science can explain the movement of the stars or even the composition of matter; it is quite another to believe that science can explain human nature itself, and all the disorderly intricacies of human life' (Levine, 2006, p. 1). Levine's statements on the issue of re-enchantment in particular highlight a potential connection with the need publicly to rethink the Victorians' own relationship to religion and science, faith and doubt. The neo-Victorian novel itself often runs the danger of debunking faith without the kind of subtleties and nuances of thought and rationality that are frequently emblematic of the nineteenth century's own debates on these matters. Harwood's text and the narrator's concluding realization, 'half a life too late, [of] the enormity of my delusion' (Harwood, 2005, p. 372), might thus reflect something about our own delusions in the faith we place in the neo-Victorian text and its in many respects too-comforting treatment of the spectral. Like the Victorian fraudster mediums pulling out all the stops in the hoax séance, we are complicit in the fakery of the text and its summoning of the haunted and haunting past.

Harwood's second novel, *The Séance*, is more firmly set in the Victorian period but this still allows for a set of spectral and textual tricks to take place in his re-visioning of the clichéd haunted mansion trope. Divided between four first-person accounts of different stages in the mystery surrounding Wraxford Hall and its history of alchemical, necromancing, and mesmerist inhabitants, Harwood's text is at its most knowing when it plays with our rationalized response to the Victorian obsession with spiritualism and the afterlife. Thus, the central female figure and first/last narrator, Constance Langton, writes of her atheist father's disapproval of the tenets of spiritualism: 'I had already begun to suspect that Papa did not believe in God [...] [when] I discovered that the book he had been writing for so long was called *Rational Foundations of Morality*' (Harwood, 2008, p. 12). Mr Langton's book is designed to demonstrate that one should behave morally irrespective of the existence of God or an afterlife, something Constance thinks is common sense. It is also something which we are encouraged to endorse in the sense that the narrative positions us to hold true to our own rationalist, postmodern, and post-Christian perspectives on such matters. Yet Langton's rationalism is undermined very early on with his decision to leave his wife and Constance. At this point, the text almost suggests that cool rationalism is what undermines human interaction, rather than the less harmful faith in spirits and the beyond.

As with *The Ghost Writer*, reading plays a key function in the narrative not only as we bring together the diverse range of stories but also in the earliest descriptions of Constance Langton's life. She views her childhood world as a 'kind of limbo state in which I was free to read whatever I wished, and walk wherever I wanted, whilst at the same time feeling that nobody would care if I vanished from the face of the earth' (Harwood, 2008, p. 12). Constance thus presents herself very much as a spectre, and later in the novel reading and mesmerism almost go together in the metatextual comment that '[i]n the deepest state of trance [...] a subject could be instructed to see scenes and persons who were not actually present' (Harwood, 2008, p. 71). It is hard not to read this as a statement about narrative and the textual nature of the spectral along the lines of some of the earlier material I have discussed. Mesmerism is closely aligned to the idea of reading in this text, with Magnus Wraxford, the key spiritualist of the novel, described by his future wife Eleanor Unwin as having 'a slightly Mephistophelean air, and dark eyes of remarkable luminosity. Though George had said he was handsome, the sheer force of his presence took me by surprise. The saying that eyes are the windows of the soul flitted across my mind as I extended my hand, but I had the discomfiting sensation, as our fingers touched, that my own soul had become momentarily transparent to his gaze' (Harwood, 2008, p. 109). Reflection and observation are central once more but within this broad conceptualization of the power of the séance is, as in *The Ghost Writer*, an emphasis on science and trickery. While necromancy, mesmerism, the 'morbid fear of death' and 'the alchemists' quest for the elixir of life' (Harwood, 2008, p. 58) are presented as themes throughout the novel, they are always delivered in a knowing, non-believing way.

As readers we are regularly encouraged to invoke both scepticism and faith in Constance's narrative and those she assembles from other characters such as the respectable village solicitor John Montague. Yet Constance has already confessed to us early in the text that she has faked spiritual trances. When her father leaves, one of the reasons for his departure is the obsessive nature of his wife's hankering for com-

munication from their dead child, Constance's sister. After Langton's
desertion, Constance pretends to enter a trance in order to reassure
her mother of her dead sister's happiness in the world beyond. But
the performance proves too strongly convincing for Mrs Langton
and she commits suicide to rejoin her child in paradise, leaving
a note beside her 'empty bottle of laudanum ... which read, "Forgive
me – I could not wait"' (Harwood, 2008, p. 31). Harwood's ironic
comment on the desire to place faith in the easily ventriloquized
and *faux* authentic contact between the living and the dead is, one
cannot help but read into it, also a reflection once more upon our
own readerly yearning for the Victorian novel itself. Just as Harwood
masquerades as Constance and the other narrative voices, so his
characters in turn imitate their parts from older Victorian narratives.
Harwood even begins his novel with a para-textual nod towards
the fakery before it starts by a quotation from *Revelations of a Spirit
Medium* (1891), a real text from the period, which explains how to
'manifest a spirit' using silk in 'a darkened room'. There is thus a kind
of suggestiveness about the functions of the spectral in these texts
and Harwood's awareness of the late-Victorian questioning both after
spiritualism and the truths it might reveal but also the investigations
into the faked performance of such séances via bodies such as the
Society for Psychical Research. Is Harwood asking us to place our faith
in his novel's ability to mimic, medium-like, the period in which it
is set? Or is he instead asking us to think about why we continue to
want these spirits to be summoned before us? Writing on A. S. Byatt's
paired neo-Victorian novellas published as *Angels and Insects*, Hilary
Schor comments that 'Byatt, like any brave New Historicist, is trying
to talk with the dead' (Schor, 2001, p. 247). It reads to me as if Palliser,
Waters, and Harwood – to name just the three I have looked at in this
chapter – are instead trying to use ghosts and the spectral to talk with
the living. Metafictional texts, by their very nature, are more about
the moment of their writing than the setting of that writing, and
metahistorical novels, the genre into which often the most interesting and stimulating neo-Victorian fiction falls, are as much concerned
with the historical moment that is now as they are with the nineteenth century. By casting the fiction and the fakery of the séance, of
the ghost and of the spectral itself back to us as contemporary readers,
Harwood and others are multilayering the notion of textual haunt-

ing, and possibly even challenging our 'faith' in the postmodern text and its own séance-like trickeries.

Towards the end of Harwood's novel our attention is turned to Whitby and the discovery of the truth of the mystery. It is of course an ideal location, being the site of Dracula's landing. The space where the classic representative of the undead and vampiric arrives in England is suitably ironic as the home of the woman everyone believes to be either dead or a murderess in Harwood's text. But this knowingness – our knowledge when reading this neo-Victorian fiction of the appropriateness of this place's literary significance for a late-Victorian reader eight years after the latest narrative within this novel is set – is part of the spectral show. For what it hints towards is that imperceptible but ever present spirit behind the best of the neo-Victorian genre of wanting to be fooled. While Wolfreys's views on the spectral may be correct for a reading of the Victorians, and Castricano's 'cryptomimetic' theory is evidently supported by these texts, neither truly accommodates the sense of s(p)ecular faith we place into the novels themselves, and our presence at the table rapping as both spirit and believer.

(W)Rapping up

What both John Harwood's novels illustrate is the duality of the neo-Victorian encounter with the spectral or ghostly. Just as neo-Victorian writers are eager to explore (and one might even say exploit) the popular perception of the late nineteenth century as a period of the séance, of spiritualists and mediums, and of arcane returns to mysteries of religious practice and faith in the possibility of immortality, so, too, they must indicate a prominent scepticism and knowingness towards any such ideas. The repeated invocation of Victorian spiritualism, mesmerism, and mediumship in these texts, even when it promotes the conclusion that the spirit realm is a false consolation for a period grappling with the disparate theories of the world embodied in religion and science, is striking. The metafictional possibilities for writers to provide a subtle commentary on their own practice in conjuring up or summoning the Victorians in contemporary fiction are clear. However, what becomes less distinct in that misted-over glass is whether these anxious alliances with a Victorian tradition of the unexplained, the ghostly, and the secular faith of the spirit world is consciously attempting to underline the spectral and in essence 'faked' nature of the neo-Victorian text. Do these novels coax us with their hoaxes just as the Selina Dawes of the 1870s to 1910s duped a susceptible public eager for ghosts to replace the debunked God of the Western centuries? Or do they represent a kind of commentary on the need to believe, to look back and to be reassured that the past lives on, continually keeping those Victorian shadows part of our present?

Ultimately, these texts all present an uneasy sense of the Victorians looking forward to us just as much as we look back towards them, and indicate, however fleetingly, the potential substantiveness of those spectres in the glass. The awkward fear of religiosity or faith in the Tennysonian sense, the exploration of true existential crises, is not at the root of the presence (or possibility) of the phantasmagoric in the contemporary text. Instead, writers are demonstrating an increasing sensitivity to the idea that their publications are the equivalent now of the séances and communications with the dead then. Through pastiche and re-visioning, through the mesmeric nature of rereading, the ghost writers of the present are playing an ambiguous game with a contemporary readership hungry for the summoned spirit of a Victorian fiction they believe in. And yet as a character in Harwood's latest novel puts it, 'Truly it is said, that he who attends a séance in the medium's house is asking to be deceived' (Harwood, 2008, p. 237).

Note

1. Keynote lecture delivered at the 'Adapting the Nineteenth Century' conference, University of Wales, Lampeter, August 2008. This essay was already in draft before Duncker's paper, but I am very grateful to her for the conversation we had about the possibilities of a 'neo-Tractarian' text, and for her confirmation concerning the perhaps troubling absence of religious crises in neo-Victorianism arising in part from our post-Christian framework.

Part II Spectral Women

3
Repetition and Eternity: The Spectral and Textual Continuity in Michèle Roberts's *In the Red Kitchen*

Agnieszka Golda-Derejczyk

> The universal teaching of modern spiritualism is
> that the world and the whole material universe exist
> for the purpose of developing spiritual beings – that
> death is simply a transition from material existence
> to the first grade of spirit-life – and that our happi-
> ness and the degree of our progress will be wholly
> dependent upon the use we have made of our facul-
> ties and opportunities here.[1]

The nineteenth century offers a captivating reservoir of topics for contemporary novelists engaged in the process of recreating and re-imagining the Victorian world, among which are: religious *angst* and the dilemmas of science; the impact of the Industrial Revolution; emerging discourses of sexuality, illness, and medicine; the myster-ies of the Victorian underworld; nineteenth-century technology; and women's emancipation. It thus seems logical that a significant part of what constitutes a Victorian zeitgeist, that is the Victorian interest in the paranormal – mesmerism, spiritualism, telepathy, or hallucination – has also found its way onto the pages of the neo-Victorian novel. Practices of spiritualism and mesmerism, and other psychic phenomena have entered the nineteenth-century plotlines of contemporary historical fiction. Novels as diverse as A. S Byatt's *Possession* (1990) and *Angels and Insects* (1992), Michèle Roberts's *In the Red Kitchen* (1990), Peter Carey's *Jack Maggs* (1997), Sarah Waters's *Affinity* (1999), Colm Tóibín's *The Master* (2004), or Julian Barnes's *Arthur and George* (2005), to name just a few – all, in one way or another, employ the themes of spiritualism and haunting. Yet, the haunting presence of ghosts or mediums in this type of historical novel serves purposes beyond merely satiating current tastes or fashions. By introducing the spiritual, the paranormal, or the supernatural into their narratives, contemporary novelists seek to bring a variety of social and cultural questions to the fore. These are often questions which, though relating to the nineteenth century, demonstrate current relevance.

Michèle Roberts's 1990 revisionist novel, *In the Red Kitchen*, introduces the themes of spiritualism and mediumship precisely to address the social and cultural politics of gender. The interpretative and metaphorical potential of nineteenth-century spiritualism and haunting furnishes here a useful tool to problematize the question of women as subjects *in* and *of* history. The novel therefore seems to have deliberately avoided a singular narrative voice, instead relegating the task of storytelling to various voices with a view to representing women's history as a sum of personal experiences. For this reason, too, and to stage a confrontation between the past and the present, the narrative is split between the contemporary age, the Victorian period, and that of ancient Egypt. The novel's central theme of spiritualism, situated strategically in the Victorian age, serves as a unifying principle, bringing other female subjectivities together, thus creating a specific spectral continuity between the past (ancient Egypt, Victorian England) and the present (contemporary London), and functions as a point of convergence between women's experiences of maltreatment, discrimination, and self-writing. This essay intends to look at the way in which spiritualism is employed fruitfully by Roberts to (re)construct the history of women as governed by the cyclical and monumental modalities of time – eternity and repetition, respectively – posited by Julia Kristeva in her 1979 essay 'Women's Time', where she discusses the stages in the development of the feminist movement.

Rosie White, in her (2004) article 'Visions and Re-visions: Women and Time in Michèle Roberts's *In the Red Kitchen*', has also noticed the interpretative potential of Kristeva's text in reading Roberts's novel. For White, both the critical text and the novel comment on the need to 'change our understanding of sexual identity in order to avoid the old order reasserting itself' (2004, p. 180). In this sense, she argues, the two works remain 'in conversation with each other' (2004, p. 180). In Kristeva's psychoanalytical reading of the historical development of the women's movement in the twentieth century, the three generations of feminism correspond to the three positions in the development of female subjectivity at the Oedipal stage before entering the social order. These positions, in short, are: paternal 'symbolic' identification; attachment to the maternal, the 'semiotic' (that is, a predominance of the maternal modality); and last – the dialogic position between the two, as Pam Morris argues, 'on the threshold between control and disruption' (Morris, 1993, p. 151). For Rosie White, the women's three temporal perspectives in Roberts's novel represent these generations of women and the three positions in Kristeva's reading of the relation between the symbolic and the semiotic. White argues that if the first generation of women (in the novel represented by Hat King of Ancient Egypt) 'privileges the masculine symbolic in the form of linear time', the second generation (represented by Victorian Flora) embraces the feminine as a space outside temporal linearity, a utopian otherness' (White, 2004, p. 185). White, however, defies an uncomplicated parallelism between Kristeva's proposition and Roberts's narrative realization of these ideas. In her understanding, Roberts's novel does not constitute a simple demonstration of these opposite strategies, but rather 'an indication of potential' (White, 2004, p. 188), in which the most contemporary character, Hattie, may represent Kristeva's third generation that 'can see beyond the masculine symbolic and the feminine a-topic' (White, 2004, p. 188).

Such a reading, where the novel's three female voices are perceived as mapped onto the three generations of feminism posited in Kristeva's 1979 essay, is clearly legitimate. However, what I wish to show in this essay are the metaphorical possibilities of exploring Kristeva's proposition on the relation between female subjectivity and the modalities of time: cyclical and monumental temporalities. I intend to demonstrate how in this context the dimensions of spiritualism, mediumship, and writing as self-inscription function to promote the history of women as a collection of shared experiences, a dialectic across time and space, one where a frequent failure at communication cannot of course be avoided, as White rightly points out in her essay. Additionally, through the reference to the mediumistic activity of passive writing, Roberts's novel also explores a textual continuity – the potent bond between writing and living, between self-inscription and self-definition. *In the Red Kitchen* may thus serve as an illustration of both spectral and textual aspects of a constructed continuity between the past and the present.

Repetition and eternity: Spectral and textual continuity

To write is to enter the mysterious, powerful world of words to partake of words' power, to make it work for me. To write is to deny the power of death, to triumph over it. To inscribe a person's name on the wall of his tomb, to describe his attributes thereupon, is to ensure that he will live forever. As the tombs cut into the rock is the doorway to eternal life [...]. Words mean life. The absence of words means death: being forgotten by men for all eternity.

Michèle Roberts, *In the Red Kitchen*

As for time, female subjectivity would seem to provide a specific measure that essentially retains repetition and eternity from among the multiple modalities of time known through the history of civilizations.

Julia Kristeva, *Women's Time*

In the Red Kitchen intertwines its various women's stories across historical and spatial divides. The historical, but at the same time personal, perspectives seem to change here like photographs in a kaleidoscope revealing, in the first person accounts, the obsessions of each temporal age: eternity and immortality in Ancient Egypt, spiritualism in the nineteenth century; and a reconstruction of identity in the contemporary age. Although dissimilar at first sight, these obsessions seem to have a common source: an attempt at defining female subjectivity vis-à-vis the prevailing social and cultural order of the specific time, whether it is the law of the father in Ancient Egypt, the male-dominated world of science and medicine in Victorian England, or the twentieth-century socio-economic milieu. The novel offers three historical perspectives, but five narrating voices, three of which belong to women in the Victorian age, the novel's historical backbone. They belong to: Flora Milk, the Victorian working-class medium;[2] her sister and assistant, but later also a rival, Rosina Milk;[3] and finally Minnie Preston, the epitome of Victorian womanhood, and the wife of William Preston. The Prestons' house becomes home for the two sisters so that Minnie can use Flora's invaluable spiritualist skills in her private séances to reconcile herself with her dead daughter's spirit, while William, an investigator into hysteria and spiritualism, can conduct his scientific research into psychic phenomena and carry out experiments on Flora. Flora, who contacts the spirits through her spirit-guide Hattie, serves also as a point of convergence for the other two women characters and storytellers in the novel: Hattie, the contemporary woman, who has just moved into the house in Bayswater once resided in by Flora Milk, and Hat King, 'sole daughter of the Pharaoh, sole princess of the blood royal of the Two Kingdoms of Egypt' (Roberts, 1990, p. 8), obsessed with securing herself an eternal life. Thus the two Hatties may in fact form a single person; the contemporary Hattie could be interpreted as a reincarnation of the Pharaoh's daughter, who thus manages to remain eternal, or, conversely, Hat of Ancient Egypt may figure in the modern Hattie's childhood fantasies as a projection of herself, a double onto whom the unacceptable experiences of the past suffered by little Hattie (sexually abused by her uncle) can be projected (Hat King is sexually abused by her father). In her account the modern Hattie recollects how after the instances of abuse 'at night, in [her] narrow white bed encircled by white curtains, [she] escaped into another country called Egypt where [she] was king' (Roberts, 1990, p. 135). Furthermore, her house is frequented by the ghost of Flora; and Hattie, encountering Flora's grave during a walk at the cemetery and realizing she once lived in the house, wants to name her daughter after the Victorian medium, thus enabling Flora's reincarnation. The novel thus displays an intention to construct female subjectivity and women as subjects in history by highlighting ideas of continuity and repetition; converting the personal into the political, collapsing the private into the public, and focusing on the ex-centric,[4] rather than the central.

In 'Women's Time', Kristeva observes that 'female subjectivity would seem to provide a specific measure that essentially retains *repetition* and *eternity* [original emphasis] from among the multiple modalities of time known through the history of civilizations' (Kristeva, 1993, p. 445). 'On the one hand', she writes, 'there are cycles, gestation, the eternal recurrence of a biological rhythm which conforms to that of nature'; on the other, 'there is the massive presence of monumental temporality, without cleavage or escape, which has little to do with linear time', but is rather 'all-encompassing and infinite like imaginary space' (Kristeva, 1993, p. 445). This latter modality of time, Kristeva further observes, evokes 'various myths of resurrection which, in all religious beliefs, perpetuate the vestige of an anterior or concomitant maternal cult' (Kristeva, 1993, p. 445). The two types of temporality she calls cyclical and monumental, and indeed the two modalities of repetition and eternity become pivotal for the novel's several themes.

The idea of repetition finds its realization in Roberts's novel on two related levels: the first, more literal level, where the modality of repetition evokes the specificities of the female body: cycles, gestation, birth-giving, as outlined by Kristeva; and the second, metaphorical level where cyclical temporality refers to the idea of shared experience that does not know the boundaries of time or space. It can thus imply eternity, or infinity, or, to use other words, it is a point at which the two modalities merge. The first level thus refers to these women's life stories as separate units, one cycle from birth to death; on the second, and more profound level, the women's stories are to be construed as a repetition of a repetition, a cycle within which an infinite number of cycles take place. The novel represents on its narrative level the points of intersection between these various individual cycles to form a history of women's experience as continuity.

In *In the Red Kitchen* the women's shared experience of the loss of a child, sexual abuse, humiliation, and passive subjection make these points of intersection. The modern Hattie loses her daughter due to a miscarriage; the Victorian Flora, who lived well into the twentieth century, loses her son in a war; while Minnie Preston, though in constant mourning, may have murdered her own child, as Flora's séances reveal. Similarly, the torment of sexual abuse manifests itself with a cyclical regularity in the novel: starting from the incestuous relationship Hat King had with her father Pharaoh, whom she finally marries, through the sexual exploitation of Victorian Flora by William Preston under the guise of his scientific researches, and ending with Hattie's childhood experience of being sexually abused by her uncle, the event which together with a difficult adolescence spent in an orphanage may have led her astray (Hattie may have had the past of a prostitute).[5] Both novels, then, chronicle individual female experiences and stage separate life stories only to collapse them into the shared history which unfolds itself like a collage of multiple personal narratives.

Also the act of narration itself involves the two types of temporality Kristeva mentions: repetition and eternity, as the act of self-writing presupposes the act of reliving, rethinking the lived experience. Repetition is thus intrinsically bound up with writing, as is eternity. The act of narrating one's life incidents is performed with a view to transcribing them onto the paper and thus freezing these memories, converting their transience into eternity. Related to the above is the idea of making one's past seem true precisely by narrativizing it. Linda Hutcheon, drawing on Hayden White, argues that what we accept as 'real' or 'true' in historiography, as in fiction, is that which 'wears the mask of meaning, the completeness and fullness of which we can only imagine, never experience' (Hutcheon, 1988, p. 143). It seems then that only once the past gets narrativized will it be accepted as 'true' (Hutcheon, 1988, p. 143). The relation of these three questions (the temporal modalities of repetition and eternity, as well as the idea of making one's past seem real) to the act of writing is skilfully crafted in Roberts's novel. What unites the three historical perspectives in the novel is the idea that writing, spinning narratives of one's own past, may provide all three key historical characters in the novel (the modern Hattie, Victorian Flora Milk, and Hat King of Ancient Egypt) with a chance to control their past, to retell it so as to give themselves a history of which women were frequently deprived. On buying a house, a hitherto homeless modern female character observes:

> I've never kept a diary before. The past, my own past, has not mattered to me. Now, in this house, the past surrounds me and holds me, and my own past leaps back at me in flashes. Impossible to hold gleaming drops of water in my fingers; the past leaps away in a trail of silver; yet I need to go on trying to hold it, second by second. *I want to tell you my stories. I want to record my life with you. I want to give myself a history. That's all.*
>
> (Roberts, 1990, p. 17; all the emphasis added)

The idea of narrativizing one's life so as to give shape to one's experience and 'make it real' resonates more strongly in the following confession made by the modern Hattie: 'I wrote these stories down. I wrote in order to find out whether I had the right to *exist*, how *real* the world was, how much it *touched* me, whether it could *include* me. Words were alive like dogs and trees and made me real too; I wove nets of words which *held* me up (Roberts, 1990, p. 27; emphasis added). In the account of Victorian Flora, who 'writing this story of [her] life', though at first undertaken 'for no reason except to please [herself]' (Roberts, 1990, p. 18), gradually assumes the ambition of saving life from the threat of oblivion – the ambition of eternity. This is prefigured by the importance of writing in Ancient Egypt, where the act itself inherently involves existence, where writing is tantamount to living (and where the Cartesian *cogito* could be transcribed into 'I write therefore I am'):

> To write is to enter the mysterious, powerful world of words to par-take of words' power, to make it work for me. To write is to deny the power of death, to triumph over it. To inscribe a person's name on the wall of his tomb, to describe his attributes thereupon, is to ensure that he will live forever. As the tomb cut into the rock is the doorway to eternal life. [...]. Words mean life. The absence of words means death: being forgotten by men for all eternity. [...]. The tomb is the first book; the house of life; the body that does not decay because it is written. Stone is cut into, cut out; this absence of stone, this concavity, this emptiness, yet means fullness: the words appearing, their presence overcoming the absence of what they denote, filling emptiness with meaning, creating the world over and over again. Writing, I live; I enter that world beyond the false door of the tomb; my existence continues throughout eternity.
>
> (Roberts, 1990, p. 24)

Yet, the promise of eternity becomes endangered the moment the inscription of a name, the sign of self-identification, becomes sub-ject to erasure: 'On the columns, all the cartouches containing the hieroglyphs spelling out my name have been savagely hacked out' (Roberts, 1990, pp. 132–3). This is the time when the threat of death, or rather self-effacement, becomes overwhelming, and the narra-tive voice bemoans: 'I have been *unwritten. Written out. Written off.* Therefore I am not even dead. I never was. I am *non-existent.* There is no I' (Roberts, 1990, p. 133; all the emphasis added).

Roberts's achievement is to add yet another powerful interpreta-tion of writing and its life-preserving attribute by introducing the dimension of spiritualism. The potent bond between writing and making 'alive' which Roberts revives in her novel is made possible through spiritualist séances and the mediumistic activity of passive writing. The timeless spiritual world which Roberts creates becomes, in a sense, the all-encompassing, infinite imaginary space of Kristeva's monumental temporal modality. To approve of one's existence, to be inscribed and resurrected is to be brought back into the realm of written language. For Hattie of Ancient Egypt, resurrection depends on being written into existence by 'a scribe who will write down [her] name and let [her] live again' (Roberts, 1990, p. 133). She intends to 'dart forward through hundreds of years, searching for a faithful scribe who will spell [her] right and let [her] rise. One whose hand will dance to [her] spelling' (Roberts, 1990, p. 133). The Victorian medium Flora Milk, with her capacity for passive writing, enables this resurrection.

The bond between writing and living, acknowledging one's life experience, seems thus to operate in *In the Red Kitchen* on two related levels. The first functions as spiritualism where the mediumistic activity of passive writing is literally bound up with the act of existing, approving the visiting spirit's existence, spirit's materialization. The second functions as the metaphorical representation of individual women's nostalgia for giving themselves a history, having their life stories acknowledged, even though only in a fictionalized form. The Victorian perspective with its theme of spiritualism and mediumship serves two purposes, then: first, it adds a new spiritual dimension to the relation between writing, repetition, eternity, and self-inscription; and second, it offers a representation of Victorian femininity which subverts the image of perfection and submission the Victorians built for their women, and demythologizes the frequently made equation between women of mediumistic skills and female deviancy or hysterical condition. The Victorian mediums were seen by many as an 'infringement of acceptable femininity, and furthermore, as one expression of the instability of gendered identity' (Owen, 1989, p. 203). Alex Owen observes that hysteria and sexuality were intrinsically linked, and though in the nineteenth century the ancient causative theory of the 'wandering uterus' was virtually abandoned, still 'the heritage of sexual association led many physicians to interpret hysterical symptoms as evidence of depraved sexual practices' (Owen, 1989, p. 148), among them masturbation, sexual excess, or rampant sexuality, and therefore as evidence of moral degeneracy. The association of spiritualism with hysteria was sufficient to evoke a paradigm of vicious immorality (Owen, 1989, p. 14), and, as Roberts's novel suggests, justified sexual exploitation of the allegedly hysterical medium.

In the novel Flora Milk travels with William Preston to Paris to be exhibited as an hysteric in Dr Charcot's Salpetrière hospital. There, she is a passive subject in the exercise of masculine power and hypnotic manipulation. She does as she is told: 'I am the girl in the white night-gown in the photograph. We undress for the doctors; slow ritual we have rehearsed so often. Their eyes examine us. They think they have guessed our secret thoughts. How can they? We don't speak. We just dance for them, which is all they want. They are delighted with our performance' (Roberts, 1990, p. 124). The potency of the scene is reinforced by Roberts's inventive deconstruction of the word 'hysteria'. Flora, not knowing French, hears Dr Charcot speak of female hysteria, but misinterprets the words for 'women' and 'history': 'I understand one word. It recurs often enough for me to grasp it, turn it over in my hand. *Isterry*. History? And then *famm*. History and women?' (Roberts, 1990, p. 124). The subversive quality of the incident lies in Flora's unconscious and unintended interpretation of women's history as hyster-y. In one innocent phrase, she lays bare the long-term association between femininity and irrationality made by patriarchal historical accounts, and challenges the persistent cultural association of women and insanity.[6] *In the Red Kitchen* offers, to use Susan Rowland's words, 'an *hysterical history* [emphasis added], employing fiction both to interrogate the apparently disinterested status of traditional accounts and to recover marginalized women in a fictional form that problematizes the concept of fiction in connection with occult and unconscious drives' (Rowland, 2002, p. 206).

Finally, as already mentioned, in *In the Red Kitchen* Roberts refrains from constructing a singular, unified account of women's history in favour of promoting plurality and a variety of historical experience by offering women's histories, rather than History. By presenting a plurality of voices, granting none a privileged position in the narrative, the novel manages to defy the totalizing, speaking-for-all singular point of view. Moreover, by allowing the historical perspectives to speak for themselves, the novel involves the reader in the process of meaning-making. It achieves this effect not only by dispersing the narrative perspective onto multiple speaking-female voices but also by introducing the personal, rather than authorial voice that tells the story. The difference is significant, as Susan Lanser claims in her study of women writers and narrative voice *Fictions of Authority*:

> The authority of personal voice is contingent in ways that the authority of authorial voice is not: while the autodiegetic 'I' remains a structurally 'superior' voice mediating the voices of other characters, it does not carry the superhuman privileges that attach to authorial voice, and its status is dependent on a reader's response not only to the narrator's acts but to the character's actions, just as the authority of the representation is dependent in turn on the successful construction of a credible voice. These differences make personal voice in some ways less formidable for women than authorial voice, since an authorial narrator claims broad powers of knowledge and judgment, while a personal narrator claims only the validity of one's person's right to interpret her experience.
>
> (Lanser, 1992, p. 19)

The assumption of personal voice in the often conflicting narratives prevents any one of them from being presented as the 'historical truth', the master narrative that operates to subordinate all the others. Thus women as subjects in and of history, and as storytellers, seem to share an insistence on the primacy of the personal experience, consciously refraining from assuming an authorial (and authoritative) voice, but rather resorting to the expression of their individuality. Nevertheless, the shift of focus from the official (official often being concurrent with male-dominated) records of history onto the personal in female narratives does not imply that women have refrained from politicizing their gendered experience. The insistence on the personal leads to a reconsideration of what once constituted the content of historical narrative to include the individual experience. Once the personal becomes the political, the existing dichotomy of male/female, public/private has to be rethought.

It can be argued that Roberts's novel in its own way politicizes the personal, and manages to rewrite, if only in fictional form, the traditional separation between private and public history. From among the number of possible forms, the novel re-appropriates personal and life narratives which were available to women in the nineteenth century and earlier: diaries, letters, journals – that is, all first-person accounts, not meant for public presentation.

Traditionally, these forms of writing reinforce the dichotomy of male/female, public/private. As Dale Spender notes, 'there is no contradiction in patriarchal order while women write for women and therefore remain within the limits of the private sphere; the contradiction arises only when women write for men' (Spender, 1980, p. 190). The reinsertion of these earlier forms of women's writing (as pastiche) within the space of the contemporary novel, setting them alongside contemporary personal accounts, seems to aim at a few ends: it evokes textual continuity, collapses the earlier separation between private and public, and promotes a gender politics of self-representation devoid of any culturally or socially determined mediations by the third person.

In the relation between spiritualism and mediumship, on the one hand, and self-writing as an act of identification and self-creation, on the other, Michèle Roberts represents the continuity of women's experiences as a sum of women's personal accounts. The dimension of spiritualism and automatic writing enables communication, though often impaired, between women's past and present, reflecting, too, Kristeva's all-encompassing space of monumental temporality. In the novel the personal and the textual counterbalance the master narratives of the novel's three temporal ages. Flora Milk's accounts of medical sessions with William Preston, for example, lay bare the falsity of the master narrative of Victorian medical science. In avoiding the singularity of the speaking voice, instead relegating the storytelling to various narrators across time and social standing, Roberts thus renounces the temptation to construct and represent one dominant discourse. She manages, instead, to unite her novel's various female voices in the spiritual timelessness of an echo chamber.

Notes

1. 'Spiritualism', *Chambers's Encyclopaedia*, 9, pp. 645–9, London and Edinburgh, 1892. Quoted in Smith (1999).
2. For an in-depth analysis of the tropes of Victorian spiritualism and Carl G. Jung's psychology in Roberts's novel, see Rowland (2002, p. 206).
3. Susan Rowland observes that the fictional Rosina was most certainly modelled on the Victorian middle-class medium Mary Rosina Showers, Florence Cook's spiritualist rival.
4. I'm using the word to convey the meaning Linda Hutcheon ascribed to it, that is the focus on the non-central, minoritarian discourse. But in

this context, the second implied meaning of eccentricity might also be applied.
5. William's researches may well have been exercises in mere pornography, as he uses Flora's spells of unconsciousness to take photographs of her in her negligee.
6. For an extensive study of cultural representations of female madness, see Elaine Showalter (1987).

4
The Maid, the Master, her Ghost and his Monster: *Alias Grace* and *Mary Reilly*

Esther Saxey

The heroines of *Alias Grace* (Margaret Atwood, 1996) and *Mary Reilly* (Valerie Martin, 1990) have much in common. Both are nineteenth-century maidservants; both experience emotionally or sexually charged relationships with their master; both masters die an untimely death. In addition, both maids tell their own story, and this retelling is sometimes prompted in each case by a doctor who has a degree of authority over the heroine. The heroines experience childhood poverty and each has a drunk and abusive father (Atwood, 1996, p. 149; Martin, 1990, pp. 22–3). Both novels also offer extensive descriptions of the long hours of physical labour maids had to perform. However, each novel also contains an element that may sit oddly alongside the rigorously researched historical details; both Grace Marks and Mary Reilly encounter a supernatural force: Grace Marks is haunted and possessed by a dead friend, and Mary Reilly is plagued by Edward Hyde, a monstrous double of her employer. So what is the purpose of this supernatural element?

The liberation plot and its limitations

My first proposition is that the supernatural functions as a form of liberation, freeing these maids from their circumstances, particularly the repressive sexual morality of the Victorian era. The supernatural is not bound by taboos or legal considerations, and can therefore allow what has been silenced in a culture to be spoken, and let desires that have been suppressed be released and enacted. It is plausible to read both *Mary Reilly* and *Alias Grace* as explorations of the sexual desires of working-class women. Grace Marks is ill-informed on sexual matters until she meets her 'ghost' Mary Whitney, who gives her a new, sexualized vocabulary. When Whitney speaks (through Grace) after her death, she revels in her sexual power, while Marks remains apparently chaste. Mary Reilly, imprisoned by sexual repression and her class status, can only speculate timidly on whether she is attractive to her master, but the existence of the monstrous Hyde brings maid and master closer together, and binds them with shared secrets. The supernatural element does not, in either novel, allow the maid's desires to be enacted in any straightforward way, but this does not prove the two are not associated; the chaos caused by the ghost and the monster suggests the increased force of a desire that has been repressed or displaced and which now resurfaces. The supernatural is a highly appropriate tool for such explorations; Victorian supernatural fiction has been read as particularly expressive of the sexual urges and anxieties of the societies producing it. The critic Christopher Craft (1984), for example, outlines the temptations and menaces of sexual licence and gender inversion in Bram Stoker's *Dracula* (1897).

The two supernatural novels discussed in this essay are part of a wider celebration of the drama of Victorian repression and liberation. Matthew Sweet argues that Hammer studio horror films (from the 1950s to the 1970s) employed a Victorian setting 'to tell parables about the pleasures of the Permissive Society, which it dramatized as a battle between the promiscuous Undead and conservative Victorians' (2001, p. xix). In the more recent neo-Victorian fiction boom, Sarah Waters's depiction of Victorian lesbians, Victorian cross-dressing, and Victorian sex toys has found a wide readership. This plot of suppression and liberation derives its pleasure from surprise and contrast. To this end, the Victorian carapace of sexual repression is reinforced so that its underbelly can be exposed. Sweet credits Hammer with acting in this way, and as having done 'the most to shape the popular perception of Victorian sensibility' as staid and repressed (2001, p. xix). The film company created the historical backdrop needed to display the liberation plot to its best advantage. Readers can even seem willing to undergo voluntary amnesia to sustain their enjoyment; Christian Gutleben asks why 'contemporary novels go on denouncing Victorian prostitution as if it were an unheard-of scandal' and accuses them of recycling 'facts which have become common-place' (2001, pp. 65–6).[1] I will be using the term 'liberation plot' to describe fictions which employ this dynamic, depicting Victorian sexual repression or social oppression, providing plot development and reader satisfaction by ultimately overcoming such constraints.

There may well be a note of self-congratulation in this depiction of Victorian repression and liberation. It fleshes out an underlying modern belief that Michel Foucault refers to as the 'repressive hypothesis' (1990, pp. 8–12). He describes how we bolster our modern self-image by asserting that we handle sexual matters far better than 'the monotonous nights of the Victorian bourgeoisie' (Foucault, 1990, p. 3). Victorians are depicted as sexually repressive, with a 'triple edict of taboo, non-existence, and silence', so that we can see ourselves as bold liberators when we speak of sex (Foucault, 1990, pp. 5–7). Neo-Victorian fiction often supports this belief by attributing benign, transformative powers to liberated sexuality;[2] desire is seen as capable of circumventing or breaking down social barriers. Working-class women characters claim the 'speaker's benefit'; this 'benefit' is the understanding that to speak of sex is to act in favour of social justice.

There are other forms of restriction at work in *Mary Reilly* and *Alias Grace* in which the supernatural might also intervene. Modern awareness of the sexual inequality of the Victorian era has made it a productive ground for fictional engagements with feminist issues. In addition, rigid class distinctions are another area of popularly perceived Victorian oppression. Neo-Victorian fiction fetishizes the elaborate rituals of class, the forms of address, and the vast disparities of income involved in live-in service; they then also celebrate those who escape or transgress these class distinctions. In these social situations, the supernatural might be precisely the tool to bridge the gap between inner, psychological liberation and outer, social empowerment; the ghost or the monster might be able to rescue the maid. *Mary Reilly* and *Alias Grace* are full of pleasurable class and gender transgressions, prompted by supernatural elements. Mary Whitney, the ghost/maid, has an advanced political critique of the landowning classes. Edward Hyde, as I will explore, catalyses the scrutiny of Dr Jekyll's upper-class philanthropy which is found wanting. Such transgressions have their echoes in the Victorian fiction of the uncanny. Lloyd Smith uses Nicolas Abraham and Maria Torok's theory of the 'phantom' (1994) to argue that as well as the individual unconscious, the 'social unconscious' can be depicted through the uncanny: 'the unconscious (that is, the concealed or silenced) knowledge of the larger historical/political culture' (1992, p. 288). This opens up the possibility of a fiction of the uncanny in which unease is created through cultural silences and contradictions. This is particularly appealing for modern authors whose project includes strong social critiques of Victorian culture.

It has become commonplace to assert that we use the Victorians to identify ourselves as contrastingly 'modern'. Kucich and Sadoff (2000), Gutleben (2001), and Sweet (2001) all make this point, with different emphases. The liberation plot, therefore, not only characterizes the Victorians in a certain way; it contrasts them with the modern world, suggesting a certain model of historical progress, and thus celebrates the victory of sexual liberation in the present day. There is a particular temptation in neo-Victorian novels to overinvest in the power of sexual liberation, connecting it (conceptually or causally) to the escape of female characters from harmful social situations. These novels often collapse the plots of social and sexual liberation into one another. Rose Tremain's *The Colour* (2003) can be read as an example of this problematic collapse. The heroine undertakes arduous travel and manual labour but her final liberation comes through a sexual relationship; the heroine finds gold deposits in the spot where her affair takes place. Comfortably wealthy, she can bring up her illegitimate mixed-race son alone. One interpretation might be that the affair symbolizes how far the heroine has come in terms of personal development. A less subtle inference is that sex brings freedom, and freedom of several kinds simultaneously. As Foucault notes, '[s]omething that smacks of revolt, of promised freedom, of the coming age of a different law, slips easily into this discourse on sexual oppression' (1990, p. 7).[3]

The liberation plot is thus a particularly tempting tool for the neo-Victorian author. However, *Alias Grace* and *Mary Reilly* are too subtle to allow it to triumph untroubled, or to allow the ghost or the monster to rescue the maid. In both novels, the notion of liberation powers the plot at points, but does not dominate. I will show how these two novels use the liberation plot, and employ supernatural elements to support it, but also demonstrate how it is complicated, undermined and haunted.

An initial consideration of both novel shows liberation plots introduced, then quickly complicated. *Alias Grace* is based on a real crime committed in nineteenth-century Canada. Much of the novel is narrated by Grace Marks, imprisoned for the double murder of her master and his housekeeper. She speaks to a doctor who has come to investigate her amnesia; the doctor has been employed to provide evidence of Marks's innocence, but the doctor's own motive is to establish himself as an expert through his work with Marks. In the first three pages of Grace Marks's narration, the idea of women's repression and potential sexual liberation is conjured up. First, there is a description of restrictive clothing (this time, the crinoline rather than the corset): '[crinolines] are like birdcages; but what is being caged in? Legs, the legs of ladies; legs penned in so they cannot get out and go rubbing up against the gentlemen's trousers' (Atwood, 1996, p. 24). This offers the reader some familiar Victorian dynamics; the sexual desires of (middle-class) women are suppressed, and clothing is both a tool of, and a metaphor for, that repression. But a page later, Marks adds: 'I think of all the things that have been written about me – that I am an inhuman female demon, that I am an innocent victim [...] that I was too ignorant to know how to act [...] that I have blue eyes, that I have green eyes, that I have auburn and also brown hair' (Atwood, 1996, p. 25).

Marks is a prisoner, and is here listing the various accounts of her given at the time of her trial, by newspaper coverage, ballads, and court statements. The list of her attributes and identities concludes with Marks asking how she can 'be all of these different things at once?' (Atwood, 1996, p. 25). This list moves us into a territory familiar to many postmodern works of fiction. The capacity of media and legal sources to comment on Marks, and on her body, is resisted. This resistance is part of the novel's attempt to problematize history; it questions the authority of historical documents and foregrounds their textuality. Critics have extensively discussed the relationships between *Alias Grace* and its historical origin and intertexts.[4] One can categorize the novel as 'historiographic metafiction', to use Linda Hutcheon's phrase defining a historical fiction which 'problematizes the very possibility of historical knowledge' (1988, p. 106). The role of the ghost may be to give this postmodern approach a final twist. The ghost taunts her listeners and the reader along with them, then vanishes and is not retrieved again; she embodies (by her very disembodiment) the impossibility of knowing the past. The reader has waited for the evidence of Marks's guilt or innocence, but the detective story is diverted into a ghost story.

The introduction of the supernatural also means the novel cannot itself be an accurate historical account; its fictiveness is foregrounded.

This destabilization of historical knowledge, made prominent through the inaccurate list of Marks's attributes, also has implications for the liberation plot. Several varieties of knowledge are displayed in this list, and more appear as the novel develops: law, branches of medicine, poetry, spiritualism, news reporting. These different discourses create multiple identities for Marks. Some come in pairs, one of which must be false for the other to be true (guilty, innocent), but the truth of others can hardly be judged against one another, as they come from entirely different registers ('inhuman demon', amnesiac patient). This represents the novel's understanding of how knowledge operates discursively which inherits much from Foucault. In terms of sexuality, it is a model which undermines the idea of sexual liberation; power in this system not only represses or releases sexuality, but also constructs it in complex ways, in part through the discourses through which it is described. Sexual desire does not transcend its social situation, but is rather always a specific, socially located experience of desire. *Alias Grace* continues to juggle and shift between these two conceptualizations of sex and power – a repressive model and a discursive, located model – to great effect.

It is also possible to read *Mary Reilly* as a case study in the oppression and sexual suppression of a young working-class woman. *Mary Reilly* is based on Stevenson's *The Strange Case of Dr Jekyll and Mr Hyde* (first published in 1886). It is presented in the form of a diary kept by Mary Reilly, a maid in the house of Dr Jekyll, and presents the reactions of Reilly and other servants to the decline of Jekyll and the intrusion of Hyde. Reilly has a deep emotional attachment to Jekyll, her master, and there are distinct moments where Reilly's sexuality seems best characterized as repressed. Every time she expresses desire she interweaves it with denial and almost comically complex assertions of propriety:

> Then I fell on thinking of [Jeykll's] cool fingers against my neck, which was a thought I knew I had no business entertaining and I gave myself a talking to on the subject of a servant's foolishness and how wrong it is ever to have fancies outside one's station as it always leads to misery, as I've observed myself often enough, and in the midst of lecturing myself I fell asleep.
>
> (Martin, 1990, p. 12)

Her few moments of class-based anger are also repressed. Her master is pleased to find she learned to read at a charitable school he had helped to found and endow, yet she tells the reader: 'I had such a mean thought it left me speechless, for it was this, that considering how rough the school was, it was a wonder I could read and had got as far as I had in the world, which surely even Master mun see isn't very far' (Martin, 1990, p. 30). She has articulated this thought but it has left her 'speechless'; it thus goes unvoiced at first, but both the thought and the self-censorship are recorded in her journal. Later, an even more extreme conflict with her master troubles her but fails to register consciously: 'Somehow the sight of [Dr Jekyll] so comfortable and relaxed, which usually makes me feel content, as if it was myself relaxing after a fine meal, run against me, why I cannot say' (Martin, 1990, p. 121). The 'why I cannot say' is a remarkable piece of false consciousness; Jekyll has recently sent her, on her single weekly leisure afternoon, to deliver a message to a brothel, where she has seen the bloody aftermath of a recent assault. Reilly is even more sexually repressed than her servant colleagues: she fails to understand sexual jokes, and has no desire for flirtation or a boyfriend. Even her most overt desires for her master are framed in terms of response and service: 'I brushed my hair down and let it fall over my breasts and I thought, is this a sight my master would care to see?' (Martin, 1990, p. 49).

But although Mary Reilly's desire for her master increases, her feelings for him are difficult to characterize as liberated, or liberating. Jekyll notes that Mary Reilly has 'a fairly profound view of social order and propriety', to which she replies that '[e]very servant knows as much if he's any wish to stay in service' (Martin, 1990, p. 17). It is Reilly's 'wish to stay in service' that complicates her life. She has a pragmatic need to stay in her job, but in addition, her emotional attachment to her master encourages both of them to go beyond their roles. Sometimes they communicate more on equal terms, but far more often they voluntarily intensify their mastery and service, with Mary serving him more, and he asking more service of her. To say that Mary Reilly's desire for her master takes tortuous paths would imply that there might be a direct path, a simple lust that sidesteps their existing relationship. It is hard to say whether Mary Reilly's desire for her master is disruptive or predictable. It leads her to make claims on him, to speak to him more freely than do other maids. She believes herself to have a special relationship with him, which is borne out by his own behaviour. However, this special relationship allows him to extract more labour from her. It is clear that the liberation plot breaks down in both these novels. To help productively complicate the notion of 'liberation' I introduce a third maid, and a third text (or rather, a profusion of texts) in the form of Hannah Cullwick (1833–1909).

Uncanny doubles and further multiples

Cullwick, a genuine, rather than fictional, Victorian maid, stands as an uncanny double for both Mary Reilly and Grace Marks. All three are maids, and all have a complex sexualized relationship with men from a higher social class. All three represent themselves in writing, encouraged do so by an upper-class man.

However, where finding a historical precursor might be expected to unlock the 'truth' of a fictional text, seeing Cullwick as a progenitor complicates interpretation still further. Cullwick was a Victorian maidservant with a passionate attachment to manual labour. Her partner, Arthur Munby, was a middle-class man with a philosophical and erotic investment in labouring women. Cullwick wrote journals for Munby to read detailing her domestic work, and the pair wrote letters to one another. Cullwick shares with Mary Reilly the dilemma described above; her emotional investment in the idea of 'service' (and her love for one particular man) increased her workload, but was also the foundation of her sense of self-worth. The most obvious question about their relationship is the one I previously posed about Mary Reilly, in a stark binary: was Cullwick oppressed or liberated; a victim of false-consciousness and exploitation, or a keen participant? In trying to answer this, more subtle secondary questions are: is it possible to eroticize a power difference which constitutes one's entire life, and have a genuine preference for playing the maid when one *is* a maid? I aim not to settle these multiple questions, but to use the intertextual ghost of Cullwick to further explore the situations of her fictional doubles, Grace Marks and Mary Reilly.

Echoes of Cullwick abound in the two novels. In an interview, Valerie Martin acknowledged Munby and Cullwick as inspirations (Brace, 2004). Both novels use class division to create erotic scenarios. In the opening chapter of *Mary Reilly*, Mary is blacking a grate and becomes 'black to the elbows' (Martin, 1990, p. 5). Despite this, her master asks to inspect her. She declines 'for shame of [her] dirt' (Martin, 1990, p. 6). 'Black' (with associated problematic racial connotations), 'dirt' and the phrase 'on my knees' (which Mary uses) are highly charged words and phrases which appear time and again in Cullwick and Munby's diaries and correspondence. Mary Reilly's master then holds Mary's hand to scrutinize it, and she notes that '[h]is fingers are long and delicate, almost like a lady's, and the nails is all smooth and trimmed even, so I thought here are hands such as should never know work, and I wanted to hide my own rough red hands away' (Martin, 1990, p. 6). Barry Reay dedicates a chapter to Munby's particular pleasure in working women's hands and their contrast to those of leisured men, which reverses the clichés of romance novels: '*his* is the small, white hand, and hers the big broad palm' (Munby, quoted in Reay, 2002, p. 126).[5] Mary Reilly's inability to remove herself from uncomfortable encounters is eroticized throughout the novel. When laying a fire for Jekyll, she experiences an orgasmic wave of embarrassment: 'So I had to kneel at his feet, which made me uncomfortable [...] a swell of heat seemed to pour out from under my hands, so I fell back on my knees while the wave rose up before me. "There," Master said, drawing close and holding his hands out before him. "Good [...]"' (Martin, 1990, pp. 50–1).

In Atwood's *Alias Grace*, Marks also seems aware of the erotic qualities of manual labour. She gives a detailed description of scrubbing the floor with her 'shoes and stockings off' and her 'skirt and petticoats pulled back between [her] legs' (Atwood, 1996, p. 319). Marks describes her employer in coarse terms: 'he was watching my bare ankles and legs, dirty as they were, and – if you'll excuse me, Sir – my backside moving back and forth with the scrubbing, like a dog waggling its rump' (Atwood, 1996, p. 320). Marks protests against her employer's voyeurism, but she then recounts the incident at length for another male authority figure, the doctor, to enjoy. In such scenes, we see immediately a flaw in the liberation plot; sexual desire is not a benign force which naturally tends towards equality. Rather, for the reader and often for the maid herself, class division, shame, and exploitation are presented as erotically pleasurable in themselves. How can desire break down such social barriers when it is invested in them, deriving energy and erotic inspiration from shame, from non-consensual encounters, and from bodies polarized by classed labour? In both novels, the supernatural enters a situation in which there are elements of repression and oppression, but also strong moments of enjoyment and erotic investment in the social order.

To interrogate this balance between transgression, conformity and sexuality further, I wish to locate Hannah Cullwick, Mary Reilly, and Grace Marks in the tradition of the 'uncanny double'. The double appears in Victorian gothic fiction, and in its close relation, the sensation novel. The gothic double is typically a splitting of the hero, as seen in *The Private Memoirs and Confessions of a Justified Sinner* (James Hogg, 1824), *The Strange Case of Dr Jekyll and Mr Hyde* and arguably *The Picture of Dorian Gray* (Oscar Wilde, 1890–1). One aspect of the hero remains socially respectable, the other commits (or urges) terrible acts. (Edgar Allan Poe's 'William Wilson' (1839) follows this pattern, but reverses the roles of protagonist and double, having the 'double' act as the conscience of the protagonist narrator.) In sensation fiction, there is often a mundane explanation for the double, but this cannot entirely remedy the air of the uncanny. For example, in two of the seminal novels of the sensation genre, *The Woman in White* (Wilkie Collins, 1859) and *Lady Audley's Secret* (Mary Elizabeth Braddon, 1862), a working-class woman is substituted for an upper-class woman, and dies bearing her name. From this a whole series of uncanny elements arises (many of the ones noted in Freud's essay, 'The Uncanny' (2003)): a woman is 'buried alive', a dead woman walks; a living woman is mistaken for a ghost; the name of the living woman appears on a grave or in an obituary, highlighting the slippage between name and identity; a resemblance between the heroine and her double is faulty, but striking enough to sustain confusion.

I asked earlier whether the supernatural could be used alongside the realist or social protest aspects of contemporary novels. The tradition of the double in Victorian literature makes it clear that this is not a new combination. The presence of the uncanny double often heralds social or sexual transgression. In *The Woman in White*, the working-class double is possibly the heroine's illegitimate sister; Lady Audley has paid a poor woman to die in her place in order to commit profitable bigamy. The gothic double explores social hypocrisy: Jekyll, not wishing his 'impatient gaiety' to disturb his 'imperious desire to carry [his] head high', reaches adulthood 'already committed to a profound duplicity of life' (Stevenson, 2003, p. 55). Robert Wringhim (the 'justified sinner') is pious, and Dorian Gray attractive, but both commit murder.[6] The plot of the double is thus highly appealing to the modern author and reader wishing to investigate inequalities of sex and class. One bestselling example is Sarah Waters's *Fingersmith* (2003), which draws on *The Woman in White* and shows how both the upper-class woman and her working-class double are exploited. The 'doubles' become lovers, and only through trusting one another overthrow the plot which would harm both of them.

In this tradition (particularly in the sensation genre) Hannah Cullwick could easily be seen as her own uncanny double. She has a 'double life', one which threatens the stability of class identities and sexual propriety. She is both the upper-class lady *and* the working-class girl who bears the lady's name.[7] Subsequent interpretations have doubled her again; the two images, of Hannah as manipulator and as exploited victim, are as different as the photographs of her as maid and mistress. Her many forms of duplicity represent the unsettled issue of how desire (particularly female, working-class desire) interacts with power structures. This is, I suggest, why Cullwick appears as the double of Grace Marks and Mary Reilly; her situation is a fascinating one to explore, pivotal to our conceptions of Victorian society, and as such it is a situation to which authors repeatedly wish to return.

I use this doubling as a starting point to examine the other doubles Grace Marks and Mary Reilly have within the novels: the ghost Mary Whitney and the monster Edward Hyde. In Marks, we have both a haunting and a haunted heroine. Marks is well qualified to be classed as a ghost; she is a genuine historical figure who has been made to speak. She seems initially to be like many ghosts, appearing in order to right a wrong done in her lifetime (her false imprisonment), although this impression is ultimately misleading. Marks is also haunted, within the novel, by her friend and fellow maid Mary Whitney. They have some doubled aspects: they share a job, and work in the same house; the reader learns early in the novel that Marks uses Whitney's name when fleeing subsequent to the murder. Whitney is described by Marks as 'an outspoken young woman, and did not mince words; and she had some very democratic ideas, which it took me some getting used to' (Atwood, 1996, p. 183). Whitney is only physically present in the book for 35 pages out of 550, but she works hard in her short existence to shake up Marks's world. She tells Marks that the Rebellion in Canada 'was against the gentry, who ran everything and kept all the money and land for themselves' (Atwood, 1996, p. 171). The ruling classes are 'feeble and ignorant creatures [...] by their own nature as useless as a prick on a priest – if you'll excuse me, Sir, but that was how she put it' (Atwood, 1996, p. 182). Marks is, as I will explore, reporting such remarks directly to a member of the ruling classes. Whitney is also a proto-feminist, undercutting the biblical and classical basis for misogyny by reframing Adam and Eve ('as soon as there was any trouble, [he] blamed it all on her' and Pandora's box, 'why did they leave such a box lying around' (Atwood, 1996, pp. 190; 168). She delivers a lesson on the double standard, and on avoiding sexual assault ('if you must, you should give them a kick between the legs where they'll feel it'), and sham promises of commitment ('if there's a ring, there must be a parson to go with it' (Atwood, 1996, p. 190).

For a short space, Marks and Whitney form a double act as the repressed naïve virgin and the self-motivated sexual woman. But Whitney cannot make the leap between one form of liberation and another; her sharp intellect and her awareness of her own sexual desires cannot lead the way to an improved social situation. There is no space for a liberated maid. Whitney switches from being the dispenser of wisdom to being an object lesson in sexual exploitation. She breaks her own cardinal rule, hiding a golden ring she has been given under the floorboards when there is no parson to go with it. Whitney's lover is the son of her employer, but he deserts her, and Whitney dies in Marks's presence after an attempted abortion.

Whitney then haunts Marks in several ways. She lives on vividly in Marks's quotations of her more earthy pieces of advice. Marks relishes these while simultaneously distancing herself from them by apologizing: 'he was of no more use – if you'll excuse me, Sir – than tits on a rooster, as Mary Whitney used to say' (Atwood, 1996, p. 138). Invariably, Marks uses Whitney's animal metaphors when expressing frustration at being exploited, even when she is not apparently consciously aware of the exploitation. Whitney thus becomes a barometer for exploitation, and even in death is more attuned than Marks to social and sexual power. Marks also uses Whitney as inspiration for original material: 'I try to think of what Mary Whitney would say, and sometimes I can say it' (Atwood, 1996, p. 72). Marks internalizes Whitney as a spikier, more savvy alter ego.

These eruptions (whether direct quotes, or original phrases inspired by Whitney) form a welcome contrast to Marks's often staid and reserved narration. Whitney is, in part, simply the salt to Marks's innocence and conformity. I see this as a solution to a recurrent problem; the neo-Victorian heroine must not accept societal norms too passively, or the reader may become bored by her, or alienated from her. But a heroine who is too consistently far-sighted and liberated becomes implausible. In *Alias Grace*, the two positions – of innocence and knowledge, loyalty and rebellion – are dichotomized into two characters. This dichotomy allows dramatic slips between the two positions. This is even more true when Whitney begins to literally haunt Marks. Marks's internalization of Whitney, and their uncanny doubling, reaches a climax near the close of the book. During a session of hypnosis, Whitney is revealed to be 'possessing' Marks. Speaking through Marks, Whitney claims to have been inside Marks's mind ever since her death, and to have taken a dominant role during Marks's periods of sleepwalking, madness, or amnesia. Whitney describes sexually manipulating Marks's codefendant and bribing him to commit murder, using Marks's body as bait: 'I'd let him kiss me, and touch me as well, all over, Doctor, the same places you'd like to touch me [...]. That was all I'd let him do. I had him on a string' (Atwood, 1996, p. 465).

This hypnosis scene is ambiguous. It shows a battle between several 'sciences' for the right to interpret Marks's symptoms: hypnosis, psychology, and spiritualism. The reader knows from the outset that the hypnotist is potentially a fraud.[8] The doctor who has been interviewing Marks scorns hypnosis as quackery, and champions new understandings of psychology. However, the doctor is himself unreliable; he is an amnesiac, a user of opium, a somnambulist who wakes to find himself having sex with his married landlady. Spiritualism is derogated both by the hypnotist and the doctor, but 'spirits' nevertheless interrupt the meeting with loud rapping noises. Séances are held on that day and the spirits are 'used to coming' (Atwood, 1996, p. 463). Their timely attendance shows spiritualism as at least superficially more reliable than the two 'sciences'. Whitney's status is thus never settled: is she a psychological phenomenon, created by Marks's denied desires; is she a conscious invention by Marks to explain her murderous impulses and behaviour, and to try to dodge punishment; or is Whitney a genuine ghost in an innocent host? The novel refuses to confirm any one explanation. This complicates the issue of Marks's consciousness in at least two senses. In psychological terms, is she aware of this internalized double? In second-wave feminist terms, her awareness of endemic cultural misogyny (her feminist 'consciousness') is equally questionable. If Whitney is an invention, Marks's naïve conformity is a pose, and her dead friend a useful cover for her murderous rebellion. But Whitney could also represent the splintering of Marks's mind under the contradictory requirements of her social class and gender. She is expected to be chaste, but sexually available to her master; she must stay conscious of his superiority, even as he undermines their roles by informal behaviour and sexual advances.

Whitney, as a supernatural agent, has the potential to be liberating. She could be the reader's representative in the text, bringing Marks into greater awareness. Instead, her existence is one element employed by the novel to confuse the very notion of liberation. She unsettles those who come into contact with her, and also the reader; this unsettling capacity emerges from the question of sexuality and ultimately disturbs the possibility of historical knowledge itself.

Whitney's failure to assist in the liberation of Grace may make more sense when read through Torok and Abraham's notion of the 'phantom' (1994). Both Marks and Whitney initially appear to be returning to right a wrong done to them – Marks returns through the medium of the novel, Whitney returns through Grace. Both, in a sense, fail to right this wrong: Marks confirms her guilt, and Whitney murders not only the sexually exploitative master but also the housekeeper he has made pregnant (Atwood, 1996, p. 466). Torok and Abraham describe a tradition of ghosts who return not to restore justice, but to perpetuate the concealment of a wrong, and to hide the shame of a previous generation. The 'phantom' deals not in genuine revelation but in misdirection and 'subterfuge' (Torok and Abraham, 1994, p. 189). The phantom is the result of a trauma not in the individual's personal experience but handed down from parents, or as Lloyd Smith elaborates, from the wider culture. Marks seems a suitable candidate for such a phantasmic haunting. Her account is riven by amnesia, and curious lacunae – for example, her inability to describe the appearance of her master (Atwood, 1996, pp. 240–41). Rather than being based solely in her own trauma, her symptoms could easily be rooted in the cultural silences which she has inherited. Her encounters with others suggest this, such as when a more experienced servant tries to warn Marks about sexual exploitation without naming it: 'she didn't like to talk [...] and least said soonest mended [...] she felt she'd done her duty by me in saying as much as she had, because I'd no mother to advise me. And I didn't have the least idea of what she was saying' (Atwood, 1996, p. 234). The fact that the older servant names Marks's absent mother in this unhelpful warning is a nod to the fractured maternal inheritance of Marks, but also more generally of Marks's culture. Mothers and other older women might prepare younger women for the truth of sexual exploitation, but instead they disguise their shame by handing on a legacy of silence: 'a gap', 'the unspeakable' (Torok and Abraham, 1994, p. 174). The phantom who appears in this context – Marks or Whitney – cannot bring restitution, only further obfuscation.

In the tradition of Victorian sensation fiction, Marks could be the working-class woman, nearly killed and imprisoned for a lengthy spell for her double's benefit (although Whitney cannot escape imprisonment, and is in fact doubly imprisoned, being trapped inside Marks). Mary Reilly's doubling is more traditionally gothic. *The Strange Case of Dr Jekyll and Mr Hyde* is perhaps the most famous fictional uncanny doubling. I will argue that in this revised version of the story, Hyde is as much Mary Reilly's double as he is Jekyll's.

Modern critical analyses and reinterpretations in film and fiction have read Hyde as an eruption of the repressed sexual desires of the protagonist.[9] Whereas the original Hyde is small, 'pale and dwarfish' (Stevenson, 2003, p. 16), and in *Mary Reilly* he remains so, other reinterpretations of the story have made Hyde monstrously large or bestial so he can more effectively embody the id or libido. In the neo-Victorian graphic novel *The League of Extraordinary Gentlemen*, author Alan Moore and illustrator Kevin O'Neill depict Hyde as gigantic and apelike. Moore has Hyde explain how he has grown, and how Jekyll has shrunk, using Freudian terminology:

> I mean, when I started out, I was practically a ****ing dwarf. Jeykll, on the other hand, a great big strapping fellow. Since then, though, my growth's been unrestricted, while he's wasted away to nothing. Obvious, really. Without me, you see, Jeykll has no drives [...] and without him, I have no restraints.
>
> (Moore, 2004, Ch. 5)

For Moore, these 'drives' are mostly homo-erotic.[10] Elaine Showalter persuasively reads Hyde as a recognizable queer figure, a working-class young blackmailer exploiting a richer, older man (1995, pp. 111–12). *Mary Reilly* makes sexual desire in the story more explicit, but also more heterosexual. Jekyll's peers discuss a racy female stage-act, Hyde interacts with female prostitutes.[11]

If Jekyll's world is feminized and heterosexualized, we can read Hyde not only as Jekyll's double, but also as Mary Reilly's. Reilly's sexual self-repression in the early scenes of the novel are echoed by a change in Hyde's crimes; he is a murderer, as in the original novel, but here his crimes are also sexualized. He has wrecked a room and assaulted a woman in a brothel. The emotionally charged scene between Mary and Jekyll, in which he examined her scars with 'cool hands', also finds its parodic repetition in Hyde. Hyde injures himself and rubs his cut and bleeding hand against Mary Reilly's mouth, his self-harm parodying Mary Reilly's scars, and his intrusive assault mocking the doctor's careful physical examination.

As noted, the process of doubling can be read as a symbol of Victorian hypocrisy, both sexual and more widespread. *Mary Reilly* uses Hyde in just such a way. Even before Hyde's arrival, Jekyll's philanthropy has already been questioned: is it a genuine engagement with social injustice or a sop to his ego? A charitable school Jeykll helps to endow, as already noted, is described by Mary Reilly as 'rough' and ineffectual. Jekyll's fellow trustees argue that educating the poor makes them dissatisfied, and equips them for more ambitious crimes. In this time of doubt, Mary Reilly becomes a touchstone for Jekyll. She is an obedient and literate ex-pupil of the school. Hyde is the opposite. He is frequently assumed by other characters to have been a pupil in one of Jekyll's charitable schools just as Mary has been. Far from showing gratitude, Hyde murders Jekyll's peer, extorts money from him, and breaks his possessions. Hyde's sexual and class transgressions provide the counterpoint to Reilly's powerful propriety. Hyde's appearance in the original novel is consistently represented as that of an unseen deformity; in *Mary Reilly* when the servants seek to define their revulsion, the comment most often made is that Hyde is not a 'gentleman' (Martin, 1990, p. 106). Hyde mocks the divergence of Mary's interests from Jekyll's, when both maid and master had assumed they were congruent. Hyde thus broadcasts the failure of the system of 'good service' and 'good works' which cast Jekyll as a 'good master'.

Speech and the silenced maid

I wish to conclude with a discussion of another telling connection between Hannah Cullwick, Mary Reilly, and Grace Marks. All three narrate at least a part of their story in their own words. But a portion of this, in turn, is prompted by an authority figure. Marks tells her life story to the doctor who is attempting to cure her amnesia; Mary Reilly writes an account of her childhood abuse for her master (another doctor); Hannah Cullwick wrote letters, and a diary, for Munby to read. Neo-Victorian fiction often gives the role of narrator to a character who is disenfranchized within Victorian society. Marta Bryk notes (drawing on R. McLure Smith) that Mary Reilly's prototype in the text is a crying maid who is silenced by Poole, the butler: 'to endow [the silenced maid] with the narrative voice clearly constitutes "an empowering act" [...] an act of historical reparation and an attempt at subverting the political bias of the original text' (Bryk, 2004, p. 205).

Speech as empowerment is a conceptual foundation of second-wave feminism. This sprang in particular from the model of the consciousness-raising group, where women described their lives for a circle of female peers. These groups aimed to interpret women's experience in ways which did not trivialize or pathologize it; ideally, experiences which women had believed to be personal and individual would become visible as widespread and political. In this context, telling one's life story (for a woman) came to be understood to be a political act in itself. Another aspect of the speaking maid's appeal, I would argue, rests on a different base – Foucault's 'speaker's benefit', which I have already briefly discussed. I note here that neo-Victorian novels seem to draw both on second-wave feminist notions of empowering speech, and 'repressive hypothesis' notions of liberating sexual speech. This is despite the fact that the two models potentially actively conflict with one another; for example, many kinds of sexually explicit speech are not seen by feminists as liberating, but rather as being used to silence women.[12] The maid's speech thus potentially has the power to fight both gendered oppression and sexual repression.

Cullwick raises complex questions because her self-representation is directed by Munby. Women's diaries have been considered a privileged medium by feminist criticism, offering an insight into women's lives with the fewest external influences or motives for misrepresentation. However, Cullwick's lengthy diaries were written in the knowledge that Munby would read them. Is Cullwick's speech, in such a case, able to liberate? Is it her speech at all, or an act of ventriloquism?[13] Both novels echo this problem. They both contain a blend of first-person accounts produced spontaneously, such as Mary Reilly's diary, and those incited by male authority figures (the doctor visiting Marks, or Jekyll). Both doctors have enormous power. The visiting doctor may be able to assist Marks's pardon or parole. Mary Reilly is wholly dependent on the master for her 'good place'. Can speaking under such circumstances produce either feminist liberation, or sexual liberation?

Mary Reilly thoroughly confuses the reader, showing speech and literacy as a source of pride in one moment, and as an additional vulnerability in the next. The novel opens with an account of Mary Reilly's childhood abuse which she has written at her Master's request. It is oddly sexualized: 'I'd only a thin skirt on [...] the creature began to work its way through the two thin layers separating us [...] I felt a claw sink into my thigh' (Martin, 1996, p. 3). Mary has to extract time from the ends of the working day to write the account just as Cullwick did ('It was hard to get up the next morning because it was so rainy and dark, but I knew I had my writing to do' (Martin, 1996, p. 12)). Even though the subject matter is embarrassing and painful to her, she states: 'I worked all day with the promise of giving my writing to Master in the evening like the promise of a fine day out before me' and concludes her work by 'feeling proud of it all in all [...] and anxious to have Master's opinion' (Martin, 1996, pp. 14; 19). She is proud of her capacity to write, and takes pleasure in it, but at the same time the reader is given an example of her submission in the face of Jekyll's authority; she allows herself to be physically examined by him, despite her extreme reluctance, and repeatedly reminds herself of his 'right and reason' (Martin, 1996, p. 6) as a doctor, and her employer. Placing the written and physical examinations side-by-side, can we accept at face value her pleasure in one when we see her self-abnegating participation in the other? To complicate the matter further, she then eroticizes the examination incident when recalling it. The 'Afterword' of *Mary Reilly* gives another twist to the maid's authority: her journal, it is stated by a fictional 'editor', always capitalizes 'Master' and never capitalizes 'i' (Martin, 1996, p. 243). This cleverly undercuts even the implied assertion of a first-person narration.

Other incidents also argue against the idea of Mary Reilly's liberation through speech. Reilly transgresses class barriers to speak early in the novel, but not for her own benefit; instead, she expresses concern about her master's health. The master tactlessly repeats her comments to another member of staff, bringing Mary Reilly under hostile scrutiny. Throughout the novel, Jekyll seeks her speech to morally justify his activities. He attempts to fit her life experiences into his discourse of public charity work, despite the limited benefit she has derived from the school he founded. Later, he tries to elicit permission for his experiments by extracting from her a fantasy of living without consequences. She does not support his position (partly because she misunderstands his necessarily indirect questions). Jekyll has Mary Reilly perform paid and unpaid manual labour, and unpaid literary labour; and it is only when he attempts to extract unpaid moral labour from her as well that she resists.

Barry Reay (2002) judges Munby harshly for abusing the power to incite speech, a power which is foregrounded in these novels. Munby was able to 'collect' the life stories of working-class women because (as Munby himself notes) '[t]o be asked bluntly "What is your name?" or 'How old are you"? by a stranger does not seem to them at all offensive' (Reay, 2002, p. 20). Intriguingly, Valerie Martin is not a stranger to using power to elicit life stories. She characterized her time working for the welfare department in Louisiana as follows: 'People come in and you ask them a lot of questions about their personal life and finances and if they're lucky they get food stamps' (Brace, 2004). She agreed, when prompted, that it was great training for a writer.

Grace Marks's life story shows explicitly the ways in which the incitement of a male authority figure affects her speech. She reveals the benefits to her as a speaker. The doctor can bring much-needed food and entertainment into the prison. She responds to his requests partly from self-interest, and partly out of gratitude: 'I set to work willingly to tell my story, and to make it as interesting as I can, and rich in incident, as a sort of return gift to him' (Atwood, 1996, p. 286). When Marks marries after leaving the penitentiary, her husband takes over the doctor's role, inciting her again to recount her suffering: 'his favourite part of the story is when poor James McDermott was hauling me all round the house [...] looking for a bed fit for his wicked purposes' (Atwood, 1996, p. 531). Marks details this in a letter she sends to the doctor, and adds: 'you were as eager as [my husband] is to hear about my sufferings and my hardships in life [...] it gave me joy every time I managed to come up with something that would interest you' (Atwood, 1996, p. 531). She concludes: 'if you'd had ears like a dog, they would have been pricked forward, with your eyes shining and your tongue hanging out, as if you'd found a grouse in a bush' (Atwood, 1996, p. 531). Although Whitney is not named here, Marks's other Whitney-inspired *bon mots* also use sexual hints and crude animal metaphors, and inspiration from Whitney usually comes when Marks is (consciously or not) being exploited. Yet Marks concludes that speaking for the doctor made her feel she 'was of some use in this world' (Atwood, 1996, p. 531). The doctor has been both a liberating opportunity for speech, and a pragmatic distraction. Overall, however, both doctors are attempting to place the maids' speech within their own discourses. To return to Foucault, his work notes that sex is discussed in the Victorian period precisely through various mechanisms of incitement (1990, pp. 23–31). Medical, religious, and political discourses all required sex to be articulated. Therefore, for the maids in these novels, who speak to their doctors, liberation seems less likely than their being positioned within various discourses of medicine, crime, and philanthropy.

In both novels, the supernatural double throws light on this tension between speech and incitement. Grace Marks's speech in the confession scene is highly significant. If one believes in her 'possession', then Whitney, an even more oppressed maid, also speaks. In fact, Whitney sobbingly protests at her lack of opportunities to speak: 'I was not heard' (Atwood, 1996, p. 468). But the effects of the speech are deeply confused; the confession reveals that Whitney is a malicious killer, that Marks (or at least her body) committed the murder, and that Marks thus has not been wrongly imprisoned. What is the purpose of this potentially liberating, but ultimately self-incriminating, monologue?

'Possession' works in this novel, to an extent, like 'madness' in *Lady Audley's Secret*. In both novels, a beautiful woman has possibly committed a decidedly unwomanly crime: murder. A fraught confession near the close of each novel seems to settle the matter. However, while each confession incriminates its speaker, it also throws doubt on her mental state, and thus complicates the mechanisms of justice which might apply to her. Lady Audley, in her melodramatic monologue, describes the cunning, ambition, and endurance she needed to commit her crimes. However, during her confession, she also states that she is mad. Marks's 'possession' functions in a similar fashion. In her 'possessed' confession she describes her agency, faking sexual pleasure to manipulate a man into murder; she also attacks the sexual hypocrisy of the doctor who has interviewed her. However, these comments can be ignored as either the malicious gabble of an unholy spirit, or the ravings of a madwoman.

Jill Matus has explored how Lady Audley's 'madness' allows feminism a voice in the text. It allows Lady Audley, during her confession, to describe the severely limited choices open to her, and to criticize patriarchy. However, it simultaneously silences these critiques by associating them with insanity, which is depicted as a physical condition rather than a social or economic state (Matus, 1993, p. 344). Braddon's text, written for a popular readership, explores female agency but cannot embrace it and ultimately demonizes it. Atwood, an author who consistently deals with feminist themes, is not motivated by any such need for reticence. Why, then, give the heroine a supernaturally disordered mind? *Alias Grace* uses the supernatural to recreate the inherent complexity of nineteenth-century class and sexuality, its internal contradictions and double binds. The novel – through dreams, amnesia, hypnosis – re-inscribes the oversimplified concept of 'Victorian repression' as unspeakable, obscure, and uncanny. The novel refuses to depict a direct route out of sexual or social disadvantage. In doing so, *Alias Grace* also refuses to support the reader's sense of liberated superiority. Grace Marks and Lady Audley's confessions, splendidly, both take place in exactly the same year: 1859.[14]

Mary Reilly's double also mocks the idea that her speech, or her writing, might lead to her liberation. In one of the most chilling scenes of the novel, Mary Reilly finds Hyde has written obscenities in books from Jekyll's library. This is an extrapolation from the original novel, in which Utterson finds a 'pious' book has been annotated with blasphemies (Stevenson, 2003, p. 64). But in *Mary Reilly* the vandalism gathers a host of new associations. Utterson is shocked, but his discovery does not endanger his right to be in the house. Mary Reilly, however, has been given special dispensation from the master to read his books. Hyde's vandalism could cause her to be punished, and her privileges to be revoked.

The scene shows the constraints of Mary Reilly's literacy. Her literacy is a source of much of her self-worth. However, like other aspects of her person, her literacy is used by Jekyll; it reassures him of the success of his philanthropy, and increases his own self-esteem. Hyde's obscene annotations on Jekyll's books are thus a useful symbol. The crude juxtaposition is similar to the revelation of illicit desire and exploitation within Hyde's benevolence. But Hyde's scribbling helps nobody, and threatens at a practical level to bring more trouble to Mary Reilly. Again, Hyde stands as her double, his futile and obscene marginalia mocking both her timid desires and her carefully kept journal.

Both novels suggest how far the stories of working-class women were *not* uniformly silenced, and how they were in fact invaluable to the Victorian social order. Journalists such as Henry Mayhew collected them for general consumption, social campaigners such as Munby himself used them to support their arguments, and emerging sciences (psychology, sexology, and psychoanalysis) established themselves by using such stories. Marks's doctor incites one working-class woman to tell her story. He will use it to set himself up in professional life and enhance his social standing. This is a microcosmic version of the operation of many aspects of Victorian society.

In Victorian fiction, the supernatural is never as constructive as a modern reader might wish. On the one hand, aspects of the uncanny are often employed when Victorian social and sexual mores are challenged. On the other hand, the supernatural is not a reliable tool for social critique. In the sensation novel, the uncanny double does not explicitly and clearly highlight social injustice. Rather, it generates a sense of the uncanny which becomes attached to acts of sexual transgression, making them more visible but also further demonizing them. The uncanny motifs continue after the double has been explained and departed (for example, the title of the chapter in which Lady Audley is incarcerated in an asylum is 'Buried Alive'). The supernatural is also often of no practical use to the disenfranchized characters. The gothic double tends to violent crime, but its violence injures both the privileged and the disadvantaged. Neo-Victorian fiction continues this ambivalent tradition. The supernatural in these novels is not the embodiment of simplistic liberation; the ghost is not a cipher for the progressive opinions of the reader.[15] Atwood and Martin employ the ghost and the monster to toy with the idea of liberation, but then to undermine it. The ghost and the monster are not introduced to rescue the maid.[16] The appeal of the double in these novels is rather their capacity to express the contradictory, infuriating (and in these works, inescapable) ramifications of the Victorian systems of class, gender, and sexuality. The success of these complex novels suggests that the current neo-Victorian boom is not an act of self-congratulation on the part of modern culture. The liberation plot is satisfying, and holds aspirational messages about the power of women's sexual desire, but it also tends to freeze the Victorians, and modern culture, in oppositional roles. By seeking fresh ways to express the nuances of the sexual landscape of the nineteenth century, authors (and readers) are also refusing to simplify contemporary sexuality.

Notes

1. I believe aspects of Victorian sexuality remain surprising to many modern readers, and that Gutleben overestimates the spread of knowledge. Also, Gutleben's suggestion that themes such as class exploitation, prostitution, race, and homosexuality have been employed for shallow excitement does not, to my mind, invalidate the continuing portrayal of characters who are not straight, male, white, and middle-class.

2. Other novels reveal Victorian sexual drives in a less approving fashion: sex work (*The Crimson Petal and the White*, Michel Faber, 2002), commercial erotica (*Fingersmith*, Sarah Waters, 2003), forced abortions (*The Colour*, Rose Tremain, 2003, adulterous incest ('Morpho Eugenia' in *Angels and Insects*, A. S. Byatt, 1992), and child prostitution (*Mr Timothy*, Louis Bayard, 2005). The focus of this essay does not allow me to explore this at more length, but I note here that both conceptualizations of Victorian sexuality – of the liberation of sexual release, and the horrors of particular forms of sexual activity – often coexist in the same novel.

3. This is a particularly thorny formula as women characters have often been confined to romance plots, finding rebellion and liberation alike through sex.

4. See, for example, Niederhoff (2000) on Atwood's historical strategy, and the *American Historical Review* 103: 5 (1998) for three historians commenting on *Alias Grace*. Atwood herself discusses her approach in the same volume ('In Search of Alias Grace: On Writing Canadian Historical Fiction').

5. Mary Reilly, oddly enough, does the most to dispel this intertextual connection when she most clearly admits her own sexual investment in the scenario. Told to wash and return to her employer, she washes 'as

vigorous as a new bride'; but Munby would not generally have required Cullwick to wash, nor would Cullwick have wished it.

6. James Hogg, *The Private Memoirs and Confessions of a Justified Sinner* (1824); Oscar Wilde, *The Picture of Dorian Gray* (1890–91). In some editions, the name of Hogg's protagonist, 'Wringhim', appears as 'Wringham'.

7. The doubling continues: Like Lady Audley, Cullwick makes a great leap of social class by marriage, but unlike Lady Audley, she continues to switch back and forth between the roles of servant and wife. She is – briefly – both the mistress of the house, and the maidservant with whom the master has sex. She is also doubled in her representations – her own writing, Munby's writing, and many staged photographs of her in various roles. In these photographs, and in Munby's erotic imagination, she transgresses the distinctions of class and gender in her single body, appearing as a masculine working woman or (with her rough hands hidden) as a middle-class lady. She is dead, but returns time and again through fresh generations of feminist debate; her outline is unclear (although through an excess of material relating to her, rather than because she has only been glimpsed obscurely).

8. The hypnotist has previously appeared as a peddler, Jeremiah, who can act out 'an imitation of a gentleman, with the voice and the manners and all [...] it was so lifelike' (Atwood, 1996, p. 179). Before the murder he asks Grace Marks to join him in a travelling hypnosis act (Atwood, 1996, p. 311). He tells her she would need to assume a French name to convince the audience – he reappears under the name Jerome DuPont.

9. Some sophisticated elaborations on this theme are provided by Veeder and Hirsch (1988), particularly in Veeder's 'Children of the Night: Stevenson and Patriarchy' which reads the novel as expressing the 'Oedipal rage' of late-Victorian male society. Linehan addresses film adaptations of the novel, noting that 'a near-constant of the major film renderings is the graphic representation of something which in the text is merely a possibility, namely, that the pivot for Jekyll's transformations into Hyde is sexual repression' (2003, pp. 86–7). She traces this back to the first serious stage interpretation of the novel in 1887.

10. The Picture of Dorian Gray and The Private Memoirs and Confessions of a Justified Sinner have also been read in this light, by critics including Sedgwick (1985) and Clausson (2003).

11. It is regrettable that in introducing female characters and perspectives to this previously tightly homosocial and male-centred novel, the potential for a homosexual reading has been diverted; one radically rewritten aspect has enabled another, less radical, change.

12. Teaching *Fingersmith* to an undergraduate group gave me examples of this divergence of interests. At the novel's conclusion the heroine becomes financially self-sufficient by writing erotica. Many students enjoyed the heroine claiming both sexual agency and authorship; others felt that this was unsatisfactory, and that rather than 'finding her voice' the heroine's speech, and her lesbian relationship, had been co-opted by the misogynist 'voice' of commercial erotica for a male readership.

13. Rust (1994) describes some of the critical positions in the debates, including Davidoff (1979) and Swindells (1989) who see Cullwick as manipulated and exploited, and Stanley (1984) who notes Cullwick's resilience and grants her more authority over her own diaries. Rust attempts to complicate these readings by discussing Munby as a 'colonizer', and Cullwick's diaries as embodying escape strategies through which Cullwick created 'a secure and flexible sense of self' (Rust, 1994, p. 102).

14. The hypnosis scene in *Alias Grace* is set between two letters, both dated August 1859; the day before Lady Audley's confession, she receives a letter dated March 1859. I believe there is no reason within the historical record for *Alias Grace* to focus on this year; the doctor is a fictional character and Grace's release does not occur until some years later.

15. By contrast, I note two novels in which ghosts are undoubtedly on the side of the maid, and liberate her both financially and romantically: Jane Harris's *The Observations* (2006), and Sarah Waters's *Affinity* (1999). However, in both these cases, the ghosts are forgeries. In *The Observations* the narrator maid blames a ghost to cover up her nocturnal activities. This haunting accidentally drives her mistress insane. The novel concludes with the mistress incarcerated and the maid employed in the same asylum, the maid thus achieving social advancement and the permanent loving companionship of her mistress. More poignantly, the heroine of *Affinity* is deceived into a belief in the supernatural by her class position; she can more easily believe that 'spirits' bring her flowers and gifts than that her maid is plotting against her. The maid steals the mistress's money and escapes to sexual contentment and financial security. It appears that the supernatural can only liberate the maid when it is faked.

16. I have briefly drawn on Torok and Abraham's 'phantom' (1994) to explain why the supernatural agents in these novels seem to aid the status quo as often as they disturb it. The shame of the heroines' mothers, disguised and passed on to their daughters, may be one source for the contradictory phantoms which appear in the novels. Both maids have trouble explaining their mother's attraction to their fathers, both violent men who drink; Mary Reilly refuses to believe that her dying mother voluntarily resumed contact with her father (Martin, 1990, p. 186–87). The pregnancies of Marks's mother (Atwood, 1996, p. 123) and the shameful poverty associated with them may resurface as a phantom through Mary Whitney's murder of an unmarried pregnant servant. The shame and death of the heroine's mother in each novel is both symptom and symbol of a wider cultural failure.

Part III Sensing the Past

5
Olfactory Ghosts: Michel Faber's *The Crimson Petal and the White*

Silvana Colella

In a general sense, all neo-Victorian novels are haunted. They are haunted by the ghosts of other texts and forms of writing, by authoritative voices from the past, by the spectral traces of Victorian characters whose actions still resonate within contemporary narratives, and by the shadows of histories and plots that resist closure. This haunting process may take different shapes. In Byatt's (1990) novel, it instigates the quest for 'possession' of the material and symbolic traces of the past. Sarah Waters's novels – *Affinity* (1999) and *Fingersmith* (2002) – are informed by 'the promise of a haunting to come' which always accompanies the spirit of the gothic, as Wolfreys claims (2002, p. 10). Clare Clark's *The Great Stink* (2005) is disrupted by moments of return which occur in the sewers of Victorian London where 'knee-deep in the effluvia of the largest city on earth' (2005, p. 10) the distraught hero, William May, finds his freedom.

In the very first paragraph of Michel Faber's *The Crimson Petal and the White* (2002), it is the contemporary reader that dons a ghostly garb. 'The truth is', warns the narrator, 'that you are an alien from another time and place altogether' (2002, p. 3) – this 'you' is imagined as a phantasmic figure time-travelling to the past in order to make 'connections'. In this respect, the present haunts the past just as much as the past manifests itself in the present. Faber's text is also haunted by what Garret Stewart calls the 'photographic moment', the visual reality of Victorian lives chemically fixed in an image (1995, p. 156). Victorian photographs are often regarded as material traces which persist in the present as documents. Their 'evidentiary force' seems undisputed (Green-Lewis, 2000, p. 31). However, in Faber's novel the return of nineteenth-century technologies of the visual is further complicated by the spectral persistence of (neo-)Victorian odours. Olfactory ghosts often intervene in this narrative to disturb the calm surface of realistic and visual representations.

Smells have an ethereal nature: they are invisible but perceptible, material and immaterial at the same time. The insistence on the olfactory modality, in Faber's novel, adds an extra dimension to the 'ghost of Victorianism' (Gikandi, 2000, p. 181). The Victorian past is made to appear concrete, contingent, and almost tangible whenever the material reality of Victorian lives is powerfully evoked through the olfactory medium. On the other hand, however, the spectrality of the past is further reinforced by the reference to historical odours that function as mute signs, or silent traces of an object world receding into an unbridgeable distance. 'Smell has an uncanny duplicity', writes Nicholas Royle, 'it can in a split-second drop us out of the erstwhile familiarity of our present into the strange, painful and/or pleasurable, impossible country of the past; and yet a smell resists being recalled, in reality, even for a moment' (2003, p. 140).

In the following pages, I shall investigate the structure of sensations upon which this novel is built, focusing in particular on how olfactory hauntings create a sense of the unfamiliar within the familiar conventions of narrative realism. Smells may haunt our memory in many unpredictable ways. Faber's high awareness of the olfactory modality is in tension with his own cultural memory and with the task of 'remembering the Victorian novel' (Schor, 2000, p. 235) – a task he shares with other contemporary writers. In his case, remembering often means displacing: interrupting the 'homely' with the 'unhomely', the familiar with the uncanny. Faber's vigorous revival of nineteenth-century realism does not simply play into the hands of nostalgia – the nostalgia for the real, which is undoubtedly a crucial component of neo-Victorianism. Olfactory references function like alien guests in the house of Victorian realism. If the uncanny is, as Royle claims, 'a crisis of the proper and natural' (2003, p. 2), the olfactory euphoria Faber's text articulates blurs the distinction between the ordinary and the weird, making the familiar strange.

The Crimson Petal and the White is redolent of historical odours. From cheap, democratic perfumes (Rakham lavender soap) to the smell of excrement and bodily fluids, odours feature prominently in the postrealist agenda of Faber's historical narrative. The 'process of reaching back' into the Victorian past (Shiller, 1997, p. 551) involves, in his case, an active engagement with the least intellectualized and most stubbornly material of our senses. In Byatt's *Possession* (1990) and Fowles's *The French Lieutenant's Woman* (1969) the visual modality predominates.[1] In Faber's novel even photographs are notable for their smell. Regardless of what they represent – consumable images to be passed 'hand to hand forever' (2002, p. 38) – Victorian photographs are material objects emitting a suspicious odour. The representational value of olfactory references in *The Crimson Petal and the White* resides at least partly in their referential backwardness: the stench of the photograph, for instance, points with unmitigated immediacy to a concrete material realm which appears more meaningful than the 'naked' reality chemically fixed in an image. It is the tension between smells and images, olfactory and visual representations that demands attention. Faber addresses a contemporary readership immersed in an atmosphere of olfactory 'silence' (Corbin, 2005, p. 329). The 'culture of the image or the simulacrum', a constitutive feature of the postmodern (Jameson, 1991, p. 6), is remarkably odourless. If the 'image fixation' of our cultural template coincides with the 'disappearance of the historical referent' (Jameson, 1991, p. 25), does the odour fixation of Faber's narrative cut through the nostalgic patina of pseudo-historicism?

Unlike *Possession, The French Lieutenant's Woman* and Graham Swift's *Waterland* (1983), *The Crimson Petal and the White* does not explicitly dwell on epistemological questions concerning the relationship between history and fiction. The textuality of history is still an issue – there are many excerpts of Agnes's dull journal and Sugar's resentful novel – but the main focus has shifted. The reader is repeatedly invited to sense the past in order to make sense of it.[2] 'Come up with me to the room where the feeble light is shining', bids the narrator, 'let me lead you through a claustrophobic corridor that smells of slowly percolating carpet and soiled linen. Let me rescue you from the cold. I know the way' (Faber, 2002, p. 5). The 'proposed world' of this novel, to use Ricoeur's expression (1988, p. 259), is sensorial and phenomenological, rather than overtly textual. In the first chapter, readers are encouraged to join a prostitute in her bed (but not to touch her), to engrave the smell of her room in their memory ('a smell of wax and semen and old sweat', (Faber, 2002, p. 8), and to follow her in the street, avoiding the dirt and the 'densely congregated' dung (Faber, 2002, p. 19). Faber's illocutive rhetoric almost compels the reader to begin the work of 're-figuration' by appealing to the senses of proximity: smell and touch.[3] Access to the past – however illusory – depends on perception rather than cognition. The senses define a liminal area between past and present where connections become possible: 'that's what I have brought you here to make: connections' (Faber, 2002, p. 4).

What kind of connections? At one level, Faber's novel seems to offer the same kind of historical 'experience' heritage sites promise to nostalgic tourists. In both cases the emphasis is on the 'rehearsal' of past realities and the 'immediacy' of personal experience (Lowenthal, 2005, p. 123). The actual past may be beyond retrieval, but heritage shapes an 'embraceable past' that is in itself consoling (Lowenthal, 2005, p. 165). *The Crimson Petal and the White* offers a more unsettling illusion of immediacy. When the reader – 'you' – is asked to stand in Caroline's room watching her 'squatting over a large ceramic bowl filled with a tepid mixture of water, alum and sulphate of zinc' (Faber, 2002, p. 6) there is no guarantee that this 'you' will be able to recall the smell of the concoction Victorian prostitutes used to avoid pregnancies. The contemporary reader can visualize the scene and absorb the historical information, but might fail to snap that smell into concreteness. The reference to a complex historical smell, in this case, shatters the illusion of immediacy and the pleasures of intimacy, even as it contributes to sustaining both. 'The olfactory with its virtual lack of recall potential for smell qua smell', writes Rindisbacher, 'seems in its textual representation to be one step further removed from reality than other senses' (1992, p. 14). In Faber's historical narrative olfactory references, for all their stubborn materiality, end up frustrating nostalgic expectations. The evanescent, invisible nature of odours signals a reality which is both densely historical and disconcertingly spectral.

This essay is divided into four sections. The first focuses on what scientists, from different fields, still call the mystery of smell. I describe some of the characteristics which distinguish smell from the other senses (characteristics which have some interesting implications on how smells are represented in literature), highlighting the uncanny duplicity of smells. I then analyse Faber's postrealist approach to the imagined world of the past and the structure of sensations upon which it is built. Smells occur with remarkable regularity in this narrative. They are not quantitatively more relevant than visual descriptions, but they are qualitatively different, especially when used to deflate the comforts of realism. Olfaction is also historicized, as the male protagonist is in the business of perfumery and therefore actively involved in the deodorizing project of nineteenth-century civilization. The final section addresses the question of the relationship between history and fiction and the present-day relevance of Victorian culture. Why is the Victorian 'real' so appealing to readers and writers alike? Faber claims that writing a Victorian novel today entails a higher degree of creative freedom than writing in the restrained, minimalist style of much contemporary prose: 'I think sometimes it is good to have a big sumptuous meal of a prose and really get lost in it [...] I thought if I did that in a Victorian novel, then people wouldn't complain, because that's what you expect in a Victorian novel'.[4] Is this a 'cannibalization of the styles of the past' (Jameson, 1991, p. 18) and therefore another symptom of the demise of history? Or is Faber's 'sumptuous meal' a nourishing fictional contribution to the history of the present?

The mute sense

Evolutionary biologists agree that smell is our oldest, most primal sense. It was there before our attention was 'hijacked' by sight and sound. In other words, 'we think *because* we smelled' (Watson, 2001, p. 12; original emphasis). In a temporal framework that reaches back to the evolutionary chasm of our own beginning, smell is more relevant than sight, providing 'the most powerful link to our distant origins' (Watson, 2001, p. 3). In human history, however, smell is the forgotten sense: 'animalistic, primitive, and therefore degraded' (Carlisle, 2004, p. 5). Not surprisingly, it lacks a corresponding art form (as painting is for vision or music for hearing) and a semantic field of its own. 'Smell is the mute sense', writes Ackerman, 'the one without words' (2000, p. 6). There are specific words for all the different colours we see, but the vocabulary for describing what we smell is rather scanty. Odours can be 'good' or 'bad', pleasant or repulsive. Beyond this fundamental categorization, they can be described only by a linguistic rerouting through the metaphoric (a *flowery* smell, a *pungent* odour) or by referring to their origins in the world of things (the smell *of* a rose).[5] Smells have a metonymic structure of reference, as Rindisbacher remarks, which 'always throws us back into the dis-order of things' (1992, p. x). It is hardly possible to describe the precise smell of a substance to someone who has not smelled it before. In this respect, olfactory perceptions are not easily communicable. Smells have an intangible and spectral quality that defies the power of language to represent reality.

The link between smells and language is feeble and indirect, but we smell things instantly: 'a whiff, and we know' (Burr, 2004, p. 22). No one really knows how we do it, whether the shape of a molecule or the vibrations of its electrons are responsible for the smell, but the range of molecules the human nose can detect is unlimited and yet recognition is instant.[6] 'Smell is the most direct of all our senses' (Ackerman, 2000, p. 10). Communicating directly with the limbic system, the lower part of the brain governed by instinct, smell has an immediate effect, 'undiluted by language, thought, or translation' (Ackerman, 2000, p. 11). Furthermore, it is the only sense we cannot switch off – we smell as we breathe.

According to Watson, this might be the reason why smells are more 'memorable' than sights and sounds (2001, p. 5): 'things you see and hear fade past, but where smell is concerned there seems to be only long-term memory' (2001, p. 79). The connections between smell and memory centres are remarkably strong, as literature, alongside science, has repeatedly shown. In fact, Engen (1982), Vroon (1997), Ackerman (2000), and Watson (2001) rely on literary evidence – from Kipling to Proust and Nabokov – to prove their point. Watson goes one step further, arguing that the sense of smell is 'the formula for time travel' (2001, p. 147) and odours are the 'guardians and gate-keepers of the past' (2001, p. 179):

> But in the end, what matters most about the madeleine effect is that it parlays a primitive pattern of conditioning into a formidable creative tool. It gives us access to the past with a clarity, and the kind of total recall, that no other memory system can match.
>
> (2001, p. 182)

We are haunted by smells that seem capable of bringing back the past, suffusing it with a special aura. However, the strong memory-triggering potential of smells is a highly individual, subjective affair, 'extremely unpredictable in its psychological, associative impact on fictional characters as well as on the reader' (Rindisbacher, 1992, p. 298). In other words, smells could hardly be used as memory aids to help readers remember a collective past they have never known or experienced. But they might function as gatekeepers of the historical 'real': the more smells are depicted or simply referenced in *The Crimson Petal and the White*, the more directly apprehensible the Victorian 'real' is made to appear – 'a whiff and we know'. This is of course paradoxical, since there are no smells on the page, just as there are no sounds. However, given what we know of olfactory *perceptions*, it is undeniable that olfactory *representations* on the written page carry with them a distinctive aroma of referentiality, more so than visual descriptions. The reference to an outside is built-in in the linguistic structure of smell. As Rindisbacher explains: 'There exists an object world to which language, however precariously, refers. The linguistic grounding of smells itself regularly tears holes into the language network, hinting at the primacy of perception and clearing the view for a reality beyond' (1992, p. 147).

Smells are 'more assertive' than the 'images we absorb willingly or unwillingly every day' (Vroon, 1997, p. 118): the perceiving subject tends to react to bad smells by avoiding or removing their cause and to good smells by approaching their source. Distance and proximity, alarm and pleasure: if in real life these are the reactions associated with bad and good smells respectively, do olfactory references in literature elicit similar responses? Characters of course respond to the smells they encounter in a variety of unpredictable ways. In *The Crimson Petal and the White* Sugar is knocked down by the powerful aroma of burning lavender (Faber, 2002, pp. 492–3), is irritated by the scent of roses (p. 271), but does not flinch when the acrid smell of William's urine hits her nostrils (p. 115). The 'sickening stink of shit' is like 'oxygen' to the disturbed conscience of William May, in *The Great Stink* (Clark, 2005, p. 10). But the reader who has been offered ten pages of vivid descriptions of putrid matter and fetid underground tunnels may indeed experience a plausible reaction of disgust. Both novels rely on the reader's memory of a few basic repulsive smells – typically the stench of excrement, the smell of blood and vomit – in order to bring their point home: the Victorian past is, among other things, a cacophony of bad odours. This basic olfactory identity renders the past more material, immediately apprehensible and familiar, albeit in a crude way.

By the same token, however, the past can also be constructed as 'a foreign country' (Lowenthal, 1985), a reality beyond reach, especially by readers – Calvino's 'noseless [men] of the future'[7] – who are likely to experience their own modernity as mainly odourless, or thoroughly and artificially deodorized. Smells have an ethereal form, they are both material and immaterial. As such, they also stand for a disembodied, evanescent reality. They are spectral ambassadors from a past that remains difficult to name: a non-thing despite its material identity. My contention is that Faber's awareness of the duplicity inherent in smells has some interesting bearings on the epistemological questions posed by contemporary historical novels. In *The Crimson Petal and the White* the textualization of the past is less relevant than its phenomenological construction. As a physiological constant, olfaction mediates between now and then, the present and the past in many interesting ways.

'The unprettified truth'

'Yes, there must be receptive minds out there in the world', muses Sugar, the female protagonist of *The Crimson Petal and the White*, 'hungry for the unprettified truth' (Faber, 2002, p. 229). Her own gory and revengeful novel never sees the light of day, never reaches those receptive minds. But the 'unprettified truth' of Victorian brothels, homes, and streets, of the intimate and the psychosexual (Stewart, 1995, p. 153) seems to be Faber's speciality. At a general level, this novel, like other neo-Victorian narratives, sets out to counteract what Simon Joyce calls 'the commonsensical "doxa" of public opinion about the Victorians' (2002, p. 4): the flattering stories, 'welcoming you as a friend', that Faber's narrator discards in the very first paragraph (2002, p. 3). The ideology of 'the Victorians' shrewdly deployed by Margaret Thatcher in the 1980s is one of those pretty truths several authors have already debunked in their fictions. Contemporary neo-Victorian novels do not find the 'doxological Victorians' (Joyce, 2002, p. 7) terribly interesting. In this respect, there are indeed 'various current-day uses of Victorian culture' as Christine Krueger argues (2002, p. xiii).

The romantic, fetishized image of the Victorian world as a dream of stability, elegance, and graciousness is often deployed as an effective marketing strategy to promote the consumption of Victoriana – a variety of objects and styles which are becoming increasingly more appealing as 'conveyors of identity and authenticity' (Green-Lewis, 2000, p. 29). The 'will to authenticity' prompting the popular fascination with the world of Victorian commodities also motivates the emphasis on sexuality – on the combination of 'sex and crinolines' (Gutleben, 2001, p. 173) – in many neo-Victorian novels. Post-Freudian readers – and viewers – are likely to find sexual explicitness more compelling and authentic than self-repression or respectability. Hence the high incidence of sex scandals in historical fiction:[8] the 'unprettified truth' of sex comes across as more accurate, in historical terms, than the pretence of prudery.

Faber's novel shares the same rhetoric of revelation, albeit with an added twist. If graphic descriptions of sexuality – deviant or otherwise – are well on their way towards becoming the new doxa of literary neo-Victorianism, Faber shifts the focus from the bed to the 'chamber-pot', from the eroticized to the physiological body, from vision to smell. The first encounter between Sugar and William Rackham, in the prostitute's boudoir, is notable for the absence of sex and the disturbing presence of a pungent, easily recognizable stench: 'The sharp stink of stewed piss wafts up, inches from Sugar's nose, but she doesn't flinch. For all the effect the stench has on her unblinking gaze, her serene brow, her secret half-smile, it might as well be perfume' (Faber, 2002, p. 115). Illicit, tantalizing sex between a Victorian prostitute and her upper-class, besotted client has been replaced by an olfactory encounter. The 'unprettified truth' of the repressed sexual body is superseded by another, more undignified and rudimentary historical truth: the smell of organic matter, of excreta and bodily fluids. The irruption of bad smells in what was otherwise a tranquil, almost cosy scene – William fast asleep in bed, Sugar reading her manuscript – functions as a shock tactic, here as elsewhere in the narrative. Lulled by the familiar comforts of realism, readers are suddenly awakened, or more specifically resensitized: the past they are 'experiencing' is so crudely perceptual that it seems to lack the conceptual cohesion they have been trained to expect. Nineteenth-century realism is a discourse of sublimation as far as smells are concerned: it is classificatory (smells are social indicators), tends to favour inoffensive smells (Carlisle, 2004, p. 16), or to disregard them altogether depicting what should be rather than what is (Rindisbacher, 1992, p. 39). In this respect, Faber's narrative is indeed postrealist, embracing the legacy of realism while exposing its repressed other: matter without spirit, the material without the abstract, the 'real' prior to classification – the smell of urine, instantly recognizable, but somehow out of place, like a relic without an archive.

The history of smell and olfactory perceptions is of course a history of acculturation, as Corbin (2005) has brilliantly demonstrated. Smells have their own archives and their – arbitrary – systems of classification. My point is that in Faber's cultural fantasy of retrieval, certain smells function as pure relics, or uncontaminated traces. It is often offensive odours that acquire this function, as if in response to Victorian novelists' preference for more subtle and nuanced smells. When the narrative seems to glide a tad too smoothly towards the certitudes of traditional realism – third-person narration, graphic descriptions of objects or domestic interiors, or not even a whiff of self-referentiality – the sudden resurgence of a repulsive odour in an unlikely place (dog-shit in the bedroom, vomit in the nursery) abruptly interrupts this circle of complicity. Not because the smell is revolting – although that too might have an impact – but because this kind of olfactory reference renders realism itself oddly unfamiliar. 'The alteration of a small detail in a well-known picture', writes Žižeck, 'all of a sudden renders the whole picture strange and uncanny' (1991, p. 53). In Faber's novels, it is often olfactory representations that activate this haunting process:

> With every sweep of her comb, a luxuriant mass of hair falls against her pale flesh, only to be swept up again a moment later. He clears his throat to tell her how [...] how very fond he is growing of her.
>
> Then he notices the smell.
>
> '*Paghh* [...]' he grimaces, sitting bolt upright. 'Is there a chamber-pot under the bed?'
>
> (Faber, 2002, p. 247; original emphasis)

The source of the stench is not the chamber pot, which Sugar has already emptied, but a 'stiff sludge' of excrement on the sole of William's shoe. The excrement is there because London streets, in the 1870s, are dirty and dark. The 'sludge' is a documentary notation as well as an occasion to re-emphasize the axiological reversal upon which this story is partly predicated: Sugar, the prostitute, is clean and 'immaculate' like her boudoir; William, the rational businessman, is messy like the city he inhabits. There is also a more basic, anti-romantic function this mess performs: the transition is from the fetishized image of Sugar's luxuriant hair and William's prospective wooing, to the contingent, mute materiality of smell.[9] If the motto of conventional nineteenth-century realism might be: 'Don't touch! Just look' (Rindisbacher, 1992, p. 33), Faber's postrealist perspective undermines this voyeurism, by raising the threshold of olfactory tolerance which is characteristically low in the literary tradition he inherits.[10] A reshaping of the reader's perception is taking place: in order to imagine what the past might have been like, we are expected to fall back on the most primitive modality for the appropriation of the object world.

The olfactory has a strong 'potential of uniqueness and freshness', remarks Rindisbacher, because it is 'unhampered by literary verbal clichés' (1992, p. 329) and even by scientific and linguistic models. Capitalizing on this lack, Faber's narrative makes sense of the past by insisting on a perceptual, sensorial modality of representation. Characters often register the surrounding world through their nostrils, just as readers are expected to connect past and present through their memories of a few basic smells. Thus packaged, the Victorian 'real' – unprettified, contingent, smelly – seems most touchable where it is most implausible: 'All the things in *The Crimson Petal* that you most strongly suspect couldn't possibly have been done or said in the nineteenth century', observes Faber (2003) in an interview, 'are most likely the things that are 100% authentic. Victorian society was an astounding chaos of extremes. Rather like the internet'.[11] What is authentic, in this Victorian pastiche, is what seems most invented. Authenticity for Faber has a lot to do with the tension between affirming and denying the historical real – the past 'wie es eigentlich war' (Ricoeur, 1988, p. 230). The olfactory references I have analysed so far signal an unequivocal desire of the real couched in the rhetoric of revelation which Faber deploys, to great effect, in more than one scene.[12] There is, however, another side to this story. At the level of 'configuration' or plot construction, smells are no longer valuable for their referential backwardness. They are not relics or traces, but signs and the standing-for operations they perform speak of absence rather than presence.

The scent of self

In Aldous Huxley's *Brave New World* (1932) bad smells characterize the old world, the fallen past, as more real and meaningful than the artificially scented, manipulated reality of the denizens of the future. A similar axiological structure is at work in Faber's narrative, where the unprettified truth of stinking matter is a certificate of authenticity – especially in relation to the 'evidentiary force' (Green-Lewis, 2000, p. 31) of photography. *The Crimson Petal and the White* contains more than one significant 'photographic moment'.[13] In the Acknowledgements, Faber thanks all those who have written about the Victorian era and in particular 'those who photographed or painted it' (2002, p. 837). The visual medium is an important tool in obtaining knowledge about the Victorians, and the promise of access to their world, because the chemical registration of images was already a Victorian technology. Thus, as Green-Lewis argues, '[w]e can see the Victorians. Not just imaginatively, but really – or at least as really as we see anyone through the agency of photography' (2000, p. 31). The special aura of Victorian photographs derives from their evidentiary force. Fixed in an image, reproduced as an image, the past is transformed into what Foucault calls 'continuous history', entailing the promise that 'one day the subject – in the form of historical consciousness – will once again be able to appropriate, to bring back under its sway, all those things that are kept at a distance, and find in them what might be called its abode' (2002, p. 12).

Faber's narrator refers to this kind of appropriation when he defines the coffee-table book of Victorian photographs (a contemporary commodity) as 'the great leveller of past outrages' (2002, p. 38). The images of Victorian prostitutes we might consume today appear 'innocuous, quaint, even strangely dignified' (Faber, 2002, p. 31), but the narrative we are reading – this is Faber's point – tells a different story. The visual is deceiving, as the several episodes of photographic manipulation, scattered in the novel, suggest. The referent does not adhere to the picture when William, a businessman, poses as a Cambridge gallant (Faber, 2002, p. 56) or when he replaces Sugar's face with Agnes's in a family picture, taken after his wife's disappearance. The representational value of visual images is also questioned when Sugar and Caroline discuss their anxiety vis-à-vis future appropriations of their images 'trapped on a square of card'

(Faber, 2002, p. 36). Having thus cast doubt on the evidentiary potential of photographs, Faber moves one step further introducing an olfactory notation: photographs stink, and as Sugar concludes, 'anything that stinks so much can't last forever'. Odours, in this case, speak of impermanence, of a discontinuous history, of a past beyond retrieval. It is hard to imagine (let alone remember) what the chemicals used in the studio of a Victorian photographer smelled like. The odour of urine is arguably familiar to contemporary readers, but the chemical stench of a photograph is more likely a mute sign. The historical accuracy of this olfactory memo depends on the realization that the distance between sign and referent, the smell and its origin, the past and the present cannot be covered. So, the odour-emitting photograph is more realistic than the visual realism of photographs themselves, more evocative of the historically real object world beyond the simulacrum. On the other hand, it is a sign without a referent, a smell too distant in time to be successfully connected to its source. In this dialectic of presence and absence resides the genuine 'retrospective dimension' (Jameson, 1991, p. 18) of Faber's neo-Victorianism: nostalgic desires are powerfully evoked through the olfactory medium and at the same time frustrated when the textual presence of the past is revealed as an absence. Photographic images have a spectral structure: the Victorians we 'see' through the agency of photography appear quite literally as ghosts, neither alive nor dead. Theirs is a 'paradoxical phenomenality' (Derrida, 1994, p. 6). To this dimension, Faber adds a further twist, shifting attention from the image to the object, from the visual representation to the olfactory identity of Victorian photographs. The result is a queering of the ocular paradigm which in turn produces another spectral effect: for all its materiality, the smell of a photograph remains a blind sign – it cannot be recalled, it is the being-there of an absence.

The search for the 'real' is also staged in *The Crimson Petal and the White* at the level of plot. This quest prompts Sugar to read Agnes's diaries – 'dull as an invalid's omelette' (Faber, 2002, p. 537) – in the hope of discovering the real Agnes, the woman behind the icon of Victorian femininity. Needless to say, words like pictures have an olfactory identity in this novel. Agnes's textual past resurfaces in the present of the plot as a pile of 'filthy' papers, smelling of mud (Faber, 2002, p. 514), which Sugar jealously stores under her bed. Sugar is portrayed as a frustrated reader until she detects the material traces of Agnes's demented selfhood: 'a smear of dried blood, in the shape of a crucifix. Nor is this blood from a pinprick on the thumb, solemnising a schoolgirl pledge; this is thicker matter, incorporating a stiff clot at the point of the crucifix where Christ's head might be' (Faber, 2002, p. 558). What Sugar finds interesting in the pages of Agnes's journals is the tangible record – menstrual blood used as ink – of William's wife's innocence, ignorance, and insanity. She looks for meanings where material relics are most tangibly inscribed and the reality of the past resurfaces as matter rather than words. In this respect, Sugar might very well be the textual representative of the novel's implied reader – a reader who is willing to engage with this narrative's obsession with crude materiality.

This is why Sugar's reactions to olfactory stimuli are particularly revealing. One of the most 'common scents' (Carlisle, 2004) in this novel is lavender, the olfactory signature of William Rackham's commercial success. He inherits his father's perfumery, but is reluctant to forego his literary ambitions until he meets Sugar. In order to set her up as his own exclusive mistress, however, he needs capital: hence his decision to turn to business, silencing his youthful aspirations. The apartment where he installs Sugar as his sole possession is impregnated with flowery odours: the smell of roses – 'they are filling the whole place with their stink' (Faber, 2002, p. 270), remarks Sugar – and the smell of Rackham's products: 'there is a mysterious surfeit of perfume in the atmosphere, as if the entire building has been sponged with scented soap' (Faber, 2002, p. 271). Sugar's reaction to these common, traditionally feminine scents – the fragrances Victorian novels like to associate with innocence and purity – is one of mild repulsion: she reaches for the nearest window, sniffing fresh air and 'the subtle odour of wet grass' (Faber, 2002, p. 271). The smell of roses, lavender, and aromatic fragrances in general are the objective correlative of the regime of 'olfactory vigilance' (Corbin, 2005, p. 17) reproduced in the plot through the agency of William. His business is the deodorization of public and private spaces: sold in big quantities, his fragrances serve to cover up human smells, the stench of decaying matter and the traces of death.

Not surprisingly, Sugar appears suspicious of these scents, despite her obsessive cleaning: Rackham soap makes her skin crack, leaving visible signs on her body of the progress of deodorized civilization. Flowery scents stand for respectability, hygiene, and the artificiality of upper-class decorum: Sugar's flat 'smells faintly of lavender soap when it should smell of food and wine and love-making' (Faber, 2002, p. 375). Her own gentrification – from brothel to home, from the streets of St Giles to the villas of Notting Hill – is portrayed as a process of progressive sensitization to the aggressiveness of bad smells. When she goes back to her old neighbourhood to visit Caroline, it is the combination of poverty, filth, and stenches she notices first: 'did it always stink like this, or has she been living too long in a place where nothing smells but rose-bushes and Rackham toiletries?' (Faber, 2002, p. 405). As if to compensate for this new sensitivity to old, familiar smells, Sugar starts emitting strong odours as soon as she is installed in William's home as the new governess: in one scene, it is the 'diarrhoea stench' that impregnates her room (Faber, 2002, p. 529), in another, the animalistic odour of her body which William's detects while looking nostalgically for the scented trail of his wife's love. Towards the end of the story, Sugar unleashes a 'noisy flux of stink', of 'blood and other hot, slick material' (Faber, 2002, p. 781) – the evidence of her miscarriage – in the ultra-modern latrine of William's soap factory.

Sugar's recalcitrant body, her uncontrolled corporeal self, is here used as a reminder of 'past outrages' (Faber, 2002, p. 38). In this novel's osmology, perfumes, scents, delicate fragrances are subtle agents of repression. The 'democratization of the soap' (Corbin, 2005, p. 279), to which William's business contributes, is portrayed as a process of containment and suppression rather than as a civilizing process of sanitation. In this respect, it is significant that Sugar unleashes a mess of oozy, smelly things (the inside of her body) while visiting William's factory, a paragon of rationalization, cleanliness, and control, where even soap bars are 'guillotined' into their rectangular shape (Faber, 2002, p. 779). In this case, once again the narrative encourages the association between foulness and truth. The inside, writes William Miller in *The Anatomy of Disgust*, 'while disgusting in its physicality, is somehow honest by not alluring us with false fronts (1997, p. 59). Faber's insistence on offensive smells could also be related to Freud's discussion of the uncanny as 'something which is secretly familiar [...], which has undergone repression and then returned from it' (2003, pp. 123–62). The advancement of the civilization of the soap, in the nineteenth-century, entailed an element of repression. Victorian writers, especially in the second half of the century, 'turned their imaginative noses away from the disgusting, contaminating stench of the poor to apprehend fainter, though sometimes distinctly distasteful odors' (Carlisle, 2004, p. 17). Faber's return to nineteenth-century realistic conventions brings to light what was previously concealed. Coming out of the darkness, Victorian smells are in this novel eerily evocative of both discursive omissions and material emissions.

There is also another side to this osmology, which relates to Sugar's own quest for the real referent beneath the high-Victorian ideal of 'porcelain femininity' (Faber, 2002, p. 130). In her role as reader, as I argued above, Sugar stands for the nostalgic subject captivated by the spoils of the past, the displaced proofs of origin, the vestiges of the real. Agnes's volatile identity is the object of both her quest and William's, especially after her disappearance. Through their separate quests the narrative dramatizes the will to authenticity (Green-Lewis, 2000, p. 29), the desire for immediacy (Shuttleworth, 1998, p. 260), the 'nostalgia for the real itself' (Stewart, 1995, p. 184) which critics identify as a powerful drive of contemporary (pseudo)historicism, especially in its popular manifestations: from costume drama and cinematic adaptations of the classics, to heritage culture and the fascination with Victorian photographs, artefacts, and styles. In this respect, it is significant that William's and Sugar's quest for the lost referent of the past ultimately fails in the novel.

Reframed in olfactory terms as an elusive and evanescent fragrance, the lost referent is the scent of self, Agnes's signature. This invisible, impalpable aroma escapes even William's well-trained olfactory organ. Fearing that his life is 'falling apart at the seams', William mourns his cherished ideal of a perfect wife (Faber, 2002, p. 595) by looking at a photograph of Agnes where her face is 'captured in sharp detail': 'Countless times he's stared at this photograph, reminding himself that it captures an incontestable truth, a history that cannot be rewritten' (Faber, 2002, p. 596). This truth, however, is one-dimensional: the image is a depthless surface with no recall potential. William's next move is to rummage in his drawer looking for a 'perfumed letter Agnes wrote to him, mere days before their marriage' (Faber, 2002, p. 596):

He rummages and rummages, through handbills of forgotten theatre performances, invitations to art galleries, unread letters from his brother quoting Scripture, threats from creditors long repaid. But the scented proof of Agnes's passion for him [...] this eludes him. Is it really possible that all trace of her devotion has vanished? He bends his face down and sniffs. Old paper; the soil on his shoes; Sugar's sex.

(Faber, 2002, p. 596)

In this episode, once again Agnes's words are odorous and therefore valued as the perfumed trail of her presence. It is the uncommon scent of her love that William identifies as the only past worth remember-ing– a past that photographs, for all their visual clarity, are ill-equipped to reproduce. The tension between the visual and the olfactory is a crucial component of the structure of sensations this novel articu-lates: smells, in both their evidentiary and evocative potential, become meaningful when juxtaposed to images and simulacra. If the past is always already archived, smells seem to communicate with memory more directly than images. However, since it is impossible to re-smell a smell in the absence of the odour-emitting substance (Engen, 1982; Miller, 1997), the olfactory, by its very nature, also refers to an object world receding into an unreachable distance. In their ethereal form, subtle scents stand for an evanescent, disembodied reality which can-not be recaptured. Both the material and immaterial side of smell's evocative potential is relevant in Faber's re-creation of the Victorian world: the proximity of matter (the dense material texture of Victorian life) and its distance (the lost referent); the familiarity of a few basic odours and the namelessness, the silence of historical smells (personal and public) which are beyond recognition.

Agnes's sudden disappearance turns her into a ghostly figure, a non-present presence which both William and Sugar try to recap-ture by literally sniffing her traces. This is where the text most explic-itly links the olfactory and the spectral. Sugar's quest culminates in an olfactory encounter, towards the end of the narrative, notable for the sense of frustration it conveys. After having been dismissed, Sugar overhears the conversation between Sophie, William and the new governess, by hiding in an oversized wardrobe – 'a wooden mausoleum for Agnes's less frequently worn dresses' (Faber, 2002, p. 802) – adjacent to the schoolroom:

The splendid array of Agnes's gowns hangs undisturbed and pungent [...] All the Agneses Sugar remembers are here [...]. Impulsively she buries her nose in the nearest bodice, to exclude the dominant odour of poison in favour of some faint residue of Agnes's personal perfume, but there is no escaping the heady odour of preservative [...]. It is too late to understand Agnes now. Too late to understand anything.

(Faber, 2002, p. 802)

In this case, the 'dominant odour of poison' blocks recollection and understanding. Designed to make things last, to prevent the work of decay and the corruption of matter, the aroma of lavender moth-repellent kills all traces of human life. Agnes's personal scent is ultimately as volatile, evanescent and unperceivable as the aroma of the past this novel strives to re-create. Agnes's wardrobe is located in a storage-room where discarded objects (her sewing machine) and rejected passions (William's photographic apparatus and his books) are disposed of. In this space – 'the room that hasn't got anyone living in' (Faber, 2002, p. 801) – the unredeemable past of the Rackham's family is randomly collected. The sense of death and loss pervading this room is reinforced by the poisonous aroma of preservative Sugar detects as soon as she steps into the wardrobe. Agnes's gowns – 'neat, incorrupt and empty' (Faber, 2002, p. 802) – are literally signs without a referent. Their artificial odour is a simulacrum of life. Turned into an immaterial essence amidst a mess of collectibles, the past Sugar wishes to evoke and perceive afresh is inscrutable. Indescribable scents, essences which no language or syntax can name directly are a powerful metaphor in this novel, of the representational imprecision of both history and fiction vis-à-vis their real or imagined referent.

'Watch your step'

Faber declares in an interview that he is never impressed when 'authors rub their reader's faces in the fact that a book is only an artificial construct [...] There is nothing new or clever in this'.[14] In *The Crimson Petal and the White* metafictional interventions do not play a pivotal role and the narrator's direct addresses to the twenty-first century, sceptical reader – 'If you are bored beyond endurance, I can offer only my promise that there will be fucking in the near future' (Faber, 2002, p. 59) – peter out after the first few chapters. This novel does not quite fit the category of 'historiographic metafiction' theorized by Linda Hutcheon (1988). This does not imply, however, that Faber's experiment is the product of a naïve understanding of historical discourse and of the complex relation it entertains with fiction. Trained as a victorianist, Faber works within the tradition of narrative realism. He balances 'inescapable sympathy' (Kincaid, 2002) and postmodern teasing, historical accuracy and playful literariness (William wants his hair cut 'like Mathew Arnold'; Faber, 2002, p. 54; while Dickens features as a client of the 'house of ill repute'), an unashamed narrative drive and abrupt cinematic transitions. Holding on to the conventions of literary realism, the narrative pushes them even further, although eschewing (but never completely) the open disclosure of their arbitrariness. Such a disclosure was indubitably a new, effective strategy when Fowles adopted it in *The French Lieutenant's Woman* (1969), the first in a long series of contemporary historical narratives which have embraced the challenge of 'remembering the Victorian novel' (Schor, 2000, p. 235). Chapter 13 in Fowles's novel – 'This story I am telling is all imagination. These characters I create never existed outside my own mind' (2004, p. 97) – would not appear as meaningfully disruptive today as it did in the late 1960s.[15]

Hilary Schor claims that contemporary *readers* and contemporary *writers* like to 'turn the novel backward' (2000, p. 234) for slightly different reasons. Most readers are arguably enthralled by narrative suspense, 'the confidence of psychological realism' (2000, p. 235) or the promise of 'moral unity and historical veracity' which the Victorian novel codified as its 'unspoken' rule. For contemporary novelists, however, the work of remembering entails above all a 'new possibility for discussion not only of fiction but of material reality' (Schor, 2000, p. 234). In other words, it is their postrealist, rather than simply postmodern, agenda that demands further attention. Byatt's postrealism, in *Angels and Insects*, is a question of 'how to render matter' and, at the same time, how to make '"mere" forms "matter"' (Schor, 2000, p. 238; 244). Faber's postrealism, as I have argued, is a question of renaming or signifying matter, the historical 'real', by appealing to sense perceptions: the character's own perceptions of their material world – amplified beyond proportions – as well as the reader's second-order perceptions of the 'proposed world' of the text.

To Victorian scientists, the senses were 'ambassadors from the material world'.[16] In Faber's novel, smell functions as a special kind of ambassador, representing the Victorian world at its most material and immaterial at the same time. Arguably, it is the paradoxical nature of smell that renders it particularly appropriate to the standing-for operations historical fiction performs. If, on the one hand, to encounter a scent is 'to encounter proof of a material presence' (Classen and Howes, 1994, p. 205),[17]on the other hand, volatile essences in their ethereal form are invisible proofs of a vanishing referent. In *The Crimson Petal and the White*, olfactory references crop up very frequently. Smells are used figuratively – 'the smell of truth' (Faber, 2002, p. 379), the 'stench of charity' (Faber, 2002, p. 410), the 'miasma of […] delusion', the 'odour of male superiority' etc. – as well as literally to render the material texture of everyday life in the 1870s. The return of Victorian odours in Faber's novel produces a defamiliarization of familiar conventions, a flickering sense of strangeness that disrupts not only the habitual and the homely codified by nineteenth-century realism, but also the flattened image of the 'doxological Victorians' that heritage culture promotes.

My analysis has focused on the polarization of good and bad smells, which is one of the few categorizations of olfactory perceptions throughout the history of the human nose. This simple structure allows for a fictional configuration of the historical past as a discontinuous realm. Victorian odours, resurfacing in the boudoir, under the bed, in the streets, emanating from bodily orifices, as well as from the jaws of manufacture and technology, delineate a segment of reality that has little in common with the largely inodorous dimension of contemporary visual culture. However, this historical framework is complicated by the reference to a temporal structure which hinges on olfaction as a physiological constant. Although nobody knows what the past smelled like, it is the act of smelling itself that connects the present and the past within a broader anthropological framework. This is brilliantly exemplified in Calvino's short story 'The Name, the Nose' (1986), where three narrative voices, from different historical epochs, recount the same quest: a male subject following the feeble trace of an indescribable scent emanating from a dead female body. In *The Crimson Petal and the White,* the act of smelling alludes to a very basic, rudimentary level of continuity and familiarity which Faber uses to shake the comforts of realism. The reader is offered a perfectly recognizable realistic tableau which becomes oddly unfamiliar when familiar smells (of urine or excrement) enter the picture. In other words, two regimes of plausibility intersect: one descends from nineteenth-century conventional realism with its excisions and its reticence, the other from the primordial past or the continuous present of olfactory perceptions. The latter poses as plausible what the former declares implausible. The imagined historical real is thus reframed by dipping into the relatively ahistorical time of sensory experience.

According to Ricoeur (1988), fiction is 'quasi-historical' just as history is 'quasi-fictional'. Both discourses share a structure of reference to the past based on standing-for operations. Fiction may act as a 'filler' vis-à-vis history by revealing (standing for) the 'hidden possibilities' of the past (1988, p. 285). Faber's novel, like other neo-Victorian texts, is revelatory in this respect. It shows the flipside of the doxological Victorians, their hunger 'for experience, for thrills' (Faber, 2003), their quirky, chaotic reality, the role of pornography in their experience, and the maddening effects of domestic seclusion. It even breaks the ultimate taboo of high Victorian fiction: not sex but business and commercial culture. Business letters and marketing strategies are often discussed and settled in bed by William and Sugar, during their love-making. 'I have focused on things' – says Faber (2003) – 'which you don't necessarily think of as being part of that age. But everything has always happened to everybody. Forever. So it's all there'. Since historical information is no longer a scarce resource in an Internet age, Faber (2003) claims, history has become all the more inspirational: 'I'm constantly discovering weird things'. For this very reason the past is never concluded. If it is a text, it is a text without closure. Faber's take on the Victorian past is open-ended in more than one sense. The ending of his novel is a sudden interruption. More to the point, the 'real' portrayed in the text has a paradoxical quality. A nostalgic aroma of referentiality lingers over the narrative, punctuated however by the recognition that the process of reaching back, like the act of smelling itself, has an inherent representational imprecision.

'In our disposable culture', writes Miriam Bailin, 'the ability to transform the discarded object of another century into the 'found' treasures of our own may offer some reassurance that here, at least, in the perdurable world of things, all is not lost' (2002, p. 45). The miscellaneous past holds out a 'promise of redemption' the closer it gets to the 'mute and glorious certainties of the material realm' (2002, p. 44). Faber's narrative follows this trajectory from the disposable present to the perdurable past only up to a point. As a neo-Victorian text, it, too, promises if not redemption, at least a 'good time', in a conventionally realistic mode. But the objectified past paraded in this novel is most intensely singularized when it takes on the ethereal form of an airborne essence, by its very nature fleeting, transitory, impermanent. The immaterial side of the neo-Victorian odours evoked in this narrative renders them particularly inapt as agents of fetishization. As the plot itself reveals, nostalgia is bound to be frustrated, especially when the historical referent is couched in olfactory terms. Sugar and William's nostalgic longing for the human scent of their own past mimics at the level of plot today's 'rash of backward-looking concerns' (Lowenthal, 2005, p. xiii) which sustains both heritage culture and historical undertakings. This longing is acknowledged and encouraged at the onset of the story, when the material identity of the textual past first hits the reader's eyes and nose. But it is also undermined whenever olfactory traces are revealed as frustratingly silent, mute signs which do not connect to their referent. The olfactory haunts the house of realism in Faber's novel. This haunting may not be frightening in a literal sense. But it contributes to tearing holes into the nostalgic veneer of contemporary representations of the doxological Victorians.

Gutleben's critique of 'nostalgic postmodernism' is based on the conviction that 'the object of retro-Victorian fiction is not a historically accurate referent but the commonly fantasized image of Victorian fiction' (2001, p. 167). All neo-Victorian narratives presuppose the tradition of Victorian fiction as part of their historical subtext. But that does not necessarily amount to a disavowal of the historical referent as such. The 'fantasized image' of Victorian culture is the starting point of Faber's reinvention of a historical referent which is, by and large, already mediated by literary and visual documents. But he dips more creatively than others into the often unfrequented and rather unsystematic archive of smells, using them in several episodes to cut through the visual patina of current fantasies, especially cinematic ones. Photographs, in this novel, are untrustworthy documents. The juxtaposition of the visual and the olfactory is of course an integral part of the rhetoric of revelation this novel shares with other neo-Victorian narratives, luring readers with the suggestion that the fictional story they are enjoying is closer to the historical 'truth' than are visual documents. This illusion of truth is sustained by tapping on the purely momentous nature of sensory experience – 'a whiff, and we know'. Working as an 'intuitive filler' (Ricoeur, 1988, p. 285), fiction does not recount the past 'als as eigentlich war', but rehearses the stories through which the 'aporetic experience of temporality' (Ricoeur, 1988, p. 193) is configured.

'If the 1950s and the 1960s were the decades of futurology', as Shelton Waldrep writes, 'then the 1990s were times for looking back in order to see ahead' (1999, p. 62). Whether the resurgence of interest in Victorian culture and its afterlife has a genuine retrospective dimension, connecting the past and the future, is still a hotly debated issue. Heeding Jameson's characterization of the present as 'an age that has forgotten how to think historically' (1991, p. ix), some critics read neo- or post-Victorianism as a nostalgic projection of contemporary anxieties and a misrepresentation of historical discourse. Gutleben speaks of an 'opportunistic appropriation' of the Victorian past: 'That the postmodern novel should emphasize its (commercial) appropriation of the Victorian tradition and appeal to its readership's nostalgia cannot be said to speak in favour of a progressive elite' (2001, p. 46). Other critics, however, emphasize how the 'ghost of Victorianism' can be used in different contexts to further programmes of 'liberation and self-identity' (Gikandi, 2000, p. 181). Historical novels, '*poietic* histories', as David Price defines them, 'reconfigure the past in ways that will help us to configure our future' (1999, p. 4; original emphasis).

Whether progressive or regressive, the contemporary fascination with Victorian culture has been accounted for in many ways. The nineteenth century is the site of a break or a 'cultural rupture' (Kucich and Sadoff, 2000, p. xv). The framework of Victorian fiction provides 'a kind of reassuring buffer which allows epistemological questioning to spread its wings without threatening to alienate the reader' (Bormann, 2005, p. 70). By counteracting the 'ballooning instability of postmodernity', the nineteenth century is alluring because it is 'fixed and over' (Green-Lewis, 2000, p. 34). Alternatively, it is the 'continuing residual force of the Victorian' that drives our 'investments' in this period (Joyce, 2002, p. 15). Finally, since 'we are in many respects post-Victorians', revisiting this past throws into relief the historicity of our own practices, experiences, and concerns (Krueger, 2002, p. xii).

Faber's narrative experiment neither mourns nor derides the legacy of Victorian fiction. It may promise the consolation of tradition, but does not endorse the ideal of stability and permanence which goes with it. The past it revives may appear domesticated and 'embraceable' just like the heritage past repackaged for contemporary visitors. Yet it does not share the 'presentism' of heritage culture (Lowenthal, 2005, p. 150).

The past does remain foreign and ultimately too distant and incomplete to be successfully possessed. 'The past is generously biddable', writes David Lowenthal, 'since few from yesterday can answer back, it harbors scope for invention denied to the present' (2005, p. 171). This creative freedom nourishes both the 'quasi-fictional' discourse of history and the 'quasi-historical' discourse of fiction. That is why their intersection is often so compelling. In light of this, the novel's three magic words – 'watch your step' – repeatedly quoted by Sugar, Caroline, William, and the narrator, might be construed as a mild warning to the historical consciousness of contemporary readers: to avoid stumbling on the uneven ground of the present and the future, you must watch your step when digging up traces of the past. Those traces might throw up unsettling images of the present. As Derrida reminds us, to live in the company of ghosts is not to give oneself up to nostalgia: 'this being-with specters would also be, not only but also, a *politics* of memory, of inheritance and of generations' (1994, p. xix; original emphasis).

Notes

1. In Byatt's *Possession*, for instance, food stands out for its colourful quality rather than for its taste or smell: 'Fresh brown bread, white Wensleydale cheese, crimson radishes, yellow butter, scarlet tomatoes, round bright green Granny Smiths [...]' (1991, p. 268). When Fowles describes 'the area of Victorian London we have rather mysteriously [...] dropped from our picture of the age' (2004, p. 291) – the area where casinos, brothels, fish shops and the like are congregated – no smell is mentioned. Attention is drawn instead to the 'torrent of colour' distinguishing this neighbourhood from other, more respectable city quarters (Fowles, 2004, p. 292).
2. David Price speaks of historical novels as narratives which make sense of the past by allowing us 'to sense the past through figurative language' (1999, p. 5).
3. I refer to Ricoeur's redefinition of mimesis in terms of 'prefiguration', 'configuration', and 're-figuration'. The act of reading is the act of re-figuring the configured world proposed by the text (1988, p. 244).
4. Interview with Jack Mottram, 12 January 2003, accessed 10 August 2007 at: http://submitresponse.co.uk/weblog/2003/01/12/michel-faber/
5. Very often smells are described by having recourse to words – especially verbs – belonging to the semantic field of a different sense modality. See Popola (2003), who argues that in Suskind's *Das Parfum* smells are depicted through visual metaphors.

6. 'Smell is unlimited, like the immune system, and yet it is instant, like the digestive system' (Burr, 2004, p. 7). Luca Turin's vibration theory, according to Burr, could solve the mystery of smell: 'If you say the nose is measuring Vibration, the mystery, which exists only because of Shape's well-understood limitation, disappears. With Vibration smell could be instant and unlimited' (Burr, 2004, p. 28).

7. Italo Calvino's short story on olfaction, 'The Name, the Nose' (2000), is addressed to 'l'uomo futuro senza naso', the noseless man of the future who has lost the ability to decipher the 'alphabet of olfaction'. The story evokes a double temporal framework, historical on the one hand, evolutionary on the other. The interlaced tales of different narrative voices, from three distinct historical epochs, delineate a common pattern: regardless of where and when the olfactory quest takes place, its unfolding and denouement are the same. Smell is the sense of sexual attraction and the completion of the quest coincides with the death of the object of desire.

8. See Gutleben's analysis carried out on a vast sample of neo-Victorian novels (2001, pp. 50–4). See also Sutherland's review (2002), where *The Crimson Petal and the White* is described as a 'sexed-up modern Victorian Novel'.

9. For an interesting analysis of the relationship between mess and contingency in nineteenth-century culture, see Trotter (2000).

10. Faber claims that the voyeuristic effect is precisely what he strived to avoid in this novel: '[v]oyeurism implies that you are watching something from a safe distance, with no emotional involvement required of you [...]. Voyeurism is spiritually cold and I try my best to give all my work genuine warmth'. See interview, accessed 20 September 2007 at: http://www.bookbrowse.com/index.cfm?page=author&authorID=82 2&view=interview.

11. See 'The Complete Michel Faber', Bookmunch Interview, September 2002, accessed 20 September 2007 at: http://www.canongate.net/News/ CompleteFaber,

12. On the real as an 'object of desire' in contemporary historical fiction, see Thiher: 'if history can still lay claim to be a discourse of the real, so writers continue to look upon history in its multiple senses as the *other* discourse, a postmodern rival, or perhaps an ungrateful sibling, endowed with Hegelian pretensions ' (1990, p. 13; original emphasis).

13. This expression is a mutated form of that used by Garret Stewart in his analysis of cinematic adaptations of Victorian classics (1995, p. 156). Photography appears in this novel as a new technology, a pastime taken up and then discarded by William, and an instrument to record the past. It is the function of photographs as documents of past events and identities that the novel repeatedly questions.

14. See 'The Complete Michel Faber', Bookmunch Interview, September 2002, accessed 20 September 2007 at: http://www.canongate.net/News/ CompleteFaber.

15. When Faber started writing his novel in the 1970s he was driven by the 'deconstructionist desire to expose the apparatus of narrative' (2003, p. 102). Later on this postmodern playfulness was replaced by the need for greater historical accuracy. Faber recounts how he revised his Victorian narrative, trying to avoid anachronisms as well as the overt disclosure of 'the shackles of bogus mimesis'. The search for historical accuracy led his narrative to '[flourish] under the discipline' (2003, p. 103).
16. See George Wilson, *The Five Gateways of Knowledge* (1860) (quoted in Carlisle, 2004, p. 7).
17. More specifically, Classen and Howes argue that this was true in the past, '[t]oday's synthetic scents, however, are evocative of things which are not there' (1994, p. 205).

6
The Haunting of Henry James: Jealous Ghosts, Affinities, and *The Others*

Ann Heilmann

In recent years scholarship on Henry James has been enriched by the influence the 'master' of the turn-of-the-century 'Art of Fiction' has exerted specifically on the neo-Victorian imagination. As Cora Kaplan (2007, p. 65) has noted, the genre of biofiction has had particular resonance: Emma Tennant's *Felony* (2002), Cólm Toíbin's *The Master* (2004), and David Lodge's *Author, Author* (2004) all invest in what John Freedman (1998, p. 1) has called 'the moment of Henry James' (and Lodge more recently conceptualized as 'The Year of Henry James')[1] in order to retrace, recreate, and refract the multiple personae of a writer whose experimentation with issues of authorship, identity, and subjectivity reflects central literary and critical preoccupations of the turn of the millennium. This essay examines four different instances of the creative adaptation not of 'the author' James himself but of his most influential, 'authoritative', novella, *The Turn of the Screw* (1898): in the medium of the gothic tale (Joyce Carol Oates's 'Accursed Inhabitants of the House of Bly', 1994), the litcrit campus thriller (A. N. Wilson's *A Jealous Ghost*, 2005), the neo-Victorian lesbian gothic (Sarah Waters's *Affinity*, 1999), and supernatural film (Alejandro Amenábar's *The Others*, 2001). Each text adds another 'turn' to James's exploration of the imagination's ability to shape reality, and in so doing engages with Jean Baudrillard's concept of the 'hyperreal': the intense psychological authenticity simulacra assume in the mind. While Oates experiments with James's novella by retelling it from the perspective of the ghosts, Wilson projects the governess's disturbed imagination into a contemporary American research student who descends into psychotic breakdown

111

and murder. Waters adopts Peter Quint's deviant libidinousness in a novel about an hysteric's lesbian awakening and in her own twists of the screw subverts contemporary readerly expectations and interpretations. The most imaginative reconceptualization of James's masterpiece is presented in Amenábar's film, which fuses the subject positions of 'governess' and 'ghost' on two levels. Like Waters, Amenábar plays with intertextual references to James's novella in order to destabilize the concepts of reality, identity, narrative point of view, self, and 'the Other'. The tensions between 'self' and 'Other', 'original' and 'adaptation' are explored in Oates's penultimate story in her collection *Haunted: Tales of the Grotesque*.

'How otherwise to know what power we wield, except to see it in another's eyes?': 'Accursed Inhabitants of the House of Bly'[2]

In contradistinction to James's triangular first-person account, which moves from the unnamed frame narrator through Douglas to the governess, Oates's third-person narrative throws into relief three of the unspoken voices in the original text: Jessel, Quint, and Miles. The story begins with Jessel's rage at seeing herself replaced by the new governess, dubbed 'St Ottery' by the ghostly couple in disparagement of her rural parsonage upbringing. Evidently, Jessel's anger is largely motivated by self-hatred since the chaste St Ottery is all she once was. Like St Ottery, Jessel began by falling in love with her employer and indulging in romantic fantasies of a 'new family' with a ready-made child, Flora (James, 1908a, p. 260). Seduction by the master's proxy, Quint, transformed innocence into experience, but brought no relief from her internalized sense of shame, resulting as it did in pregnancy, disgrace, and dismissal. While the act of 'crossing over' to the spirit world has freed Jessel from her moral inhibitions, enabling her to give unabashed expression to her passion, her new incarnation deprives her of the physical basis for bodily enjoyment. Beside herself with rage at seeing her material desires trapped in her immaterial body – the reverse of St Ottery's caged mind – Jessel projects her self-revulsion onto that mirror image of her earlier self, and enters into a deadly contest with the new governess for the possession of Flora, the emblem of her union with Quint. Like Jean Rhys in *Wide Sargasso Sea* (1966), Oates thus offers us the perspective of the 'other' woman demonized in the original text. Both Oates and James are haunted by Brontë's novel and its Cinderella romance; Miss Jessel, Oates tells us, 'had avidly read her *Jane Eyre*' (Oates, 1994, p. 260), and so, presumably, has James's governess when she indulges in daydreams of 'some one' observing her actions and appearing on garden paths or gazing from towers to offer his benign approval (James, 1908a, p. 37). Just as in Brontë the face-to-face confrontation between wife and bride leads to a final explosion of violence followed by the collapse of the first Mrs Rochester, so James and Oates dramatize the disintegration of the first governess when she is challenged by the gaze of her successor: it is this commanding gaze which prompts Jessel in both texts to resign her ghostly presence.

Quint, by contrast, finds his failing spirits revitalized by his encounters with the governess. In her revision of James's text Oates retains Quint's womanizing proclivities but turns him into a much more caring individual: until St Ottery's arrival his passion for Jessel is genuine, as is his compassion for Miles; in contradistinction to the not-so-veiled hints in *The Turn of the Screw* about Quint's 'secret disorders, vices more than suspected' (James, 1908a, p. 51), this is not a story about potential child abuse. Instead it is the Harley Street uncle who comes under attack: not only does he ignore the children's desperate need for affection, he also demands of Quint that he stamp out any signs of unmanliness in his nephew:

> 'I want [...] this boy [...] to be a boy; and not, you know', here he paused, frowning, '– *not* a boy [...]. These boys' schools – notorious! All sorts of –' Another pause, a look of distaste. A nervous stroking of his moustache – 'Antics. Best not spoken aloud. But you know what I mean. [...]. A nephew of mine, blood of my blood, bred to inherit my name, the bearer of a great English lineage – he must, he *will*, marry, and sire children to continue the line to –' Another pause, and here a rather ghastly slackening of the mouth, as if the very prospect sickened, ' – perpetuity [...] I would rather see the poor little bugger dead, than *unmanly*'.
>
> (Oates, 1994, p. 261, original emphases)

The uncle's extreme discomfort with the idea of marital reproduction, along with his own manifest bachelorhood, his blatant indifference to the governess and Flora, and his disintegrating speech may signal his own condition, hinted at in his loaded choice of diminutive ('the poor little bugger') and the sheer force of his physical revulsion at the thought that Miles might turn out to be a 'degenerate' (Oates, 1994, p. 261). James, too, insinuates the uncle's deviant sexual proclivities when he has Mrs Grose refer to his quasi-Wildean penchant for lowly company and his exaggerated concern for his valet's health (James, 1908a, p. 50): a reminder to contemporary readers of the wealthy and cultured Dr Jekyll's inappropriate affection for the loutish, distinctly lower-class Hyde in Robert Louis Stevenson's 1886 novella (a partiality which his bachelor friends associate with same-sex desires). In Oates the figures of the responsible and irresponsible adult change place; here it is the uncle who exudes the air of savagery previously projected onto Quint. Oates's Miles has no wish to have his uncle summoned but only, and exclusively, wants to be loved by Quint. Traumatized by the loss of his parents at the age of five, Miles finds himself orphaned for a second time at Quint's death and, grief-stricken, begins to search for signs of him. Oates develops the story of Miles's quest for Quint in close analogy to James, but infuses James's dramatic conclusion with profound irony when, in a poignant volte-face, she has Miles run outside, desperate to rejoin Quint, only to become distracted from his life-and-death pursuit by the sound of bullfrogs:

> Into the balmy-humid night the child Miles runs, runs for his life, damp hair sticking to his forehead, and his heart, that slithery fish, thumping against his ribs. Though guessing it is futile, for the madwoman was pointing at nothing, Miles cries, in a hopeful, dreadful voice, 'Quint? – *Quint?*'
>
> The wind in the high trees, a night sky pierced with stars. No answer of course.
>
> Miles hears, with a smile, bullfrogs in the pond. Every year at this time. Those deep guttural urgent rhythmic croaks. Comical, yet with dignity. And so many! The night air is warmly moist as the interior of a lover's mouth. The bullfrogs have appropriated it. Their season has begun.
>
> (Oates, 1994, pp. 282–3, original emphasis)

The bullfrogs' mating calls deflate the expectation that the story might 'turn the screw' on James's conclusion. Oates's denouement determinedly refuses to address the mystery of 'what really happens' at the end of James's text. (Does Miles suffer a heart attack because he does, or does not, see the ghost?) Instead, the new 'season has begun': just as nature renews itself, so, it is implied, might Miles; and so, too, might the nature of James's tale. This idea of literal and literary renewal is central to the twenty-first century context of Wilson's *A Jealous Ghost.*

'[N]ow, in quite a different way, she was inside *Turn!*': *A Jealous Ghost* [3]

At the end of her experience of retracing the steps of James's governess, Wilson's third-person protagonist, 27-year-old Sallie Declan, reflects that:

> She had certainly changed *Turn*. Poor old Henry, he'd hardly recognise it, her version. Maybe that was it, maybe Hell's Bells [Helstone, her traditional-minded PhD supervisor] was one of those people who thought you could get back to the *Turn* that Henry had written and maybe that could never be done. There was the old house down in the country, and the two children, and the housekeeper, and the ghosts. But they were never going to be the same again. That was certain.
>
> (Wilson, 2005, p. 186)

They are never going to be the same again, first, because to the doctoral student Sallie, schooled in poststructuralist thought, any rereading of a text must of necessity effect its transformation. Second, any reorganization of the 'raw material', the textual building blocks, will make for a radically different dynamics of interaction. The old country house, the children, the housekeeper, the ghosts depend for their overall effect and impact on the reader on the central consciousness through which events are filtered and (mis)represented: the governess. Without Wilson's metacritical twists to this pivotal character and her singular 'imagination working freely, working [...] with extravagance' (James, 1908b, p. 120) the novel might read like pastiche: Staverton is believed to be the country seat on which the anecdote which inspired James was based (Wilson, 2005, p. 24); eight-year-old Frannie (Frances) and her ten-year-old boarding-school brother Mike (Michael) are the master's children in literal as well as literary terms since James's Harley Street uncle here assumes the guise of Charles 'Masters', high-profile international attorney and absentee father; the physically imposing, self-assured, and happily married housekeeper Gloria, on the other hand, could not be further removed from the unassuming, motherly Mrs Grose. An American in England, working on a poststructuralist thesis on 'Metanym and Anonym in Henry James' (Wilson, 2005, p. 54), the narrator, Sallie, is both an all-too-knowing subject of her fantasies and the hapless captive of a deeply disturbed psyche. Whereas James purposely withheld all but the most essential details of his governess's character and previous life history, even denying her a name ('Anonym') in order to capture in his story 'the tone of tragic, yet of exquisite mystification' (James, 1908b, p. 120), Wilson contextualizes Sallie's psychosis within a history of childhood and adolescent alienation punctuated by episodes of mental breakdown and assault. At the same time the novel draws on her critical reflections on the 'ur-text' to conceptualize the 'copy' she is attempting to inhabit: '*Turn* was itself a turn, in which metaphor and the nominal, the real and the imagined, imploded classically; hence "metanym", a change or turn of name' (Wilson, 2005, p. 54). The complex relationship of 'ur-text' and 'copy' is analogous to the increasing dissociation between 'reality' and 'fantasy' in Sallie's life. Underplayed in James, the trauma of parental loss and geographical displacement is here transposed into the long-term effects of family breakdown and cultural dislocation: with her father lost to divorce, her mother to tranquillizers, Sallie, an only child, from the age of eight (Frances's/Flora's age) formed a habit of escaping into the world of the mind. As an undergraduate she found a precarious refuge in her American student peer group, but now she discovers herself entirely unprepared for the loneliness of her postgraduate life in London. Her infantile psyche, visually manifest in fleece tops adorned by teddy bears, yearns for a substitute family; hence her disappointment at meeting Gloria: 'Sallie had wanted a homely body, not this tall, self-confident and, yes, sexy person. She realised that some of the moments in the James tale that touched her most were those when the terrified governess takes the old housekeeper into her confidence, and the two women embrace and clasp one another. Sallie had been in quest of such a figure' (Wilson, 2005, p. 37). Unable to recover the longed-for, imaginary mother, she stakes out her claim on the father, furtively taking possession of Masters's pyjamas, toothbrush, and bedroom from her first night at Staverton: a gratification which prompts a 'mysterious sense of belonging' (Wilson, 2005, p. 100). These acts of libidinal appropriation notwithstanding, Sallie insists on disavowing any sexual element to her desire. Just as the repression of James's governess manifests itself as an obsession with reading sinister sexual meanings into innocuous gestures, so Wilson's protagonist is painfully absorbed by the thought of the possibility of any physical encounter with the sexual. Thus when fantasizing about becoming Staverton's mistress, she reassures herself that, as Masters has fathered two children already, '[t]here was absolutely no need, ever, for him to do that thing again' (Wilson, 2005, p. 100). In James's novella the governess notoriously displaces her horror of sexuality onto that of spectrality: Peter Quint makes his first appearance on a phallic tower, Miss Jessel at the side of a lake, and when in the latter situation the governess observes Flora fitting a mast onto a boat made out of sticks, she responds with extreme revulsion: 'They know – it's too monstrous: they know, they know!' (James, 1908a, p. 54). The children's knowledge refers both to the existence of the ghosts and the sexual act: the two are interchangeable in the governess's mind. Sallie will have none of this classic Freudian interpretation: 'with her absolute dread of that activity, her disgust at the very words used [...] she had tried to discount what these truly filthy-minded critics had seen' (Wilson, 2005, p. 98). Much more pointedly than in the case of James's governess, the urgency of her desire to turn her wish-fulfilment fantasies into tangible reality leads to extreme misinterpretations of her interchange with others. Thus she returns from her short interview with Masters in the conviction not only that he lost his wife (in actual reality he has had an injunction placed on her contact with their children after discovering her affair with a drug dealer), but that he intends her, Sallie, for his 'trial bride' (Wilson, 2005, p. 23): 'He was auditioning her, not for the role of temporary nanny, but of [...] the kids' mother!' (Wilson, 2005, p. 18) Her misrecognition of her employer's agenda to suit her infantile needs is exacerbated by her projection of literary figures onto real-life contexts: Masters reminds her of Byron, Mr Darcy, Mr Rochester, and Max de Winter (Wilson, 2005, pp. 16, 19, 13). Even as she is awaiting trial for the murder of his daughter, Sallie still deludes herself with thoughts of Masters's marital intentions.

For all her inability to function within and interpret effectively actual social interaction with others, in her thesis Sallie ironically reflects with considerable lucidity on the collapse of reality and fantasy in epiphanic moments of 'hyperreality': 'Baudrillard had argued (*Simulations*, 1983)', writes Sallie, 'that in hyperreal situations, what is real and what is imaginary implode into one another. We experience "reality" and "simulations" as "hyperreality", without being able to distinguish between them' (Wilson, 2005, p. 51). Sallie's 'turn' on *Turn* is of course that she knows only too well that Staverton is *not* Bly (she is dismissive of her supervisor's efforts to connect James's text to a tangible locality and history), but deliberately exults in conflating reality and fantasy à la Baudrillard. From the moment of her arrival in Staverton, she treats the simulacrum as having assumed reality status: 'she was inside *Turn*!' (Wilson, 2005, p. 55). She continually refers to Staverton as Bly and addresses the children as Flora and Miles, not because she *cannot* but because she does not *want* to do otherwise. Unable to make sense of her life other than through literary models, Sallie is determined to raise literary fantasy to the level of literal reality. Ironically, Staverton thus takes on the significance of what Baudrillard calls a '*third-order simulation*' (1983, p. 220; original emphasis). If, as Baudrillard argues, 'Disneyland is there to conceal the fact that it is the "real" country, all of "real" America, which *is* Disneyland' (1983, p. 220; original emphasis), then the dramatic emphasis of the collapse of Staverton into Bly, 'reality' into 'literature', highlighted as it is in Sallie's emails to her American friend Lorrie (Wilson, 2005, pp. 76–7), serves to obscure the Derridean dictum, so applicable to Sallie, that 'il n'y a pas de hors-texte' (Derrida, 1976, p. 158): outside of literature Sallie has no life.

Sallie's real problems arise when literature stops being a matter to be shaped by her fantasies and takes on a life of its own. When on one of her walks through the grounds she comes face to face with Rosie Masters, whom she recognizes from a picture in Masters's bedroom, her intense shock reaction and 'air-rending screams' (Wilson, 2005, p. 102) indicate that now, for the first time, she feels out of control. She had derived great pleasure from placing herself in the position of James's governess, especially from taking the governess's reveries about her 'master' much further, thus creating a new direction for the text; but she never expected to come across the equivalent of Miss Jessel, her predecessor and rival: to discover a 'real' ghost. A neighbour's revelation that Rosie is very much alive and therefore anything but a ghost tips Sallie's mind over into the Baudrillardian hyperreality she previously simulated experiencing: 'All day, since realising that Rosie was still alive, Sallie had been in this hypertense state, this condition where reality was fading in and out of fantasy, where she could not breathe or swallow or eat with ease' (Wilson, 2005, pp. 174–5). The day ends with an extreme moment of hyperreality: in Sallie's fatal misrecognition of Frances as Rosie, which results in her bludgeoning the child to death.

There is a sense in which Sallie's collapse of fantasy and reality is prompted by her naïve acceptance of poststructuralism's dismissal of all truth claims in favour of a relativist model in which thought – the imagination – represents the only reality worth taking seriously. Literary theory, in Sallie's case, literally turns into an instrument of execution:

> Rosie was meant to be dead. One of the important texts of critical theory for her – Todorov? Stanley E. Fish? They were a little muddled right now in her head – said how reading is a creative act, thinking is a creative act. Maybe it was Barthes. We make our own text. [...]. There is no such thing as a concrete reality [...]. We make reality. For her, the reality had been, ever since she came to Bly, that Rosie was dead.
>
> (Wilson, 2005, pp. 170–1)

If James's text questions and dramatizes the nature of storytelling and the processes of fiction, then *A Jealous Ghost* interrogates the impostures of literary theory.

In furnishing his protagonist with an identity and detailed personal history, Wilson surrenders the instability of James's text to a psychological exploration of the violent impulses which possess his 'governess'. As Sallie reflects, *Turn of the Screw* 'wasn't just scary because it was a story about ghosts. It was scary because of the suppressed violence that shimmered beneath its elegant sentences' (Wilson, 2005, p. 67). Indeed, the violence which erupts in full force at the end of James's story in the governess's fierce struggle for the control of Miles presents a tangible threat throughout. Early on in the story she admits to a distinctly aggressive impulse towards Flora after discovering that the child has got up in the middle of the night to look out of the window, presumably to commune with the ghosts: 'I must have gripped my little girl with a spasm that, wonderfully, she submitted to without a cry or a sign of fright. Why not break out at her on the spot and have it all over? – give it to her straight in her lovely little lighted face?' (James, 1908a, p. 67). In *A Jealous Ghost* this impulse towards violence is no longer a mere threat, but is revealed as an essential part of Sallie's previous history. Staverton is her first experience neither of childminding nor of assault. When at the age of James's governess she was entrusted with looking after the seven-year-old son of a friend of her mother, the boy barely escaped with his life when she banged his head against the bathroom faucet. A few years later, at university, Sallie hospitalized a fellow student by battering her with an iron. Her dogged denial of responsibility and insistence on her sanity and the common-sense nature of her behaviour forge a chilling voice of madness:

> Why could neither Lorrie nor Sallie's mom see that the incident in the bathroom with Jakie had nothing to do with her present little vacation job in Kent? The idea that the incident would repeat itself with Miles and Flora was simply ridiculous. Sallie Declan was not a child batterer. She was not mentally disturbed. The way Mom and Lorrie spoke, you would guess she had been both. [...]. Look, all that happened was, for a split second, she had lost control. That happens to anyone dealing with kids.
>
> (Wilson, 2005, p. 30)

In contradistinction to James's governess, there can be no question about Sallie's insanity when she continues to refer to her brutal murder of Frances as a tragic mishap, nothing but an, admittedly horrible, 'accident' (Wilson, 2005, p. 185).

It is just such an 'accident', albeit not a homicidal one, which in Waters's *Affinity* leads to the incarceration of the spiritualist medium Selina Dawes in Millbank Prison, where she is befriended by the middle-class visitor Margaret Prior, an hysteric and repressed lesbian recovering from the trauma of her father's death, the loss of her lover, and her own attempted suicide. On the rebound from a secret love affair which ended with the other woman's marriage to her brother, Margaret falls deeply in love with Selina and helps her to escape to Italy, only to find herself defrauded of lover, money, future, and even identity when Selina absconds not with Margaret herself but with Margaret's maid Ruth Vigers. Ruth, who now assumes Margaret's name, has been Selina's long-standing lover and the impersonator of Selina's 'spirit guide', Peter Quick: the 'ghost' whose manhandling of an hysterical girl resulted in Selina's prison sentence.

'How my mind runs to ghosts these days!'[4]

An accomplished neo-Victorian novel, Waters's text constructs itself through its numerous 'affinities' with Victorian culture and literature. Margaret Prior lives in Cheyne Walk in Chelsea, a street with impressive literary credentials, the one-time home of, among others, George Eliot, Elizabeth Gaskell, Dante Gabriel Rossetti, Algernon Charles Swinburne, and also Henry James. But Margaret's aspirations for an intellectual life are buried in her father's grave: 'You are not Mrs Browning, Margaret', her mother cruelly reminds her when she attempts to avoid a social gathering by claiming ill health (Waters, 2000, p. 252). Yet it is precisely the epic feminist poem *Aurora Leigh* (1856) which proves Margaret's greatest inspiration when she asks Selina to call her 'Aurora', has Selina's passport made out for 'Marian Erle', and dreams of a romantic future together in Italy; the Italy she had hoped to visit with her art historian father, and her then lover Helen. Instead of travelling to Italy she becomes a lady visitor at Millbank. The Victorian prison looms large in Waters's novel in its Gothic architecture and disciplining regime, and also in its cultural resonances: Margaret prepares for her visits by studying Henry Mayhew and John Binny's *Criminal Prisons of London and Scenes of Prison Life* (1862), and later grudgingly reads Charles Dickens's *Little Dorrit* to Mrs Prior. The clandestine relationship between the 'lady' Selina Dawes and her lowly servant Ruth Vigers and their spiritualist theatricals echo the secret marriage and 'private theater' (Green, 1991) conducted between the middle-class diarist, poet and photographer Arthur Munby and the maid-of-all-work Hannah Cullwick, whose physical strength and gift for multiple masquerades Ruth shares. (Where Cullwick posed as a 'chimney sweep', Ruth impersonates 'Peter Quick', and both excel at performing ladyhood.)[5] The paraphernalia of the master–slave relationship – the padlocked chain Cullwick wore around her neck in tribute to her 'Massa' (Stanley, 1984, p. 13)[6] – are represented in Selina's dog collar. That class hierarchies are reversed is indicated in the closing line of the novel where Ruth ominously impresses on Selina to 'Remember [...] whose girl you are' (Waters, 2000, p. 352).

While not conceived as a direct reconceptualization of *The Turn of the Screw*, Waters's novel imaginatively recasts the signifiers of 'governess', 'children' and 'ghosts' against the context of a radically different gothic setting, the urban panopticon[7] of Millbank Penitentiary, a place initially as unfamiliar and disorienting to Margaret Prior as Bly is to the governess. The figure of the uncle is discarded; the only male love-object present at the outset of the text is Margaret's late father, a supportive figure in her life who (like Stephen Gordon's father in Radclyffe Hall's 1928 novel *The Well of Loneliness*) may have had an understanding of her nature and insight into the futility of attempting to 'correct' it. The power struggle between the governess, the children, and the ghosts is inscribed into Mrs Prior's unsympathetic, all-too-knowing awareness of her daughter's 'condition' and her watchful guard of Margaret, whose illness acts as a marker of her sexual difference: Margaret's persistent physical ill health here signals her moral disequilibrium and perverse refusal, in her mother's eyes, to recover from her improper proclivities. The conflation of physical and moral health in *Affinity* bears some analogies with the homosexual innuendo in Miles's expulsion from school in James's story: what did Miles say to the boys he liked that was so scandalous? The governess at first suspects a charge of dishonesty but after her sightings of the ghosts fears much worse. Just as she is particularly apprehensive of the children's activities at night, so Mrs Prior's careful monitoring of Margaret increases at bedtime. She strongly disapproves of Margaret's desire for solitary and unsupervised contemplation, and makes every effort to stop her visits to Millbank and its ghastly/ghostly inmates who threaten to (and indeed do) take her daughter away from her. As Margaret is the novel's primary narrator, we sympathize with her exasperation and the urgency of her need to break free from a system of surveillance as persistent and relentless as that experienced by the prisoners in Millbank. Read against the context of James's novella, Margaret's plight provides some insights into the intense frustration suffered by Flora and especially Miles of never being able to shake off the governess's iron control.

If in her troubled relationship with her domineering mother Margaret bears some resemblance to James's children, she more manifestly displays the nervous condition of the governess. Resonances with James emerge from Margaret's complex interaction with the 'ghosts' in her life. Initially, the prisoners strike her as 'ghostly' (Waters,

2000, p. 20): condemned to the 'dim half-world of the wards' (Waters, 2000, p. 134), an existence tantamount to death in life, and dispossessed of a voice by injunctions of silence, they assume the aspect of apparitions, but when looked at closely appear 'suddenly terribly real' (Waters, 2000, p. 20) because they mirror her own predicament. As Margaret gets to know Millbank's inmates individually, the divisions between 'ghost' and 'person', the subject and the object of the gaze, begin to blur. Margaret's first glance at the prisoners is from the top of the pentagon's tower, the central observation point in the panoptical architecture of the Benthamite institution. Positioned like Peter Quint in his first confrontation with the governess, she stares down into the exercise yard where the women take their daily silent walk, but meets with no challenge to her gaze; the only woman to raise her eyes 'gazed blankly' at the window behind which Margaret and the prison matrons are stationed (Waters, 2000, p. 14). However, Margaret soon realizes that she too is subject to invasive scrutiny, and not only at home. Her increasing sense of affinity with the prisoners leads her to see herself as one of the ghosts haunting Millbank. Indeed, as a Victorian spinster and 'apparitional lesbian', Margaret already experiences herself as insubstantial (see Castle, 1993; Arias Doblas, 2005, p. 101). At first Millbank represents a nightmarish world which she observes as if in a dream, while Cheyne Walk is the reality; then Millbank takes over in its stark reality; in the end both locations reflect her increasing sense of hauntedness. At the end of the novel, as she waits for Selina to be brought to her by spirit hands, weakened by laudanum, insufficient sleep, and lack of food, and in a state of extreme excitement, she exults at her quasi-spectral state: 'My flesh is streaming from me. I am becoming my own ghost! – I think I will haunt this room, when I have started my new life' (Waters, 2000, p. 289). She is horribly right, of course: the suicide intimated at the close of the novel will indeed cast a haunting shadow over the house. Like Miss Jessel in Oates's 'Cursed Inhabitants', Margaret will drown herself in close proximity to the site of her greatest disgrace.

Waters's narrator thus at various stages assumes the divergent roles of James's governess, children, and ghosts. However, Margaret is unable to recognize the true spectre in her life until it is too late. Aware of the power and omnipresence of surveillance, she is blind to the most potent gazes of all: those of Selina (who in her very performance of stillness deliberately draws Margaret's gaze on her first visit to

Millbank) and above all of Ruth Vigers. Where James's governess is confronted with the ghosts with no prior warning and has no control over when and where Quint and Jessel will appear next, Margaret forever misses the crucial moments of Peter Quick's interventions: when Ruth reads her diary, thus being able to instruct Selina in how to manipulate her; when she removes objects (such as Margaret's locket with Helen's hair), or places Selina's 'spirit gifts' (orange flowers, her severed hair, her velvet collar) in her bedroom. Ruth is the agent and puppet-master of them all: the birth of Peter Quick, the invention of private séances to seduce hysterical young women into parting with their money and participating in lesbian exchanges, Selina's unwitting downfall when one of the séances goes wrong, the manipulation of the Priors' previous maid to gain access to a house situated within walking distance of Millbank, Margaret's seduction and momentous deception are all Ruth's work. Like James's Quint, Quick knows no qualms of conscience and 'did what he wished [...] with them all' (James, 1908a, p. 57). In the course of her prison-visiting Margaret has become sensitive to the interchangeability of 'lady' and 'prisoner' and has developed a social consciousness: 'Don't you think that queer?' she shouts at her mother's dinner guests: 'That a common coarse-featured woman might drink morphia and be sent to goal for it, while I am saved and sent to visit her – and all because I am a *lady*?' (Waters, 2005, p. 256; original emphasis) In her own home, however, she is as unobservant as the guests she attacks. When she comes across a portrait of Peter Quick in a spiritualist newspaper, his 'dark eyes [...] seemed – how odd it sounds! – they seemed familiar to me, as if I might have gazed at them already – perhaps, in my dreams' (Waters, 2000, p. 154). Even though she repeatedly studies the bust of Quick's muscular arm, an arm which daily helps her in and out of clothing and lays her fires, she fails to recognize her maid because as a working-class servant Ruth is well and truly non-existent to the eyes of her employers: she is as much of a ghost as James's under-servants are to the governess when she records as an impression of her first night at Bly that there was 'something undefinably astir in the house' (James, 1908a, p. 65).

This 'something undefinable' is also a central feature of Amenábar's award-winning film *The Others*. More than in *Affinity* and even *A Jealous Ghost*, the indefinable which haunts the protagonists, Grace Stewart (Nicole Kidman) and her children Anne and Nicholas, in a Jersey country house in the aftermath of the Second World War is the extreme discrepancy between consciousness and 'reality'. The characters' confusion is pinpointed in the intermeshing of historical time periods – the immediate postwar era is steeped in reminders of the Victorian past – and the frozen time and perpetual darkness of the Stewart household. Here, too, the protagonists are haunted by Victorian servants who turn out to be ghosts; but in contradistinction to *Affinity*, not only are these ghosts 'real', they also represent our own subject position as viewers: it is with their eyes, with the eyes of the dead, that we, the audience, see events unfold. Nor are the servants the only ghosts: Grace and her children, as the séance at the climax of the film reveals, are dead, too: though unknowingly so. The 'Others', the intruders to the house, are, in fact, the only characters who are 'alive'; they find themselves driven out by the ghosts.

'We're not dead!': *The Others* [8]

Amenábar's ingenious play with point of view and subject/object positions offers the most powerful and striking reflection to date on the narrative conundrum of James's text via an engagement with Jack Clayton's *The Innocents* (1961).[9] If James critics have been exercised by the question of whether the ghosts have an independent existence or are the product of the governess's hysteria – whether to regard her as a reliable or profoundly untrustworthy narrator – then *The Others* illustrates the compelling force of identifying even with a spectacularly unreliable narrative perspective. It never occurs to us to question the living reality of the Stewart family because the camera makes us share their vision. In James the governess's story is prefaced, therefore diluted, even destabilized from the start by the double frame narrative controlled by male narrators entertaining each other with suggestive ghost stories featuring inexperienced young women while the female audience is dispatched back home, thus alerting readers to the questionable reliability of all levels of the narrative (see Hutchison, 2006, p. 33). *The Others*, while offering clues throughout, deconstructs the central point of view only at the very end. It is only at this late stage that we become aware of the twofold illusion involved in believing in the 'reality' of the characters: for the protagonists' delusion of being alive offers an ironic metacritical commentary on the fantasy, or Baudrillardian hyperreality, created by film, a medium which can only ever bring 'dead' images, or simulacra, to life. Like Sallie's fantasies in *A Jealous Ghost*, *The Others* operates a third-order simulation in the sense that the revelation of the central characters' spectral status conceals the fact that they never were 'alive' or 'real' in the first instance. This is also implied in the triadic manifestation of the servants who, because in death they were captured and represented together by the camera which furnished the pictures for the Victorian 'Book of the Dead' which Grace discovers in the lumber room, can only return to the semblance of life in their collective shape.

In an additional turn of the screw, the illusion (that the simulacrum constitutes reality and the dead are alive) is maintained even as the opening of the film, as if in an adjustment to James's frame narrative, subtly signals the fairytale aspects of the story which is to follow: 'Now children, are you sitting comfortably? Then I'll begin. This story started [...] a long long time ago'. The drawings which accompany the voice-over of the mother and draw attention to the textual origins of the film we are going to see (Burkholder-Musco, 2005, p. 211) represent key scenes which are to follow; among these the image of a candle held up while a key is being placed in a keyhole and another of a girl playing with a puppet are of particular significance. The latter, a figurative reference to audience manipulation in the style of William Thackeray's *Vanity Fair* (*Affinity*, too, features a puppet, here operated by Mrs Prior; see Waters, 2000, p. 290), relates to a major episode in the second half of the film in which Anne, dressed in her white Communion outfit and playing with a puppet, narrowly escapes being strangled by her mother who believes her to be possessed by the spirit of an evil old woman: a scene which may act as a reminder of James's governess and her final, fatal, encounter with Miles. The strength of Grace's hallucination and near-homicidal response, combined with Anne's terror ('She won't stop until she kills us!'), point backward to the events preceding the beginning of the film and forward to its final disclosure: that in a fit of madness Grace smothered her children and afterwards shot herself. Throughout the film Anne makes dark allusions to something ominous having taken place – 'Then it happened [...] Mummy went mad' – a point which Nicholas, Anne's younger brother, who has a greater emotional attachment to the mother, consistently disputes ('Nothing happened'). So does Grace, even though the first shot of the film shows her starting up, screaming, from a nightmare (or recovered memory?), the initially upright angle in which she is placed by the camera and which is then corrected to the horizontal position which she has held all along again hinting at the inherent instability of any perspective, since what we see may be from the wrong angle altogether. The idea that multiple meanings are encoded in seemingly concrete contexts is also invoked by the drawing of the candle and the key pointed at a keyhole: a gothic trope about metaphorical light being shed on darkness and secrets waiting to be disclosed, the image is also a more direct reference to the fifteen keys Grace keeps with her at all times to open and lock the fifty doors of the house (representative of the 15 sets of mysteries and 50 beads of the rosary Grace is in the habit of clutching)[10] in order to ensure that her photosensitive children are never exposed to the daylight. The locked doors and semi-darkness Grace imposes on everyone are an apt reflection of her closed mind; a mind which clings to religious doctrine as a means of circumventing illumination.

When enlightenment comes it is ironically embodied in the Victorian servants, who have been dead for more than half a century. They materialize on Grace's doorstep at the precise moment when she is looking for domestic staff. In ironic inversion of *The Turn of the Screw*, Mrs Mills, who like Mrs Grose comforts the girl during the excesses of her guardian's hysteria, not only sees the 'Others' where Grace is struck with blindness, but is a 'knowing' ghost who, together with Mr Tuttle and Lydia, has arrived with the express intention of putting things in order and shedding light on Grace's spiritual darkness. Subtle intimations of the servants' and also their employers' 'condition' abound throughout: on approaching the house to ask for work they reminisce about friends who are most likely 'dead like all the rest', shortly after Bertha Mills admits to Grace that they all worked here before (those were 'the best years of [her] life') but had to leave 'on account of the tuberculosis'; Lydia 'is older than she looks' and was not born a mute, having stopped talking as a result of some unspecified shock. Later Bertha explains the 'Book of the Dead' to Grace, impressing on her that 'sometimes the world of the dead gets mixed up with the world of the living'. When the 'master', Grace's husband Charles who has been missing in action, mysteriously emerges from the fog which envelops the house, Grace, instead of reading the signs of his tragic confusion ('Sometimes I bleed'), instantly responds by redrawing the old lines between 'normality' and prohibitive 'fantasy'. After his departure and the disappearance of the curtains, she repudiates Bertha's suggestion that the children's allergy to light 'could have cleared up' and orders the servants out of the house at gunpoint. Since Grace refuses to listen, the servants decide to 'bring all [...] out in the open', leaving their 'Book of the Dead' picture in their room and uncovering their gravestones. The night-time scene in the garden in which Anne and Nicholas are approached by what Anne has by then realized are ghosts is one of the most effective and frightening invocations of James's story and the only time the servants take on the threatening dimensions of Jessel and Quint. Reduced to passive objects of possession in James's story, the children are given a much more active role in *The Others*; this is particularly the case for Anne. The position of the siblings is here reversed: it is Anne who is the elder, feistier, more self-confident, and rebellious character who consistently challenges Grace's authority, whereas Nicholas is timid, obedient, and all-too-easily terrified; prior to this scene she decided to explore the garden, and Nicholas only followed because he was too frightened to remain behind. In contradistinction to her brother and especially her mother, Anne is able not only to see but to communicate with the 'Others'. Anne's difficult relationship with her mother reworks the governess's power struggle with Miles and Flora: a struggle which results in death in each case, but in *The Others*, despite the greater overall casualty rate, ends on a more hopeful note. After she has acknowledged her acts and asked for forgiveness, Grace makes peace with her daughter. The closing scene of the film shows the mother and children trio seeing off the 'intruders' and asserting that 'This house is ours'.

'Of course we've the others': Returning (to) *The Turn of the Screw* [11]

When at the end of James's story Mrs Grose takes Flora away to London, Miles comments that now 'we're alone', and in response to the governess's reference to 'the others' still left at Bly affirms that 'they don't much count, do they?' (James, 1908a, p. 109). He's wrong, of course, for it is the governess's endeavour to protect Miles against precisely one such 'Other', Peter Quint, which costs him his life. If we apply this to *The Turn of the Screw* and its own Others, it might be argued that the innovative reworkings and revisitations of the last 15 years are a marker of how much we remain fascinated by the issues James explored. For all their differences, the texts discussed in this essay are all structured around six categories in crisis or transformation at the turn of the century: social architecture, the family, the question of (narrative) authority, femininity, sexuality, and identity. Irrespective of whether it is the historic country house or the urban prison context, the setting proves a central contributory factor in the disintegration of the protagonist's psyche because it pinpoints key anxieties about the clash between individual experience and social expectations, or because it imposes repressive boundaries and hierarchies which inhibit agency. Architecture and setting are experienced as a threat in these texts since they reflect a house or institution, thus family or society in crisis, typically because of the absence or inadequacy of the father and the instability of authority. The 'master' is dead, missing, in perpetual flight, or defunct, and the women expected to fill the vacant position are neither happy in the old nor ready for their new role; they are all afflicted with hysteria rooted in nervous exhaustion, intense frustration, or sexual repression. In denial of their condition and its underlying causes, they either overcompensate for their lack of an internal sense of control with the imposition of a rigid discipli-nary regime which prompts resistance, or suffer a mental breakdown with homicidal or suicidal consequences. Like James's governess, all the central characters experience a terrifying crisis of consciousness which manifests itself in the dissolution of boundaries – between self and other, reality and fantasy, the living and the dead – and which is reflected narratologically through the device of spectral doubles, inter-textual echoes, split narratives, spectacularly unreliable perspectives. The appeal to the late twentieth and twenty-first century imagina-tion resides precisely in the multiple instabilities of James's novella: a narrative about the nature of narrative, the text lends itself to illim-itable metafictional experimentation and thus always returns us both to itself and to ourselves: a literary game with boundless opportunities for narcissistic authorial and critical pleasure. Spectrality, in *Turn of the Screw* and its complex adaptations and reworkings, serves as a prism through which we continue to view and review the triangulated relationship between narrator, reader, and text.

Notes

1. See Lodge (2006) for the gestation of *Author, Author* and the Jamesian coincidences which led to the publication of two – and the submission

of three (Michiel Heyns, *The Typewriter's Tale*. Johannesburg: Jonathan Ball, 2005) – novels on James in the same year.
2. Oates (1994, p. 269).
3. Wilson (2005, p. 55).
4. Waters (2000, p. 126).
5. See Hiley (1979, pp. 27–31); McClintock (1995).
6. See also Munby's photograph of Cullwick as a semi-naked slave in McClintock (1995, p. 136).
7. For panopticisim see Foucault (1991); panopticism in *Affinity* is discussed by Llewellyn (2004), and Armitt and Gamble (2006).
8. Amenábar (2001).
9. While Amenábar has not commented on any links between his film and James's story, as Nicole Burkholder-Mosco (2005, pp. 211–12) argues an indirect influence may have been provided through Jack Clayton's 1961 film *The Innocents*.
10. Thanks are due to Mark Llewellyn (Liverpool) for drawing my attention to this symbolism.
11. James (1908a, p. 109).

Part IV Ghosts in the City

7
Haunted Places, Haunted Spaces: The Spectral Return of Victorian London in Neo-Victorian Fiction

Rosario Arias

> Dirt is dirt and squalor is squalor.
> — D. J. Taylor, *Kept: A Victorian Mystery* (2006)

In December 2006 the United Nations General Assembly declared 2008 the International Year of Sanitation. It is, perhaps, in keeping with this declaration that sewers, filth, disease, and sanitation have become the focus of interest in cultural histories of Victorian London. The city has proved an intriguing site for analysis in critical and literary discourses, where it is often suggested that London maintains a fluid dialogue with the dead through the traces of past times in haunted places and spaces. More particularly, Julian Wolfreys has been concerned with the spectral nature of the city of London at the *fin de siècle* and in the twentieth century, as deployed in the work of writers such as Elizabeth Bowen, Maureen Duffy, Peter Ackroyd, Iain Sinclair, and Michael Moorcock, in whose novels 'there is registered a sense that the past is transformed, but has never disappeared' (Wolfreys, 2002, p. 195), a past that can still be accessed through spectral/textual traces. However, very little critical attention has been given to the haunting presence of the city of London in neo-Victorianism. This essay will demonstrate the relentless presence of London in neo-Victorianism through the spectral recurrence of the river.

Steven Barfield has stated: '[t]he river can [...] act as a means by which writers envision change and transformation and *revisit the half-forgotten traces of London's past*' (2007, p. 1; emphasis added). One of the first critics to explore the textual traces of the Victorian past in contemporary literature is Dana Shiller who, in contradistinction to those who stress sheer nostalgia in recent novels which look back to the Victorian past,[1] anticipated neo-Victorianism's dual project, or what the editors of *Victorian Turns, NeoVictorian Returns* have categorized as 'an informative dialogism' (Johnston and Waters, 2008, p. 10). According to Shiller, neo-Victorianism aims at 'questioning the certitude of our historical knowledge', but, most tellingly, neo-Victorian novels also 'manage to preserve and celebrate the Victorian past' (Shiller, 1997, p. 541). Similarly, Cora Kaplan mentions another reason for the popularity of what she calls 'Victoriana' in a larger sense: 'the degree of affect involved in reading and writing about the Victorian past '; for Kaplan, '[t]he Victorians are at once *ghostly* and tangible' (Kaplan, 2007, p. 5; emphasis added). These ghostly traces of the Victorian past, neither present nor absent, can be discussed in the light of haunting and spectrality. This trope proves to be an apt critical tool in the examination of the intersections between contemporary historical fiction and the Victorian age. Since the 1990s, prompted by the publication of Jacques Derrida's *Specters of Marx: The State of the Debt, the Work of Mourning, and the New International* (1994), theories about the spectral presence of history in current fiction have pervaded contemporary criticism. Although haunting and spectrality as modes of analysing the relationship between past and present can be applied to a number of literary contexts, works and periods, they provide an interesting theoretical backdrop to consider the impact of the Victorian age on the twentieth and twenty-first century, as this essay and the present volume demonstrate.

The trope of haunting owes much to Sigmund Freud's 'The Uncanny' (1919), and his notion of the *Unheimlich*. One defining characteristic of the ghost is its capacity to return, and Freud's concept of the uncanny is based upon the return of a fear that had been once repressed: 'this species of the frightening would then constitute the uncanny' (Freud, 2003, p. 147). His comments on the return of the dead constitute a starting point from which to analyse Derrida's substantial contribution to the theories concerning haunting and spectrality. Both Freud and Derrida share a preoccupation with ghosts, doubles, revenants, and spectres. In this respect, Nicholas Royle has argued that deconstruction bears striking similarities with the notion of the uncanny: '[d]econstruction makes the most apparently familiar texts strange [...], [w]ith a persistence or consistency that can itself seem uncanny' (2003,

p. 24). However, rather than show an interest in the actual existence of the ghost, Derrida takes up its in-between status, as it hovers between the world of the living and the world of the dead, to address 'the notion of ghostliness [...] [and its] elusiveness' (Buse and Stott, 1999, p. 10). In this sense, Derrida utilizes the notion of the spectre to explain the pervasive influence of Marx and communism in Western Europe, despite the efforts of hegemony to expel his power. In doing so, Derrida theorizes about the relationship between past, present, and future proposing the term *hauntology* (1994, p. 51) to describe the intervention of the spectre which dissolves the boundaries of temporal linearity. As Colin Davis suggests, 'Freud acknowledges ghosts in order to demystify our belief in them [...] whereas Derrida [...] wants to put into question the intellectual tradition to which Freud, like Marx (ambiguously) belongs and to allow for the possibility that the spectral other might speak' (Davis, 2007, p. 17).

Another significant theory of haunting and spectrality is that of the phantom, the secret, and the crypt; notions which derive from Nicolas Abraham and Maria Torok's *The Wolf Man's Magic Word: A Cryptonymy* (1976) and *The Shell and the Kernel: Renewals of Psychoanalysis* (1987). Less widespread than Derrida's work, Abraham and Torok's concepts shed light on the scarred past of individuals, communities, and even nations. The phantom underlines a concealed secret which has not come to light as yet, but still has to be acknowledged: 'what haunts are not the dead, but the gaps left within us by the secrets of others' (Abraham and Torok, 1994, p. 171). In addition, they propose an interpretive model based on their theory of the crypt. In their rereading of the case of the Wolf Man, they qualify Freud's conclusions and support the existence of a place within the unconscious, a topographical space, where concealed secrets and wounds in the divided self are stored: '[i]t is a kind of "false unconscious", an "artificial" unconscious lodged like a prothesis [*sic*], a graft in the heart of an organ, within the *divided self*. A very specific and peculiar place, highly circumscribed' (Derrida, 1986, p. xiii; original emphasis). The notions of the crypt or vault, secrets, incorporation, and the phantom are crucial in Abraham and Torok's interpretive method known as 'cryptonymy'. Allan Lloyd Smith considers the full potential of their method in the understanding of how cultural forces and outside influences can silently determine one's psychic identity (Lloyd Smith, 1992, p. 294).

Drawing on these suggestive ideas about the ghostly nature of one's past, I utilize the trope of haunting and spectrality in the analysis of the spectral traces of the river Thames, the mid-nineteenth-century sanitary movement, and the hauntedness of the city of London in neo-Victorianism, through a comparative study of Matthew Kneale's *Sweet Thames* (1992) and Clare Clark's *The Great Stink* (2005), set in mid-Victorian London. Beneath the metropolis lie encrypted symptoms and traces of its physical and spiritual 'sickness', which come to the surface in the portrayal of the Victorian underworld, as well as in the persistent presence of disease and waste in the world above. Despite mid-Victorian efforts to displace human waste and excrement to a verticalized space, the Victorian age is haunted by that which it has managed to hide and repress, namely, filth and contamination. Therefore, I will concentrate on the spectral traces of Victorian London's buried history as reflected in the literary representation of its sewers and the discourse of sanitation and cleanliness in the above-mentioned neo-Victorian novels. In order to do so, I will investigate three interconnected aspects: first, the Great Stink; second, the sewer and the city as haunted spaces; and lastly, the leaky body and the sanitary map. The unifying element in all of these aspects is the River Thames.

The Thames and the Great Stink

The River Thames has always been a source of interest for writers, Londoners and non-Londoners alike, including the Romantic poets William Blake and William Wordsworth, nineteenth-century writers such as Charles Dickens and Joseph Conrad and, in the twentieth century, Iain Sinclair and Peter Ackroyd, to name but a few. Ackroyd has even published a biography of the river, *Thames: Sacred River* (2007), which shows a long-lasting fascination with the Thames, and one reviewer connects the structure of the book with the meanders of the river, suggesting that it 'twists and turns into an entertaining historical and geographical account redolent of England's very heart' (Hawtree, 2007, p. 31). In *Writing London: Materiality, Memory, Spectrality* (2004), Julian Wolfreys discusses briefly the presence of the Thames (and that of London's lost rivers such as the Fleet) in Ackroyd's *London: The Biography* (2000) and in *The House of Doctor Dee* (1993). In a succinct analysis of the relevance of rivers in these texts, Wolfreys seems to foresee Ackroyd's next project about the city of London – the biography of the Thames to be published in 2007. That '[r]ivers are of undeniable significance to the identity of London' (Wolfreys, 2004, p. 141) proves true in the novels discussed in this essay. Like *London: The Biography*, Ackroyd's *Thames: Sacred River* is a timely publication, considering the recent upsurge of interest in the Victorian Thames (Dobraszczyk, 2005; Halliday, 2006).[2] The literary representation of the unsanitary condition of the river and cholera-stricken London in the mid-nineteenth century – the period of the Great Stink – is gaining unprecedented attention in cultural studies of the Victorian period. The two novels under consideration, *Sweet Thames* and *The Great Stink*, to a lesser or greater degree, are concerned with the themes of pollution, sanitation and cleanliness in mid-Victorian London, with special emphasis on the construction of the main sewage system by Joseph Bazalgette (1819–91), a civil engineer whose projects and 'the infrastructure that he built for London ha[ve] long outlived Brunel's [achievements]' (Halliday, 2006, p. 4). The modernization of the whole system of sewers under the city of London, the largest city in the nineteenth century, was duly motivated by the material condition and state of the river. By the nineteenth century the Thames, a tidal river, had turned into a great cesspool in which all the bodily waste of three million Londoners was emptied. The whole city felt contaminated by its insufferable smells. There was then a belief, labelled 'miasma theory', that emanations from the river Thames (and also from diseased bodies and putrefying organisms) could cause illnesses such as cholera and typhoid fever (Choi, 2001, p. 566), which was further substantiated by several outbreaks of cholera during the nineteenth century – the second and most important of them in London in 1848–49 (Allen, 2008, p. 39). In the hot summer of 1858, the stench was unbearable and this period was known as the Great Stink; the smell 'was that of hydrogen sulphide created by the removal of all the oxygen from the water' (Ackroyd, 2007, p. 273). The House of Commons introduced a bill and established the Metropolitan Board of Works to undertake sewage treatment, as Matthew Kneale explains in the epilogue to the novel, 'The Real End' (2001a, pp. 315–16). Cultural historians like Michelle Allen and David L. Pike are now paying close attention to this period of sanitary reform which radically changed the urban landscape of London, not only to celebrate an astounding feat of civil engineering, but also to unsettle and counterbalance sanitized versions of Victorianism.

In glamorized accounts of the Victorian age, which purport to romanticize the period by cleaning and cleansing what is regarded as unpalatable or unsavoury, as well as in the collecting and replicating of Victoriana, there seems to be a nostalgic impulse towards the past, assuming what can be called a 'theme-park approach to the Victorians' (Gardiner, 2004, p. 167).[3] However, it is debatable that all neo-Victorian cultural forms are intrinsically nostalgic revivals of the Victorian age; such a sweeping generalization would produce a restrictive view of the complexities of this contemporary phenomenon. I agree with Dianne F. Sadoff and John Kucich who assert that some of the essays in their edited volume 'have defined potentials for historicized self-understanding in post-Victorianism, potentials that argue for the ideological efficacy of postmodern image-production' (Sadoff and Kucich, 2000, p. xxvi). As mentioned above, recent cultural historians and critics subscribe to an inquisitive attitude towards the Victorian past and look at the unresolved contradictions, hidden desires and fears, and fractures within traditional accounts of the mid-Victorian system of sanitation and purification. By focusing on 'very different, often antagonistic, visions of and responses to sanitary progress' (Allen, 2008, p. 17), Michelle Allen, for example, attends to alternative viewpoints that have been previously marginalized in historical and literary analyses of Victorian concerns with the sanitation, purification, and cleanliness of the city. Similarly, it could be argued that neo-Victorianism sets out to discard all romanticism about Victorian conditions and relishes unpalatable scenes and topics, such as the great stink of the river, in order to lay bare, debunk, and destabilize the 'romantic' visions of the Victorian sanitation movement. D. J. Taylor's *Kept: A Victorian Mystery* (2006) is a case in point since the narrative voice acknowledges the modernizing process of the city of London, but clearly criticizes what he calls 'this transmogrifying hand': 'our idea of London has altered somewhat, and [...] a metropolis previously known for its stink and its monotony has blossomed forth in all kinds of unexpected colours. In short, the place has been taken up and turned romantic' (Taylor, 2006, p. 140). *Sweet Thames* and *The Great Stink* also offer ample space to explore these alternative versions.

Matthew Kneale's *Sweet Thames*[4] is set in London in the summer of 1849, when the second cholera epidemic swept across the city and killed 14,000 people (Kneale, 2001a, p. 313). Joshua Jevons, an engineer, who recalls his dreams of 'a London unobstructed by effluent' (2001b, p. 11), devises drainage system for a competition established by the Metropolitan Committee for Sewers (the fictional counterpart of the mid-Victorian Metropolitan Commission of Sewers). While cholera attacks the city, Isobella, his wife, disappears. In a journey to the criminal underworld in search of her, he discovers the true causes of the disease, the reasons behind his wife's disappearance, and gains an insight into the underground level of the city. Clare Clark's *The Great Stink* delves into the story of William May, a mapmaker and surveyor who, traumatized by his experience in the Crimean War, returns to London in 1858 to take part in the project of 'intercepting sewers' designed by Joseph Bazalgette. Clark takes her cue from Kneale's novel, as it were, and explores the world of the sewers in the summer of the Great Stink. Interspersed with the story of William May are the adventures of Long Arm Tom, a tosher, one of 'the city's workers in filth' (Allen, 2008, p. 32), who risks his life searching for valuable items in the sewers. Both stories blend and fuse at the end as William's sanity – he is wrongly accused of murder, declared insane, and imprisoned in a private asylum – and life depend on the discoveries Tom makes in the world of the sewers.

Sweet Thames is dedicated to Henry Mayhew, whose *London Labour and the London Poor* (1861–2) provides exact, although at times romanticized, portraits of the London poor and of dispossessed people who tried to earn a living in the Victorian city, including 'the labourers engaged in collecting, sifting, or shipping off the dust of the metropolis' (Mayhew, 1985, p. 230). It is interesting to note that in Kneale's novel competing versions of the sanitation movement are at play: on the one hand, Joshua Jeavons, the male protagonist, represents an attempt to modernize the sewage system, just before the cholera outbreak of 1848–49: 'I was caught by an urgent wish that all [...] might be won to the brave cause of drainage reform' (Kneale, 2001b, p. 15); and on the other hand, the portrayal of scavengers, toshers, nightmen, drawn from Mayhew's work, underlines the sentimentalized vision of things past. Clare Clark's *The Great Stink* further insists on the nostalgic view of an activity which is already a thing of the past, as the tosher Long Arm Tom states: '[t]hose had been the glory days, when toshing was a business passed down father to son' (Clark, 2005, p. 21). Even though the protagonists of these novels,

Joshua Jeavons and William May, engineer and surveyor respectively, defend and align with the sanitary reformers of the Victorian period, their plots also unravel alternative stories and anxieties about the sanitation movement. Long Arm Tom, an old tosher, able to 'separate the city's stench into its various layers and components' (Cokal, 2005, p. 1), seems to discard the newly technological advances and engineering projects undertaken in the city of London: '[t]he speed with which everything was changing these days it seemed like there was a new dodge come along every day of the week to knock the bread out the mouths of ordinary men' (Clark, 2005, p. 18). Statements like this may come to represent expressions of conflict and resistance to a rapidly changing city, which were submerged in the prevailing view that Victorian sanitary progress was universally supported, thus proposing counter-narratives to the authorized versions of the Victorian reform period. In both novels this resistance to the modernizing process can be understood in terms of the haunting presence of the past which unsettles the 'discourses of Victorian improvement' (Nead, 2000, p. 32). Even though Wolfreys supports the argument that 'never before the end of the nineteenth century had a single site or topography so effectively served as the focal point for the exploration and expression of cultural anxiety, as had London' (Wolfreys, 2004, p. 54), it is arguable that neo-Victorianism brings to light cultural fears and uncertainties which lay submerged under the romanticized versions of Victorian ideas of progress, as cultural historians are now striving to show.

The Great Stink is full of olfactory moments since the backdrop of the novel is the summer of 1858 when the stench from the river became unbearable due to, among other reasons, a sustained heatwave and the accumulation of human waste and excrement:[5]

> London, the largest metropolis in the world, was poisoning itself. That was the consensus reached by doctors and scientists as the century passed its midpoint. As the filth pooled and putrefied in local sewers, many of which were hardly more than open ditches, it exhaled highly poisonous gases. When these poisons were diffused into the atmosphere and carried by corrupted air and water into the lungs and stomach, they entered directly into the blood, spreading deathly disease.
>
> (Clark, 2005, pp. 28–9)

According to miasma theory, disgusting emanations and odours were the cause of infection. Sewer gases and waste disposal were thought to have an insalubrious effect on people, as Edwin Chadwick posited in his 'influential sanitation report of 1842 [which] was dominated by the rhetoric of danger, filth, and alienness' (Pike, 2005b, p. 67). The key term here is filth and its effect, disease, since it was believed that these odours could clearly cause serious illnesses. The social meanings attached to foul smells were particularly forceful in the summer of 1858, to the extent that Parliament approved a plan for London's sewage system under the support of the Metropolitan Board of Works. This project, which took almost twenty years, was carried out by Joseph Bazalgette, who 'proposed a network of main sewers, running parallel to the river, which would intercept both surface water and waste' (Halliday, 2006, p. 77), as well as the construction of the Embankment. Bazalgette's plan put an end to the pollution of the city, which had haunted Londoners in the previous decades with three cholera attacks (and other infectious diseases) which had ravaged the city.

The two novels under consideration focus on pollution, disease, and illness, in a literal and a figurative sense. Cholera plays an important role in *Sweet Thames*, for example, since the city of London is described in metaphorical terms as a diseased body, a commonplace analogy in the nineteenth century. According to Lynda Nead, the city was often described 'as an immense open-mouthed body, consuming everything that comes within its grasp. If the city was a body, it might also sicken or become aberrant' (Nead, 2000, p. 15). Similarly, Julian Wolfreys in his discussion of Wilkie Collins's 'I Say No' (1885) argues that the 'figure of circulation' metaphorically describes the city as a body, contaminated by the dysfunctional system of flow into the polluted river (2004, p. 34). It is, then, fitting that the construction of a new sewage system in London (as well as in Paris) was meant as a 'response to the urban pathologies both physiological and psychological that haunted the modern city' (Pike, 2005a, p. 4). This representation of pollution and filth as metaphorical illness and moral degeneration is particularly highlighted by Joshua Jeavons in *Sweet Thames*: '[a] smell of effluent hung in the air [...] seemingly stronger since my unintended arrival in the district. I sensed the odours as in some way feeding the criminality above, acting as a fertilizer of evil, luring me to misadventure'

(Kneale, 2001b, p. 24). Pollution as human waste and pollution as criminality were indistinguishable in the mid-Victorian period since filth was equated with social and moral degeneracy. Among the marginalized urban figures culturally associated with contamination and filth was the prostitute, who embodied a physical danger – that of contracting venereal disease – and implied moral corruption as she dissolved all boundaries between filth and cleanliness, slum and middle-class environment (Allen, 2008, p. 63). Liminal as she is, the prostitute marks 'thresholds between above and below, between purity and filth' (Pike, 2005a, p. 193). In the opening pages of *Sweet Thames* Joshua has his first sexual encounter with Katie, a prostitute, a contaminated figure who, ironically, will prove to be central in his convalescence following cholera, providing him with nourishing food and drink in the last episodes of the novel. The intrinsic relationship between contamination and cleanliness is further explored in the character of Isobella, Joshua's wife, who obsessively cleans and dusts the house before her disappearance: '[o]ur home was, at least, wonderfully clean. My wife kept it so, with fireplaces swept, tables polished, and windows freshly wiped; free of all but the most lately arrived film of soot. It was her fancy to do so. In fact more; it was her passion' (Kneale, 2001b, p. 25). This passage deserves more attention in the light of the discoveries Joshua makes concerning his wife's disappearance. Isobella has turned to prostitution and the reasons behind her moral degradation are kept hidden until the tragic denouement. Isobella continually keeps her house tidy and clean, metaphorically cleansing all traces of pollution and contamination from her 'filthy' body as she is a victim of incest: her father, Augustus Moynihan, a well-known and well-respected engineer associated with important Members of Parliament, sexually abuses his own daughter who eventually murders him in a final moment of retaliation. The apparent security of Isobella's life complies with a prerequisite of ghost stories (the appearance of normality and safety), but her disappearance shatters all seeming stability in the Jeavons household. Incest, an unspeakable act, haunts the whole novel as Joshua's journey to the underworld is not only a journey to the underground level of the city of London, but also a journey into the repressed unconscious, where fears, desires, and traumatized events are held at bay. The mind is likened to the city since both are haunted by occluded secrets and by the spectral presence of the past. Joshua's first investigations into his wife's absence lead him to a Metropolitan Police station, described as uncannily familiar:

> It was one I had passed many times [...] but never ventured inside. Waiting there, among the crowd of blue-coated fellows hard at work, I was struck by a sense of something obscurely familiar [...]. The bow windows, too, were as of some other place, with their tiny panes of glass, resembling melted bottoms of bottles. Then I realized the building must have previously been an alehouse, probably converted hastily to its new purpose [...]. *Its previous life seemed to linger* [...].
>
> (Kneale, 2001b, p. 160; emphasis added)

The conflation of the familiar and the unfamiliar or strange characterizes the sense of haunting and spectrality and represents an experience of the uncanny, defined by Freud as the return of the repressed: 'the uncanny is that species of the frightening that goes back to what was once well known and had long been familiar' (Freud, 2003, p. 124). In the city of London, built up layer upon layer, buildings possess a historical past and bear the traces of past events, characters, and locations. Much has been written on the subject of the hauntedness of the past in the literary representation of London in contemporary fiction.[6] What interest me here are Joshua's explorations into a maze-like city in the process of searching for his wife, in what can be considered a narrative of the return of the repressed, of 'an unmistakingly modern configuration, recalling any number of haunted voyages of middle-class wanderers into those areas of the city that seem to threaten surface consciousness with repressed fears and desires' (Gunning, 1995, p. 44). In traversing the city, Joshua acknowledges a dark element which lurks behind the seeming opulence of the Haymarket cafes:

> These were splendid affairs [...] Alongside the grandeur, however, a darker element was also discernible; thus the young women who sat alone at tables, many of them possessing beauty and dressed in the finest crinolines, but who conjured up a sense of the unexpectedly familiar – recalling to mind night-time alleys.
>
> (Kneale, 2001b, p. 171)

Kneale's novel seems to endorse a palimpsestic vision of the city. The image of the palimpsest is a frequently used trope in literature on London (Wolfreys, 2004, p. 95); in other words, 'the *palimpsestic* nature of a metropolitan literature viewed across texts cutting across earlier texts' (Stotesbury and Onega, 2002, p. 17; original emphasis) has been the concern of contemporary writers. The image of the palimpsest uses several layers of meaning at all times: 'several figures and several meanings are merged and entangled together, all present together at all times, and which can only be deciphered together, in their inextricable totality' (Genette, quoted in Dillon, 2007, p. 5). As far as the modern city is concerned, Walter Benjamin has interpreted it as 'an accumulation of historical traces, experienced through chance associations of the present with dreams and memories of the past' (Benjamin, quoted in Nead, 2000, p. 6). In the light of Benjamin's theories about the modern city, Lynda Nead has delved into the multi-layered nature of modernity, and has developed his thoughts on an 'archaeology of modernity, in which the sites of the modern city stand on layer upon layer of an underground city, which maintains a hellish and ghostlike presence within modernity' (Nead, 2000, p. 6). I would like to argue that by focusing on the subterranean London, the novels under consideration offer a verticalized vision of the city which cuts through the present and the past, and that functions as a powerful metaphor for the return of the repressed and the uncanny.

Haunted places/haunted spaces: The sewer and the city

Sarah Waters recently stated in an interview published in the inaugural issue of the on-line journal *Neo-Victorian Studies* that she is very much aware of how we use the city of London and that 'it just felt natural to have that in *Tipping the Velvet*, where [Nancy] is often *at street level*, in all sorts of ways' (Dennis, 2008, p. 49; emphasis added). In contrast, the novels under examination, *Sweet Thames* and *The Great Stink*, concentrate on a verticalized reading of the city, notwithstanding the horizontal vision Joshua supplies when searching for Isobella in the underworld. Peter Ackroyd also approaches London from a vertical perspective in the figure of the walking/wandering subject (Hartung, 2002, p. 162), but for Matthew Kneale and Clare Clark the vertical space of the sewer plays a significant part in the disclosure of occluded meanings and secrets. In *Subterranean Cities: The World Beneath Paris and London, 1800–1945* (2005a) David Pike compellingly argues that the nineteenth century saw the emergence of a verticalized conception of the city not only in London, but also in Paris, both epitomes of modernized cities in the Western world: '[t]he conception of the city as a vertically divided space began to dominate urban representations as the lives of the inhabitants and the spaces they inhabited began to be divided in increasingly manifest ways' (Pike, 2005a, p. 196). He suggests that the nineteenth-century vertical reading of the metropolis haunts our contemporary urban experience. Among its subterranean spaces the sewer, a site metaphorically associated with marginalized urban categories such as prostitution, crime, and homosexuality, motivated one representation of Victorian London – that of disposal (Pike, 2005b, p. 55). Like the urban categories mentioned above, the sewer was the space in which to locate what was not acceptable or unsavoury, lending itself to a spectral topography of the city of London which 'occludes, marginalizes, and erases the quotidian realities and horrors of poverty, of working-class and immigrant experience' (Wolfreys, 2004, pp. 40–1). The sewer is a liminal place, as it collects everything that is in between life and death, health and disease, cleanliness and pollution. In Clark's *The Great Stink* the outcast, the marginal, and the criminal are represented in the characters of Long Arm Tom, and Hawke/the Captain. These urban characters, like the prostitute in *Sweet Thames*, make visible the contradictions between public and private, exterior and interior, filth and cleanliness, and they are placed 'in particular spaces within a verticalized conception of the city, in spaces consequently identified as more or less subterranean' (Pike, 2005b, p. 54). In this sense, *The Great Stink* provides several examples of displaced urban characters connected with the underground level of the metropolis. One such figure is the criminal 'the Captain' who lives a double life as 'Hawke', a controller of finances at the Metropolitan Commission of Sewers; he takes advantage of his position and coaxes William May into signing a contract with a particular brick firm in exchange for money. Blackmail contributes to the deterioration of May's precarious mental state, prompted by his continuing traumatic experience as a veteran of the Crimean War. This fact precipitates a series of unfortunate circumstances for his mental health and own life – the discovery of the body of Alfred England, the owner of the brick firm, not only secures his internment in an asylum, but also his confinement on a prison ship as May is accused of his murder. Hawke, the criminal involved in England's death, transgresses boundaries as he appears in both the suburb and the seedy underworld, making even more explicit the liminal nature of this urban character. In cheating Long Arm Tom to obtain Lady, a rat-killer dog in the still-profitable business of ratting, he conflates criminal and gentleman-like behaviour: '"Tom, Tom, listen to yourself," Brassey cajoled. "The Captain's not one of your ruffian associates. He's a gentleman, with a gentleman's honour. Ain't that right, sir?"' (Clark, 2005, p. 191) The criminal underbelly of the metropolitan streets 'as ugly a world as the sewers themselves' (Robson, 2005, p. 1) and the sewage system are conflated as there is no clear distinction between the levels above and below. The blurring of boundaries in spatial terms is best illustrated in the way the two plots mingle and fuse at the end of the novel – May's lawyer discovers the connection between sewer and street level in the character of the Captain/Hawke. When Rose, the lawyer, recognizes Hawke's handwriting in a signed paper given to Tom, he asks his help to save May's life; it is at this precise moment that the two plots join and fuse together:

> 'He signed himself Smith. But the hand is the same, there's no mistaking it'. Rose pointed, his eyes shining [...] He's cheated you out of your dog [...]

> 'Well then', Rose said, triumphantly, seizing the old man's sleeve. 'You want your money, don't you?'

> 'Rather have me dog back', Tom muttered [...]

> 'Very well', Rose said hastily. 'The dog, then, if that's what you want. But I need to know everything, if I'm to help you. You have to tell me everything you know about the man you call the Captain. You see, I know him too. But his name isn't Smith, I'm afraid. His name is Hawke'.
>
> (Clark, 2005, pp. 304–5)

Significantly, the vertical space of the sewers provides the final resolution, when Rose unwillingly inspects the sewage system (Clark, 2005, p. 338), which accords with the notion that '[t]he vertical framework [...] can resolve [mysteries] only in underground commonplaces of plot' (Pike, 2005a, p. 18). Nevertheless, the fact that the key element (the signed paper) in solving the mystery is found in the city's underbelly and the world of the taverns at street level emphasizes the connection between above and below, between filth as contamination and filth as moral degeneration.

Similarly, in *Sweet Thames* Joshua's desperate search for Isobella and his investigations into the causes of cholera disrupt and dissolve all limits and boundaries between filth and cleanliness, overground and underground, innocence and corruption, slum and suburb, surface consciousness and repressed anxieties and fears. He traverses the city horizontally and vertically since he travels across the metropolis, but also visits the underground in his studies of the sewage system. In these novels, the two levels become at some point indistinguishable and both of them are necessary for an understanding of the city. In other words, 'the low – what is marked as dirty, disreputable, or excluded from official culture – is itself crucial to culture's self-constitution' (Cohen, 2005, p. xvi). In terms of Derrida's hauntology, it could be argued that: '[h]egemony still organizes the repression and thus the confirmation of a haunting. Haunting belongs to the structure of every hegemony' (1994, p. 37). It is possible to contend that what is disreputable or has been marginalized and hidden from sight – physical and metaphorical pollution and secrets – finally erupts onto the surface (of the city, of the mind), revealing the occluded meanings that the city/mind had previously contained and repressed, and, consequently, they are neither absent nor present. In sum, the underground world presents a vision of London as both familiar and unfamiliar, 'the inscription of the unconscious on conscious life' (Lloyd Smith, 1992, p. 287), in what can be considered a spectralized reading of the city. By erasing binary opposites, the metropolis acquires a spectral quality since, according to Derrida, 'one must ask oneself whether the *spectrality effect* does not consist in undoing this opposition, or even this dialectic, between actual, effective presence and its other' (1994, p. 40; original emphasis).

Expanding the notion that the metropolis is haunted by the presence of the past, Julian Wolfreys argues that 'London is thus acknowledged as a cryptic space' (2004, p. 186). Concerned with revealing the processes which inhibit signification in the unveiling of a family secret or trauma, Abraham and Torok's theory of the crypt can be applied to the reading of the city of London as a haunted text in which occluded meanings, symptoms of secrets, are cryptically inscribed. A useful definition of a 'secret' in Abraham and Torok's sense has been offered by Esther Raskin: 'a situation or drama that is transmitted without being stated and without the sender's or receiver's awareness of its transmission' (1992, p. 4). The phantom is therefore that secret silently transmitted that needs to be exorcized. London's Victorian past, considered as a phantom, produces areas of slippage and fractures which are transmitted silently in a sort of 'transgenerational haunting'. In this cryptonymic analysis the blurring of boundaries between above and below, inner and outer, public and private in the portrayal of the river and the sanitation movement in the two neo-Victorian novels under examination draws our attention to Victorian London as a storehouse of concealed secrets and unresolved conflicts. The palimpsestic notion of the city now acquires a further significance if London is understood as an encrypted structure, haunted by its traces. Sarah Dillon has lucidly brought together the trope of the palimpsest and Abraham and Torok's concept of the crypt to discuss the 'palimpsest of the mind' in Thomas De Quincey's autobiographical *Suspiria de Profundis* (1845). She suggests that 'the impressions made on the palimpsest (of the mind) live on as a cryptic incorporation on its surface' (Dillon, 2007, p. 29) in what she calls 'the spectralization of the self' (Dillon, 2007, p. 33), closely related to Derrida's spectral theorization. In what follows I would like to develop the notion that in *Sweet Thames* and *The Great Stink* the two protagonists' minds are represented 'as a textual structure actively haunted by its encrypted traces' (Dillon, 2007, p. 37).[7]

Joshua Jeavons suffers from terrible nightmares and dreams (Kneale, 2001b, pp. 93–4), in which he always harms relatives and acquaintances with knives and other cutting objects. These dreams erupt as symptoms of the unspeakable secret his wife conceals. Isobella's unwillingness to speak to Joshua is all the more revealing about the trauma she experiences, although Joshua is completely unaware of the reason behind this silence: '[o]ne action, one instant, and so much seemed changed. Already I could sense the quiet – that quiet I knew so well – beginning to descend. Speak before it could encircle us both. Say anything' (Kneale, 2001b, p. 33). Interestingly, her father Moynihan is described by Joshua in similar terms: '[t]here was to him a kind of charged silence, so that even when charming

[...] he possessed an aura of things unsaid' (Kneale, 2001b, p. 52). These silences and gaps haunt Joshua's mind as traces of the secrets of his wife and father-in-law, and they surface in dream-form. Moreover, Joshua suffers from several traumatic experiences: first, the disappearance of his wife; second, the loss of all his possessions and belongings; third, his physical deterioration which leads him to contract cholera. It is especially significant that the narrative shifts from the first person to the third at some points, when there is the suggestion that the traumatized subject ponders on his past as if he were another person and those events were happening to someone else: 'Joshua Jeavons quietly emptied of faiths on the soft mud of the Thames bank. A haunting, stilled moment, and one I will carry with me always' (Kneale, 2001b, p. 270). His mind appears to be encrypted by the secrets of others that impinge on his life and emotions, as well as his own fears, desires, and contradictions.

Trauma and haunting are linked in Marie-Luise Kohlke's introduction to the inaugural issue of the on-line journal *Neo-Victorian Studies*, since the Victorian age 'is configured as a temporal convergence of multiple historical traumas [...] [which] include both the pervasive traumas of social ills, such as disease, crime, and sexual exploitation, and the more spectacular traumas of violent civil unrest, international conflicts, and trade wars that punctuated the nineteenth century' (Kohlke, 2008, p. 7). She goes on to suggest that '[h]aunting itself, of course, can be read as indicative of personal and cultural trauma' (Kohlke, 2008, p. 9). *Sweet Thames* and *The Great Stink* are both narratives in which both personal and cultural traumas hauntingly pervade the lives of the main characters. As regards *Sweet Thames*, not only personal trauma, mentioned above, but also outside cultural forces are at play in the haunting presence of pollution and contamination in the city, a secret Joshua tries to unlock (Kneale, 2001b, p. 189) and finally unveils in the last pages of the novel. In *The Great Stink* the trauma of the Crimean War features prominently since William May, an ex-soldier described as a 'haunted man' (Clark, 2005, p. 72), is psychologically scarred and bears the traces of his wounded self. William, prone to having blackouts, is permanently resurrecting the encrypted traces of his traumatized past by cutting his flesh. He slashes his arms and thighs in the sewers to regain some control over his mental balance. However, his mental deterioration prompts him to blur the two spaces, the levels above and below, as in the following passage:

> While he was awake his head crammed with questions and the
> ghosts of answers rose in a sweaty chill over his skin. There were
> certainties, he insisted to himself. Immutable certainties. He
> was in Lambeth. The war was over. He could not have walked
> the frozen trenches [...]. They were no more than dreams [...].
> He was surveyor to the Commission of Sewers. The word sent
> a terrible spasm of dread through his chest, dislodging fragments
> of memory.
>
> (Clark, 2005, p. 160)

If his mind is presented as a crypt, created out of violence, where the
haunting traces of the war linger on, the crypt and the surface (plus
inside and outside, sewer and city) are so closely knit together that
they become interchangeable and indistinguishable. Like the layered
cityscape of London, the palimpsestic (or palimpsestuous, in Dillon's
terms) vision of the mind, 'the spectralization of the human subject'
(Dillon, 2007, p. 36), offers an approach which challenges time and
space as their limits are dissolved in the fractured self. As Dillon
notes, '[t]his spectral structure of the self is also inevitably involved
with a spectralization of temporality [...] the spectrality of any
"present" moment which always contains within it "past", "present"
and "future" moments' (2007, p. 37). A sense of fluidity flows
through the pages of *The Great Stink* and *Sweet Thames* since the blurring of boundaries (topographical, psychological, and metaphorical)
seems to be the defining characteristic of both novels. William's acts
of self-harm, the shedding of his blood, symbolize the fluid nature
of mid-Victorian London, contaminated by the waters of the River
Thames, and are significant for the following discussion of the leaky
body in connection with containment and sanitary mapping.

The leaky body and the sanitary map

Fluidity, then, is central to both *Sweet Thames* and *The Great Stink*. In
the latter William, contaminated by the social ill of the Crimean War,
attempts to cleanse his body by means of self-injury – in the opening
scene William cuts his flesh in the world of the sewers and the novel
is packed with references to blood pouring out of his body (Clark,
2005, p. 41). Bodily fluids, including his loss of bowel and bladder
control in the asylum episode, have far-reaching implications in

a novel about the diseased Thames and its threats to contaminate the whole city. William's internment in the asylum and subsequent imprisonment on the ship are also meant to exert control over his diseased body and mind. Arguably, the novel narrativizes Victorian medical maps and the sanitary movement in that Victorian London, because of its polluted water supply, is portrayed as an incontinent body which needs regulation and order. In her in-depth study of Charles Dickens's *Our Mutual Friend* (1865) Pamela K. Gilbert (2005) proposes a model of circulation and fluidity vs containment and mapping. The Thames and the sewage system become crucial in a novel which precisely opens with the river and its connection with filth and contamination:

> In these times of ours, though concerning the exact year there is no need to be precise, a boat of dirty and disreputable appearance, with two figures in it, floated on the Thames, between Southwark Bridge, which is of iron, and London Bridge which is of stone, as an autumn evening was closing in [...].
>
> Allied to the bottom of the river rather than the surface, by reason of the slime and ooze with which it was covered, and its sodden state, this boat and the two figures in it obviously were doing something that they often did.
>
> (Dickens, 1971, pp. 42–3)

Gilbert contends that Dickens's novel gives voice to Victorian sanitary progress and that the city, as an organism, sickens with pollution and filth. Medical mapping, seen in this light, is used in the novel to control and impose limits on the polluted city, under the threat of the dissolution of the self and its physical and psychological boundaries. Bearing in mind the connections I have already established between disease, morality, and the city as a body, I suggest that the overwhelming presence of water and bodily fluids in *The Great Stink* and *Sweet Thames* is intimately related to the sanitary ills and diseases of the Victorian period. Although cholera swept across mid-Victorian London on three occasions, the outbreak of 1849 featured in *Sweet Thames* was by far the most virulent. The dissolution of boundaries is made particularly visible in cholera, which functions as a social leveller, affecting all social classes, and making no distinctions. Joshua contracts the disease and his fits of vomiting and diarrhoea leave his body dehydrated: 'the vomiting and diarrhoea worked upon my body like great hands squeezing dry a cloth; my arms, legs and gut became subject to sudden fits of cramp, while, with my fingers, I could feel the surface of my skin strangely altered [...]. I observed [...] how wrinkles had broken out across most of my body' (Kneale, 2001b, p. 238). Gilbert relates cholera and the leaky body to the incontinent city, since the disease 'literalized this undisciplined evacuation of fluids and linked it to the uncontained human fluids associated with improper drainage, mapping the individual body onto the built environment' (Gilbert, 2005, p. 83). The city and its vital fluids, the water supply and the sewage system, would be regulated and contained with the help of sanitary mapping, established to point out sites of infection, dirt and contamination. Edwin Chadwick led the sanitary movement in the 1850s, and his opinions and actions are scrutinized in *Sweet Thames* through his fictional counterpart, Edwin Sleak-Cunningham. Chadwick, who provides 'the critical link between maps and sewers' (Nead, 2000, p. 18), was officially removed from his position at the Metropolitan Commission of Sewers with the 1849 outbreak of cholera. After this attack, there was further research into the origins of the disease and in the 1850s Dr John Snow investigated the causes of cholera. He famously recommended that the Broad Street pump be removed as a possible source of infection, since people were drinking contaminated Thames water from it (Choi, 2001, p. 567). He developed his thesis that 'water polluted by sewage might be the vehicle by which cholera was transmitted' (Halliday, 2006, p. 130) in a series of articles and reports. His (and all) sanitary maps served a twofold purpose. According to Gilbert:

> Sanitary maps sought to make transparent or visible the hidden and therefore intractable social or sanitary ills of the day, and representation itself performed a kind of containment, while providing a guide for reformers to achieving that clean, well-lighted translucency that was the ideal of sanitarians.
>
> (Gilbert, 2005, p. 8)

Joshua Jeavons, partly modelled on the real Dr Snow, proposes the same hypothesis for the causes of cholera. He is presented both as an engineer who wants to regulate London's water circulation, and as a sanitary reformer when he turns to living in St Giles and observes the ravages of the cholera in that part of the city. He loses all his money and possessions in his search for the missing Isobella: the only thing he still owns is a leather sack containing a copy of the sewage map he intends to present in the Metropolitan Committee of Sewers contest: he carries 'on his back a strange and battered leather sack, fitting so well to his frame that he might have been carrying it since birth' (Kneale, 2001b, p. 181). Like London, he has indeed become 'a mappable body' (Wolfreys, 2004, p. 34); Joshua's destiny and that of cholera-stricken London are interdependent in the novel. In other words, Joshua embodies London, and their fates are inextricably linked. The interplay of fluidity and containment is very much present in both the character of Joshua and the novel as their body/city boundaries are dissolved in their organic circulation – Joshua is contaminated literally as he suffers from cholera, but also psychologically as he bears the traces of the secrets of others; London, in turn, is polluted by the Thames and its sewage, and morally contaminated by its human waste. The narrative functions as a form of organizing principle in the rottenness of the characters' lives and, as Gilbert suggests in relation to Dickens's *Our Mutual Friend*, 'it is the novelist who can map the hidden contamination, while the reader must yield to his expert construction of the city's space' (Gilbert, 2005, p. 94).

Despite the efforts to contain the fluid city/body, the novels under consideration display an overall concern with fluidity, perhaps because 'the drainage system is defined by its state of flux' (Pike, 2005a, p. 190). The notion of fluidity, of things permanently in motion, resonates with the image of the river and its tidal flow and, more interestingly, with mid-Victorian London which is caught in a process of modernization, where the spectral traces of the old past and the present reality of modernity are merged and blended in the Victorian discourses of filth, sanitation, and cleanliness. In this sense, competing versions of the sanitary movement and sewage reform metaphorically describe a city in flux 'with destructive and constructive forces working in an uneven rhythm to yield a landscape never wholly new, yet never entirely old' (Allen, 2008, p. 4). For Wolfreys, London is 'a fluid city, a city of singular, endless flows (both spatial and temporal)' (2004, p. 4), an image particularly fitting for the examination of *Sweet Thames* and *The Great Stink*, two neo-Victorian novels which feature the river Thames. The fluidity of the river cancels out notions of fixed time and space and, to a certain extent, represents the haunting presence of Victorianism and, specifically, Victorian London in contemporary fiction. Dissolving binary oppositions of all sorts, the fluid nature of the river/the city highlights the elasticity of time; so much so that our contemporary age can revisit the Victorian social and spatial crises, and resurrect the encrypted traces of unresolved tensions, contradictions, fears, and desires and grant them full significance.

As this essay has shown, *Sweet Thames* and *The Great Stink* place the Victorian past and the present in dialogue through a re-imagining of the mid-Victorian cultural crises concerning the River Thames, its pollution and contamination, and the associated sanitary movement. I have argued that these neo-Victorian novels present not only prevailing views about necessary improvements on the river, but also alternative stories, cultural fears, and anxieties which lie submerged in the normative versions of sanitation. By paying attention to pollution and cleanliness both in a literal and figurative sense, these novels establish the interdependence of surface and underground, suburb and sewer, thus dissolving the spatial boundaries of the city of London, understood as a diseased body. This conflation of above and below endorses the view that the city possesses a multi-layered structure, a palimpsestic nature. In this vision of a verticalized world of the sewers and the underbelly of the metropolis, where cultural, as well as individual, repressed fears and desires are lodged, there is a sense of haunting and spectrality. London appears to be haunted by encrypted traces of the cultural (and personal) past. The palimpsestic notion of London is further complicated as the city and the self are spectralized in the novels discussed; in other words, there is 'a spectralization of temporality' (Dillon, 2007, p. 37), a disjunction of temporal linearity which precisely characterizes the spectre. There is no hierarchical order in this palimpsestic reading of the city, as all temporal and spatial boundaries have been challenged. This dissolution at all levels is expressed through the fluidity of the river/city, set against attempts at regulation, order, and containment, which would fix the protean nature of the metropolis in sanctioned versions of a sanitized past. Victorian London, permanently in motion as a living organism, functions as a 'phantom' in neo-Victorianism in that it reclaims secrets to be unveiled and disclosed, transmitted silently in 'transgenerational haunting'. Neo-Victorianism, seen in this light, aims to disclose the unspeakable secrets that have been kept hidden in a crypt. Following Sarah Dillon's model of the palimpsest, it could be suggested that writing *about* the Victorian sanitation movement perpetually reconfigures the Victorian city, adding new layers to a palimpsestic relationship with the representation of Victorian London. Although Wolfreys refers to the act of writing the city, I would finally emphasize not only the act of writing the city, but also the act of writing *about* the city: '[t]he act of writing London is then a double act: of reading as rereading and rewriting, of invocation and disclosure of the hitherto invisible, whereby what comes to be remarked is what is already at work, and which, in returning, appears as the traces of multiple cultures, histories, and events' (2004, p. 129). In rereading and re-imagining the topography of the mid-Victorian city, and in unearthing the encrypted traces of a spectral past, these neo-Victorian writers attempt to add a new layer to our own interpretation of Victorian London, thus rebuilding (both in Victorian and contemporary fashions) the Victorian urban landscape. Haunted as we are by the gaps and silences of the Victorians in a phantom-like manner, neo-Victorianism purports to direct our energies towards the hidden secrets, but also allows us to enjoy the process of recovery along the way.

Notes

1. Among those critics who stress nostalgia in contemporary historical novels which look back to the Victorian past are Sally Shuttleworth (1998), who coined the term 'retro-Victorian' to refer to novels set in the Victorian age, and Christian Gutleben (2001) in *Nostalgic Postmodernism: The Victorian Tradition and the Contemporary British Novel*.
2. The March 2007 issue of the online journal *Literary London: Interdisciplinary Studies in the Representation of London* was entirely dedicated to the River Thames and several essays were concerned with the state of the river in the Victorian period.
3. I am indebted to the anonymous reader of the volume proposal who indicated the potentialities embedded in the theme of sanitation.
4. The title derives from Edmund Spenser's 'Prothalamion' (1596) and, more specifically, from the line 'Sweete Themmes runne softly, till I end my Song' (Barfield, 2007, p. 2). Julian Wolfreys also mentions Spenser's line, and T. S. Eliot's *The Waste Land* (1922), in his analysis of Maureen Duffy's *Capital* (1975), as a way of gesturing both towards the past and the present (2004, p. 94). It is also noteworthy that Fred D'Aguiar published

a long poem with the title 'Sweet Thames', broadcast in 1992. In choosing such a title, Kneale erases all temporal boundaries, which is one of the characteristics of the spectre in Derrida's hauntology.

5. For an in-depth study of the spectral quality of the smell in Michel Faber's *The Crimson Petal and the White* (2002), see Silvana Colella's essay in this volume.

6. Julian Wolfreys has offered in-depth analyses of the city of London and the spectral traces of the past in a number of writers, but he is not concerned with neo-Victorianism. In turn, Roger Luckhurst has paid attention to the notion of the contemporary London gothic, but, again, neo-Victorianism is not mentioned. For a thorough examination of Peter Ackroyd's *Dan Leno and the Limehouse Golem* (1994) and Iain Sinclair's *White Chapell, Scarlet Tracings* (1987) from the point of view of the haunting presence of the past in various guises, see Patricia Pulham's essay in this volume. Heike Hartung has also considered how the city of London is (re)written in the fiction of Peter Ackroyd and Iain Sinclair, but from the perspective of a walking subject.

7. I wish to express my gratitude to Carmen Lara Rallo for drawing my attention to Sarah Dillon's work on the palimpsest.

8
Mapping Histories: The Golem and the Serial Killer in *White Chappell, Scarlet Tracings* and *Dan Leno and the Limehouse Golem*

Patricia Pulham

On 15 May 2008, an exhibition entitled 'Jack the Ripper and the East End' opened at the London Museum of Docklands: a large display containing artefacts from the late-Victorian period including photos of abject poverty; filmed 'talking heads' commenting on immigration and the social history of the area; police reports on the discovery of the victims, and, in the final room, pictures of suspects and the well-known, disturbing photographs of the victims' corpses. The exhibition attempted to construct a history of Jack the Ripper in time and space, yet ultimately failed; the result, a fragmented experience and at the heart of it a lacuna, a lack which can never be filled by the murderer's name but which has given rise to the myth that has prompted innumerable histories, fictions, and films. Iain Sinclair's *White Chappell, Scarlet Tracings* (1987) and Peter Ackroyd's *Dan Leno and the Limehouse Golem* (1994) form part of that body of work, yet the centrality of the Ripper narrative is undermined in both by the presence of the Golem myth via which Jewish history functions as a subtext. Ackroyd's novel is set in the East End of the 1880s; Sinclair's drifts between the Victorian past and its own twentieth-century present. Both are examples of what Linda Hutcheon has described as 'historiographic metafiction'.

In *A Poetics of Postmodernism: History, Theory, Fiction* (1988), Hutcheon, responding to Fredric Jameson's critique of postmodern 'depthlessness' and the consequent 'weakening of historicity' (Jameson, 1991, p. 6) writes, '[d]espite its detractors, the postmodern is not ahistorical or dehistoricized, though it does question our [...] assumptions about what constitutes historical knowledge' (1988, p. xii). She argues that 'historiographic metafiction'– postmodern historical novels which lay 'claim to historical events and personages' – 'both install[s] and then blur[s] the line between fiction and history', playing upon 'the truth and lies of historical record' (Hutcheon, 1988, p. 5; pp. 113–14). Furthermore, she suggests that it 'self-consciously reminds us that, while events did occur in the real empirical past, we name and constitute those events as historical facts by selection and narrative positioning [...] [and] only know of those past events through their discursive inscription, through their traces in the present' (Hutcheon, 1988, p. 97).

Amy Elias and Dana Shiller each identify a subgenre of historiographic metafiction. In *Sublime Desire: History and Post 1960s Fiction* (2001), Elias uses the term 'metahistorical romances' to describe texts that rework traditional historical romance novels, and Shiller calls works that 'adopt a postmodern approach to history and that are set at least partly in the nineteenth century', 'neo-Victorian novels' (1997, p. 558, n. 1).[1] She argues that 'neo-Victorian fiction is motivated by an essentially revisionist impulse to reconstruct the past by questioning the certitude of our historical knowledge' (1997, p. 541), while Elias claims:

> The historical fiction written after 1960, that fiction that I call *metahistorical romance*, is narrative that bears striking similarities to those produced by the traumatized consciousness: it is fragmented; it problematizes memory; it is suspicious of empiricism [...]; it presents competing versions of past events; it is resistant to closure; and it reveals a repetition compulsion in relation to the historical past.
>
> (Elias, 2001, p. 52; original emphasis)

In that both Ackroyd's and Sinclair's texts figure historical Victorian personages, and play intertextually with Victorian writings, their novels might be described as neo-Victorian, and their fragmented narratives exhibit many of the features of the metahistorical romance as defined by Elias: they present 'competing versions of past events', employ repetition, and resist closure.

Shiller's article focuses on readings of A. S. Byatt's *Possession* (1990) and Peter Ackroyd's, *Chatterton* (1987) which she refers to as 'novels about literary detectives' (Shiller, 1997, p. 556). Elias observes that this is common in historiographic metafiction, and notes that many metahistorical romances include 'detectives as actual characters in their plots' (Elias, 2001, p. 132). Yet, as she points out, 'in metahistorical romance, these detectives must sort out not the workings of a criminal mind but the message of history' (Elias, 2001, pp. 132–3). I would argue that the neo-Victorian novel and, indeed, the metahistorical romance, is, in some sense, implicitly or otherwise, always a form of detective fiction: a crime, event, personage, or text from the past functions as the catalyst for the retrieval/revision of that past in order to discover some new clue that will change our perceptions in the present. Yet in metahistorical romances, such a process of detection is often complicated by conflicting models of history:

> On the one hand [...] the metahistorical romancers recuperate a sense of mythic, spatialized time that preceded Western scientific, linear time [...]. At the same time, however, the metahistorical romance correlates a sense of mythic time to Einsteinian quantum time/space, which (like myth) also dismantles Newtonian categories of time, space and history. Again and again [...] quantum space/time can become a metaphoric referent for historiographic inquiry.
>
> (Elias, 2001, p. 58)

In this quotation, Elias refers to concepts of 'space/time' in which empirical events occur in a particular place at a particular time but arguably remain unpresentable. According to Lyotard, such 'events', always interpreted in different ways, are paradigmatic of the plurality of 'truths' posited in postmodern narratives and, in Elias's view, replace 'historical sequence with a field of ruptures' (Elias, 2001, p. 29).[2] As a result, the 'act of historical telling becomes refocused on the event that is unpresentable rather than on the minute study and empirical reconstruction of past actions; history becomes more about testifying to the unpresentable than about re-presenting the past' (Elias, 2001, p. 29). Both the metahistorical romance, and detective fiction share a desire for 'truth', but in the former, the search for 'truth' is continually obscured by the unpresentability of that 'truth'.

In *White Chappell, Scarlet Tracings* and *Dan Leno*, Ackroyd and Sinclair are ostensibly concerned with a key 'event' in nineteenth- century history: the Jack the Ripper killings of 1888, which, in both texts, figure as repetitions of an earlier 'event': the Ratcliffe Highway murders of 1811.[3] Both novels are concerned with the nature of inscription and its role in representing the past. However, this interest is expressed both implicitly and explicitly via the mythical figure of the Golem, suggesting that, underlying the focus on the nineteenth-century mass murders that took place in the East End, is the spectre of Jewish history embodied in the creature which functions as the 'unpresentable' 'truth'. This chapter examines the Golem's significance for the recuperation of a 'sense of mythic, spatialized time' and Jewish history in these texts, and its implications for the retrieval, and unpresentability of the past in the neo-Victorian novel.

In his essay, 'Pursuing the Golem of Prague: Jewish Culture and the Invention of a Tradition', Hillel J. Kieval quotes from a letter written in 1674 by Christoph Arnold which explains how Golems were created by the Jewish community in Poland at that time. Whereas, initially, the Golem appears to have been benign, simply a servant created to perform menial tasks, over time, he becomes a more sinister figure, 'a source of *danger*' (Kieval, 1997, p. 3; original emphasis):

> After saying certain prayers and holding certain fast days, they make the figure of a man from clay, and when they have said the *shem hamephorash* [the explicit – and unmentionable – name of God] over it, the image comes to life. [...] On the forehead of the image, they write: *emeth*, that is, truth. But a figure of this kind grows each day; though very small at first, it ends by becoming larger than all those in the house. In order to take away his strength, which ultimately becomes a threat to all those in the house, they quickly erase the first letter aleph from the word emeth on his forehead, so that there remains only the word *meth*, that is, dead.
>
> (quoted in Kieval, 1997, pp. 3–4; original emphasis)[4]

The Golem, then, is activated by, and labelled, 'truth' and, deactivated, becomes a 'dead truth'. According to Kieval and Sinclair, the Golem is increasingly associated with one particular creator, Rabbi Judah Löw [or Loew] ben Bezalel (c. 1520–1609), a 'leading figure in the institutional history, intellectual life, and popular culture of Central European Jewry' (Kieval, 1997, p. 4; Lichtenstein and Sinclair, 2000, p. 180). Sinclair notes that there is a 'cycle of tales in which the creature acts as a primitive detective, solving local mysteries, revenging injustices, [and] false accusations' against the Jews; here, 'Rabbi Leow and Joseph Golem' function as 'early prototypes of Sherlock Holmes and Doctor Watson' (Lichtenstein and Sinclair, 2000, p. 187). In Gustav Meyrink's famous novel, *The Golem* (1915), set in Prague, the creature becomes a ghost-like figure which returns periodically, approximately every 33 years, to haunt the inhabitants of the Jewish ghetto, sometimes appearing as the double of he or she who sees him (Lichtenstein and Sinclair, 2000, p. 183). The question of history is implicit in the figure of the Golem. Created by Rabbi Löw and activated by 'truth', it emphasizes the Rabbi's importance as an historical figure and points to the importance of a cultural 'truth'. The Golem's erstwhile detective role, and uncanny presence in Meyrink's novel, also relate to issues of narrative and historical realism which I will return to later.

The Golem appears in Ackroyd's title and surfaces briefly in Sinclair's novel. The Jewish myth also features in *Rodinsky's Room* (1999), a later work Sinclair co-wrote with writer and artist Rachel Lichtenstein. Here, Sinclair and Lichtenstein meditate, in different ways, on the discovery in 1980 of a room above a synagogue at 19 Princelet Street, Spitalfields, formerly inhabited by the mysterious David Rodinsky, a Jewish scholar who vanished in 1969, leaving behind him notebooks and papers which revealed his interest in the cabbala, and his knowledge of numerous languages, as well as 'hand-drawn maps [...] of journeys around London' (Lichtenstein and Sinclair, 2000, p. 28). When Lichtenstein arrives at the synagogue to investigate, she finds students from the National Film School filming a production, *The Golem of Princelet Street*. Later in the book, Sinclair devotes a chapter, entitled 'Mobile Invisibility' to 'Golems, Dybbuks and Unanchored Presences' as he traces Rodinsky's existence in the popular consciousness (Lichtenstein and Sinclair, 2000, pp. 172–90); and in an article published in *The Guardian*, 22 May 1999, Lyn Gardner observes how 'the Jewish scholar [Rodinsky has] entered the mythology of the East End as surely as Jack the Ripper or the Kray twins' (1999). These allusions to the Golem in Ackroyd's and Sinclair's texts, and Gardner's placement of Rodinsky's name alongside notorious East End killers in her article, suggest a relationship between the Jewish myth and the murderers discussed in the novels. Both are also significant in regard to the temporal and spatial labyrinths posited by the novels' setting in the Victorian East End.

Golems and serial killers

In his 1994 novel, Ackroyd creates his own 'Golem', Elizabeth Cree, whose murderous adventures recall those of Jack the Ripper and John Williams, the Ratcliffe Highway murderer. Ackroyd's novel is composed of a third-person narrative which incorporates other texts by, or citations of, Gissing, De Quincey, and Marx; transcripts of the trial of Elizabeth Cree; her husband's [John Cree's] diary entries; and Elizabeth's autobiographical narrative. The novel makes use of the underlying theme of London's Victorian Music Halls to destabilize gender, identity, and sexuality, while simultaneously staging its own textual 'theatre' of voices. Jeremy Gibson and Julian Wolfreys note that:

> At stake through this novel are the ways in which particular texts belong to a greater textual network or structure, and the uses to which textual evidence is put in searching for meaning or framing the definition. If anything is 'on trial' before the reader as witness, it is the reliability of the city's texts, none of which are allowed any greater validity than any of the others in Ackroyd's performative and playful structure. In *Dan Leno*, the city, formed of endless repetitions and palimpsests [...] is performed as an already transformed series of texts, having always already become [...] 'the scene of writing'.
>
> (Gibson and Wolfreys, 2000, p. 201)

The city is also 'the scene of writing' in *White Chappell, Scarlet Tracings* and, here, a similar 'textual network' of 'textual evidence' is at play in the search for meaning or 'truth'. In his discussion of the novel, Alex Murray notes that 'at the heart' of Sinclair's Victorian London is an 'obscene violence'; the 'violent acts of Jack the Ripper haunt' its pages, and are influenced by the Ratcliffe Highway murders that preceded them (2007, p. 54).[5] Sinclair, like Ackroyd, mentions the Ratcliffe Highway killings, and also plays with, and adds to, the Ripper myth, drawing on the 'narratives' of Jack the Ripper suspect

Sir William Withey Gull, and James Hinton, as well as concurrent characters such as Sir Frederick Treves and Joseph Merrick, the 'Elephant Man', in relation to whom the Golem is discussed. His novel centres on a group of book-dealers who discover a rare copy of *A Study in Scarlet* (1887) and within its text seemingly detect hidden – and, indeed, prophetic – clues to the Jack the Ripper murders of 1888. The narration oscillates between fiction and history and ostensibly seeks spiritual redemption in the present by mapping and retracing the locations and events of the past. Both novels consider the repetition of violence across temporal, and within geographical, boundaries.

The Ratcliffe Highway murders took place on 7 and 19 December 1811. The first victims were the Marr family of 29 Ratcliffe Highway; the second were John Williamson, publican at the King's Arms Tavern, New Gravel Lane (now Glamis Road, near The Highway in Wapping), his wife Elizabeth, and their barmaid Bridget Harrington. The accused murderer, John Williams, a seaman, was arrested, and later committed suicide. His corpse was dragged through the streets and buried, with a stake through the heart, at the junction of Commercial Road and Cannon Street Road, and his skeleton later excavated in August 1886 by a gas company digging a trench in the road where Cannon Street and Cable Street intersect at the Hawksmoor church, St George in the East.[6] The details of the Ripper murders are, of course, more commonly known. With the exception of one, which occurred within the boundary of the City of London, the murders of five prostitutes – Mary Ann Nichols, Annie Chapman, Catherine Eddowes, Elizabeth Stride, and Mary Jane Kelly (also known as Marie Jeanette Kelly) – took place within a quarter of a mile of Whitechapel, East London, between 31 August and 9 November 1888.[7]

In *Lud Heat and Suicide Bridge* (1975) Sinclair makes a spatial connection between these two events based on the position of two of Nicholas Hawksmoor's churches in London's East End. He points to what he defines as 'the unacknowledged magnetism and control-power, built-in code force, of these places' and adds that '[t]he whole karmic programme of Whitechapel in 1888 moves around the fixed point of Christ Church [Spitalfields]', while 'St George-in-the-East was host' to the Ratcliffe Highway murders (Sinclair, 1998, pp. 21–2).[8] The Ratcliffe Highway killings, like the Jack the Ripper murders, are embedded in London's history and exist textually as well as historically. The Ripper murders feature prominently in *White Chappell, Scarlet Tracings,* which plays with their visceral nature in the images of mutilation, dissection, vivisection, and body metaphors which litter its pages.[9] In contrast, the Ratcliffe Highway murders are mentioned only briefly. We are told that:

> The staked heart of John Williams, the Ratcliff Highway Murderer [sic], beats evenly at the quadrivium [four roads], at peace, from the shuntings of the work ethic, connected in a mysterious and unspoken thread to the recently scoured white stone blocks of St George in the East.
>
> (Sinclair, 2004, p. 34)

In *Dan Leno* and *White Chappell, Scarlet Tracings,* the Golem of the Polish ghetto reappears in Whitechapel, Limehouse, and Spitalfields, areas frequented by the famous East End serial killers, and which, as we have seen, Sinclair associates with a mystical significance which hinges on Hawksmoor's churches.[10] In Ackroyd's novel, the first murder of a prostitute occurs on 10 September 1880, in Limehouse Reach; the second, six days later, takes place in the same area; on 17 September, a Jewish scholar, Solomon Weil, is murdered in his room in Scofield Street situated in 'Old Jerusalem', the Jewish quarter of Limehouse, surrounded by 'old volumes and manuscripts of Hasidic lore' (Ackroyd, 1995, pp. 5–6). The body of a fourth (another female prostitute), is discovered propped 'against the small white pyramid in front of the church of St Anne's' on which 'the word "golem" had been traced in the blood of the dead woman' (Ackroyd, 1995, p. 6). Four days later, 'an entire family is found slaughtered in their house beside the Ratcliffe Highway' in the adjacent parish of Stepney (Ackroyd, 1995, p. 7). The killings do not end there, but the concentrated location of these first incidents allows Ackroyd to allude to East End myths of murder and mayhem, acknowledging the dark forces embedded in the location.

What has been described as the 'layering of *Dan Leno and the Limehouse Golem*' functions on two levels: one textual, the other spatial. Both, however, have an historical dimension (Gibson and Wolfreys, 2000, p. 173). Gibson and Wolfreys write:

> While it [the layering] insists on the cultural and psychic accretion of recurring and similar events over a period of time in the same

location within the city [...] it also recognizes the textual aspect of this recurrence. Writers return repeatedly to particularly violent and shocking events [...]. *Dan Leno* knowingly invokes not merely history but also textual or literary history.

(2000, p. 173)

They also acknowledge that 'the text is disjointed by the return of a trace always connected, however obliquely, to the city' so that the '"return" of violent acts, of serial killing and mass murder' function as 'particularly violent traces of the city's disturbing identity' (Gibson and Wolfreys, 2000, p. 205). 'Such traces', they suggest, are 'both indelible and spectral, and given particular, exemplary "form" in the imagined shape of the Golem' (Gibson and Wolfreys, 2000, p. 205). They proceed to argue:

the Golem never exists, as such. It is only a textual trace, a shared, communal memory, given life only through the articulation of its possibility. This possibility of resonance extends from the novel to the murders identified as those committed by Jack the Ripper. The resonance between Ackroyd's novel and the Ripper murders is enough to seduce certain readers into seeking further correspond-ences, even though these are not necessarily there. Indeed, [...] given that the prostitues, a Jewish scholar, Solomon Weil, and a family are murdered, it is as true to say that the scene of Ackroyd's novel in no way resembles the Ripper murders, other than in the coincidence that they occur in the East End of London.

(Gibson and Wolfreys, 2000, p. 205)

While this may be true, the significance of 'layering' in the pal-impsestic overlay of one East End myth over another seems to have been momentarily forgotten. If one looks at the 'murders' of 1880 in Ackroyd's novel, it is clear that they are meant to foreshadow the Jack the Ripper killings of 1888, to recall the Ratcliffe Highway mur-ders of December 1811 in which two families were killed and, in the slaughter of the Jewish scholar Solomon Weil, anchronistically, to point forward to the 1980 mystery of David Rodinsky.

Moreover, as Gibson and Wolfreys suggest, the Golem is – like the Ripper, Williams, and Rodinsky – intrinsically related to the city. According to Gibson and Wolfreys, 'the city, like the Golem, only comes into being through the multiplicity of enunciations and inscriptions, while never remaining the thing itself' (2000, p. 207). The creature is, as Ackroyd states, a protean 'thing without form' (Ackroyd, 1995, p. 4); it embodies not only the shape-shifting murderess Elizabeth Cree, Ackroyd's 'Lambeth Marsh Lizzie' who springs from the London clay itself, whose geological strata bear the multiple histories of the city's violent past, but also the elusive, shapeless, Jack the Ripper, the summarily exhumed Ratcliffe Highway killer John Williams, and the weight of Jewish history. Drawing on the original 'Golem' myth, where the written word activates the creature, Gibson and Wolfreys observe that '[t]he act of writing the novel gives the Golem shape [...]. Indeed, the novel is itself Golem-like, formed in its various true shapes according to the forms of inscription' (2000, p. 206). Both Ackroyd's and Sinclair's novels seemingly play with the creation of myth, the significance of location, and the power of writing to animate dead histories. At the same time, however, the novels function as anti-detective fiction, works that frustrate the search for narrative and/or historical 'truth'.[11]

Detecting labyrinths

In *The Doomed Detective: The Contribution of the Detective Novel to Postmodern American and Italian Fiction* (1984), Stephano Tani discusses the rise of the postmodern anti-detective novel and observes:

> The traditional detective novel presents a reconstruction of the past and ends when this reconstruction has been fulfilled. To reconstruct the past is to go back to a point (the one of the crime) about which the detective is concerned. There must be a fixed point; otherwise the regression in time would be infinite. So to go back in time is equal to finding a criminal, to unravelling a mystery. There is no free time in a detective novel: the present is employed to explain the past, the past has already happened before the story started, and the future is not even taken into account. The detective 'wins' the past, unravels it, but only to be doomed to go backwards in time in the next story.
>
> (Tani, 1984, pp. 45–6)

Using the Minotaur myth, Tani demonstrates how a set of mythological elements, the mirror, the labyrinth and the map recur 'both at a literal and at a symbolic level in some early anti-detective fiction' such as Borges's 'La muerte y la brûjula' ['Death and the Compass'] and 'how it contributes to relate time to the development of the detecting process' (Tani, 1984, p. 47). He explains that the past figures as the 'creator' of the labyrinth in that it complicates the possibility of solving the crime committed and that the present is the 'mirror-maker' which 'changes and distorts' the image of the past (Tani, 1984, p. 48). The mirror (in the form of doublings), the labyrinth, and the map feature interestingly in Ackroyd's and Sinclair's retrieval of the East End's nineteenth-century history.

The labyrinth figures covertly in Elizabeth and John Cree's traversals of the city streets in *Dan Leno*, and overtly in George Gissing's meditation on Thomas De Quincey which is quoted extensively in Ackroyd's novel. Gissing, commenting on *Confessions of an English Opium Eater* (1821) and De Quincey's vision of 'the mighty labyrinths of London', notes that it is in Oxford Street that De Quincey first purchased laudanum and states: 'it could be said that the old highway led him directly to those nightmares and fantasies which turned London into some mighty vision akin to that of Piranesi, a labyrinth of stone, a wilderness of blank walls and doors' (quoted in Ackroyd, 1995, p. 39).[12] Early in Sinclair's novel, Joblard and 'Sinclair' go out onto the streets to pursue the Ripper story. The narrator writes: '[t]he zone was gradually defined, the labyrinth penetrated. It was given limits by the victims of the Ripper' (Sinclair, 2004, p. 27). In a section on James Hinton, he is described as turning 'toward annihilation, the labyrinth again, the secret heart' and, later, in an allusion to Joseph Merrick, the Elephant Man, we are told '[h]e walked the labyrinth for fifteen years, never encountering the minotaur' (Sinclair, 2004, pp. 128; 137).

In both texts blood functions as an unacknowledged scarlet thread which guides, or misguides perhaps, the protagonists' labyrinthine journey through the physical city and the city's history, and in *White Chappell, Scarlet Tracings*, bloody inscriptions activate Sinclair's own 'Golem' which emerges from the 'geology of time' (Sinclair, 2004, p. 102). Like Ackroyd's, Sinclair's Golem is 'formless' and shape-shifting.

In his astute and fascinating discussion of Sinclair's oeuvre, Robert Bond analyses what he calls 'the double sense of the novel's subtitle, associating it with the author's poem, 'Painting with a Knife' from an early collection –*The Birth Rug* (1973) – in which this process is described as 'the carving of forbidden words/on clean fresh pages', and with a quote from 'The Prima Donna's Tale' section of

Downriver (1991) in which an imaginary version of Jack the Ripper's victim, Marie Kelly, 'follows the heat path of scarlet tracings' she has inflicted on her victim's white skin with a scalpel (Bond, 2005, p. 100). Bond argues that:

> these usages of the phrase 'scarlet tracings'; do not just bizarrely recast sexual violence as body art. The poem from *The Birth Rug* already associates the inscription of scarlet tracings with 'the dissection of time'. In the light of Sinclair's claim, in *Lud Heat* for instance, that his own writing engages in 'a sequence of heated incisions through the membranous time-layer', we can see that the later novel's subtitle not only refers to the surgical violence of the Ripper, but also intimates the way in which Sinclair's novel performs a dissection of the historical traces of that violence, as part of its broader forensic examination of the period.
>
> (2005, p. 100)

The mass of codes and allusions in Sinclair's novel suggests that the 'carving of forbidden words' is central to his retrieval of secret histories. In the text, as mentioned above, the Golem figure appears in connection with Joseph Merrick, the 'Elephant Man', and his relationship with Sir Frederick Treves, the doctor who investigated his condition and afforded him shelter at the London Hospital in Whitechapel. Visiting the hospital museum to see Merrick's skeleton, the narrator posits Treves as a Golem-maker who animates his creature using arcane rituals and secret words:

> By the collaboration of the four, Aysch [fire], Mayim [water], Ruach [air] and Aphar [earth], was made the Golem of the fourth element. Red clay of the brickfields, complete in all his members, laid out in the field of Matfellon, in that absence, where a church had been.[13] Treves walking seven times through the labyrinth, from right to left, so that body grew dark, red like fire. Treves again, returning into the spiral, from left to right, seven times around the body, through Lion Yard, Old Montague, Bakers, Buxton, Spicers, Brick, Hanbury, Great Garden, so that the redness was extinguished, and water flowed through the clay, hair sprouted, nails grew. Then Treves placed in its mouth a piece of parchment, with the secret name; he bowed to the East and the

West, the South and the North, reciting the words of the ritual. He blew breath into its nostrils and the Golem opened his eyes.

(Sinclair, 2004, p. 98)

Treves's ritual entails the traversal of the city's labyrinthine streets, streets which are later to be walked by Whitechapel's famous killer, and at one point in the narrative the Golem's behaviour resonates with that of Jack the Ripper: '[u]ninstructed, the Golem [Merrick], like one mad, began running about in the Jewish quarter of the city, threatening to destroy everything' (Sinclair, 2004, p. 99).

Bond also suggests that the subtitle 'scarlet tracings' carries a further meaning which 'hints at the novel's relation to *A Study in Scarlet*' (2005, p. 100). According to Bond, Conan Doyle's text is both textually and symbolically important to Sinclair's novel in that it not only foregrounds its concern with detection, but also 'because in *White Chappell, Scarlet Tracings* Sinclair pursues, detecting and examining forensically, textual traces of *A Study in Scarlet*' (2005, p. 100). In classical detective fiction, 'the conflict between irrational and rational forces' is formalized, and 'the latter is always the winner, exorcising the former' (Tani, 1984, p. 10). This focus on the detective story might therefore imply a rationalization of the Golem motif which underlies Sinclair's novel. The narrator, 'the Late Watson' (also known as 'Sinclair'), whose appellation suggests an existence between life and death, functions as an implicit double of the creature in the Golem tales, referred to by Sinclair above, in which he 'acts as a primitive detective', an 'early prototype of [...] Doctor Watson' (Lichtenstein and Sinclair, 2000, p. 187). In *White Chappell, Scarlet Tracings*, he comments on the Golem-like nature of literary creations that become uncontainable, thus linking myth, fiction, and empirical reality:

Accepting the notion of 'presence' – I mean that certain fictions, chiefly Conan Doyle, Stevenson, but many others also, laid out a template that was more powerful than any local documentary account – the presences they created, or "figures" if you prefer it, like Rabbi Loew's Golem, became too much and too fast to be contained within the conventional limits of that fiction. They got out into the stream of time, the ether; they escaped into the labyrinth. They achieved independent existence.

> The writers were mediums; they articulated, they gave a shape to some pattern of energy that was already present. They got in on the curve of time, so that by writing, by holding off the inhibiting reflex of the rational mind, they were able to propose a text that was prophetic.
>
> (Sinclair, 2004, pp. 117–18)

In what I would argue is a key moment in the text, the 'Late Watson' dissects the first page of *A Study in Scarlet* in the hope of detecting a hidden mystery concerning the identity of Jack the Ripper. Initially, he treats the text 'like a prison censor, carefully blacking out' the words, to uncover its 'mantic' or prophetic nature (Sinclair, 2004, p. 49). Deciding that this offers 'too blatant a reading', he dictates instead 'single words' and 'cut phrases' from the text to his co-detective, Joblard, to 'let it build its own chain' of associations (Sinclair, 2004, p. 49). In attempting to locate, in Conan Doyle's text, published the year before the Ripper murders took place, fragmented words and images which might prophesy it, the narrator highlights the non-linear narrative and textual fragmentation of Sinclair's own novel, thus undermining the rationalizing influence of the classic detective story. This particular process, as the narrator explains, reverses 'the conventions of detective fiction where a given crime is unravelled, piece by piece, until a murderer is denounced whose act is the starting point of the narration', a process which is also in evidence in Ackroyd's novel, which is similarly unconventional in its refusal to unmask its murderer (Sinclair, 2004, p. 52). 'Our narrative starts everywhere', he declares, and adds '[w]e want to assemble all the incomplete movements, like cubists, until the point is reached where the crime can commit itself' (Sinclair, 2004, p. 51).

As if to represent graphically its intention to reverse 'the conventions of detective fiction', an image of Conan Doyle's text with blacked-out sections is depicted within Sinclair's own. In doing so, it recalls an important moment in Wilkie Collins's *The Moonstone* (1868), generally considered the first detective novel in English. The culprit of the crime committed is seemingly revealed when Ezra Jennings reconstructs his colleague Mr Candy's delirious ramblings and turns them into a comprehensible text by filling in the gaps. Franklin Blake duly expresses his '[a]dmiration of the ingenuity which had woven this smooth and finished texture out of the ravelled skein' and the mystery is apparently solved (Collins, 1982, p. 430). Yet, as the reader later learns, Jennings's conjectures offer only a partial solution. As in the text he reconstructs, unacknowledged gaps remain, leaving invisible spaces for the existence of a further mystery. In his anti-detective novel, Sinclair deliberately loses his readers in a textual labyrinth, unravelling the skein, or the scarlet tracings of *A Study in Scarlet* and the conventional detective story to create those gaps and fissures which disrupt textual and historical continuity.[14]

Mapping scarlet traces

The significance of the labyrinth in Sinclair's text becomes clear if we consider the nature of the anti-detective novel which 'frustrates the expectations of the reader [...] and substitutes for the detective as central and ordering character the decentering and chaotic admission of mystery' (Tani, 1984, p. 40). Bond notes that *White Chappell, Scarlet Tracings* is 'preoccupied with processes of detection and decipherment' (2005, p. 88), yet, as Murray observes, this preoccupation results in a subversion of traditional detective fiction and produces instead 'a parody of the Victorian detective novel' which undermines the genre's conventional narrative trajectory (2007, p. 55). In his discussion of the anti-detective novel, Michael Holquist explains that in 'the palimpsest of old and new detective fiction',

> the new metaphysical detective story finally obliterates the traces of the old which underlie it. It is non-teleological, is not concerned to have a neat ending in which all the questions are answered, and which can therefore be forgotten. No, the new story is purged of such linear teleology [...]. It is rather a fresh sheet of paper, on which the reader [...] must hand letter his own answers.
>
> (1971, p. 153)[15]

The image of the palimpsest employed by Holquist highlights a tension between materiality and immateriality, body and spirit, which informs *White Chappell, Scarlet Tracings*, and *Dan Leno*. The reader, then, is encouraged to carve his own 'forbidden words/on fresh clean pages' to activate his own version of the text (Bond, 2005, p. 100). Holquist argues that, 'instead of familiarity', the metaphysical detective story 'gives strangeness, a strangeness which more often than not is the result of jumbling the well known patterns of classical detective stories. Instead of reassuring, they disturb' (Holquist, 1971, p. 155).

The narrator's dictation of fragmented words and phrases from *A Study in Scarlet* in Sinclair's novel is compared, by Bond, to 'the technical strategy of quasi-automatic writing' (2005, p. 97). In doing so, he raises the crucial image of the poet/writer as medium, also mentioned by Sinclair's narrator above, which associates the novel with a Victorian occult practice which destabilizes and disturbs the rational trajectory of the detective novel.[16] Ackroyd's novel, too, in its use of the past, and of fragmented narrative forms (e.g. diary entries, trial transcripts), and various narrators might also be said to channel 'dead' voices. Voices, figures, and literary works of the past are mediated through the body of the text. In addition the past emerges through the body of London's 'geology of time' (Sinclair, 2004, p. 102) and through the figure of the Golem; the ghosts of the city's own history are discernible within its physical body. This conflict between the material and the spectral in Ackroyd's revision of the Ripper myth, and in the purportedly redemptive search for clues to the Ripper mystery in Sinclair's text, posits both a palimpsest of the city's history, and a spectral evocation of the serial killers who haunt the city's past and present. Generally defined as 'a manuscript [...] that has been written on more than once, where the earlier writing is incompletely erased and often legible', the palimpsest can also refer to a place or an area that reflects its history (*OED*). Both these definitions are suggestive in relation to Sinclair's and Ackroyd's works.

On a textual level, these novels express a concern with erasure and exposure which relates, as I intend to show, to questions of historiography. Ackroyd's novel both exposes and hides the identity of the killer; it begins with the hanging of Elizabeth Cree for the murder of her husband, whose diary entries seem to suggest he is the Limehouse Golem. However, the novel's interest in Music Hall theatre and cross-dressing, and Elizabeth's skill in both, undermine any simple allocation of guilt. In *White Chappell, Scarlet Tracings*, Joblard declares, 'I want to make tracings of unseen acts [...]. To cover all the marks of my own complicity. I want erasures [...] I want acts to repeat [...]. To erase time and to bend its direction of flow', and the narrator acknowledges, 'I know there is nothing to be written: all writing is rewriting' (Sinclair, 2004, p. 136). In wishing to 'make tracings of unseen acts', in wanting 'acts to repeat' and yet seeking 'erasures', Joblard foregrounds the simultaneously material, and yet spectral nature of the protagonists' project which revisits the Ripper murders even as it wishes to exorcize them. Similarly, in Ackroyd's novel, Elizabeth Cree both traces her own 'unseen acts' in what is supposedly her husband's diary, and simultaneously erases them from her own conscience and common knowledge by attributing them to him. Sinclair's subtitle, 'scarlet tracings' is apt and can also be applied to Ackroyd's text: in addition to the meanings of 'tracings' suggested by Bond, the word defines copies of a map, drawing, or text which are obtained by superimposing translucent paper over the original, as well as signs which mark the former existence of something. *White Chappell, Scarlet Tracings* and *Dan Leno* trace over recorded versions of violent events which are themselves haunting echoes of those which have taken place before them.

I would argue that, in the context of the novels' concern with erasure and exposure, the blood spilled in the Ratcliffe Highway murders seeps through in both texts' scarlet tracings of the Ripper killings, and that the blood spilled by the Ripper victims seeps through to the subtext of Jewish history which underlies the novels. Implicit in Sinclair's reference to John Williams is the discovery of his skeleton in 1886, which figures as a metaphorical rupture in the 'geology of time'. Unearthed only two years before Jack the Ripper begins his own murder spree in 1888, Williams functions as his spectral forerunner. *A Study in Scarlet*, published in 1887, in which Sinclair's protagonists seek prophetic clues, acts as an interesting link between the two sets of events. In his essay, 'On the Knocking at the Gate of Macbeth' (1823), De Quincey, commenting on Williams, writes: 'All other murders look pale by the deep crimson of his' (De Quincey, 2006, p. 4).[17] The Ratcliffe Highway murders feature briefly in *A Study in Scarlet*. Watson notes that, in response to the first of two murders: '[t]he *Daily Telegraph* remarked that in the history of crime there had seldom been a tragedy which presented stranger features' and that it mentions 'the Ratcliff Highway murders [*sic*]' alongside a series of others (Doyle, 1999, p. 48). As in the case of the Ratcliffe Highway killings, *A Study in Scarlet* features two murder events, and though the victims, in this case, are not hacked or slit, 'marks of blood' feature in the narrative and, more importantly perhaps, *as* narrative. In the case of each murder, a single word 'RACHE' meaning 'revenge' in German, is written on the wall 'in letters of blood' (Doyle, 1999, p. 59). It is, in part, a 'track of blood' which enables Sherlock Holmes to identify the murderer, and to unravel 'all the threads which have formed such a tangle' (Doyle, 1999, p. 60).[18]

A similar scarlet trace of blood appears in textual and metaphorical form in both *White Chappell, Scarlet Tracings* and *Dan Leno*. In Ackroyd's novel, Cree's first act of violence is prompted by the onset of menstruation. As her mother tries to stem the flow with rags, Cree stabs her in the wrist and elicits '[b]lood for blood [...] [n]ew blood for old' (Ackroyd, 1995, p. 13). Anticipating his first murder, 'John' Cree relates in his diary how the prostitute's room is to be his 'red room' (Ackroyd, 1995,p. 28). He recalls how, in his schooldays, he 'mourned' when the 'first line of ink spotted the purity of a new book of exercises', and notes how he now intends to use his knife 'to write [his] name again, but with a different instrument', and his victim, found at St Anne's, Limehouse, is 'baptised' by Cree, in her own blood (Ackroyd, 1995, pp. 29; 126). In Sinclair's novel, the narrator's books are referred to as 'stigmata of guilt'; he and Joblard share 'a bottle of menstrual wine'; a young girl is 'outlined in scarlet varnish'; Eves, a Ripperologist, has the 'victims' names printed in red on brittle vinegar-coloured cards'; the Victorian medium, Robert Lees, holds hundreds of prophecies 'in blood and ink' and in his visions sees a 'scarlet' room (Sinclair, 2004[, pp. 16; 42; 39; 153). Even more interesting perhaps are variations of the enigmatic sentence reputedly written by Jack the Ripper in white chalk on a wall close to the body of Catherine Eddowes : 'The Juwes are The men that Will not be Blamed for nothing', versions of which appear in Sinclair's text, for example: '[t]he men that will not be blamed for nothing'; 'I will name nothing'; and '[n]ot blamed, the woman, for nothing' (Sinclair, 2004, pp. 153; 26; 124; 129). While the original Ripper sentence was not written in blood, it carried the scarlet trace of the murderer's bloodied hand, and suggested either that the perpetrator might have been Jewish, or that he wished the Jews to be blamed for his actions.

Tracing unseen acts

In Ackroyd's novel, Karl Marx, interviewed by the police following the demise of the Jewish scholar, learns that the murderer is popularly labelled a 'golem' and exclaims:

So they absolve themselves of their responsibilities, and declare that the Jew is killed by a Jewish monster! Make no mistake about it, gentlemen. It is the Jew who has been killed and mutilated, not Solomon Weil. It is the Jew who has been violated, and now they wash their own hands clean!

(Ackroyd, 1995, p. 92)

The allusions to the Jew in Ackroyd's and Sinclair's novels point, on one level, to the racism which led to the suspicion that the Ripper might have been Jewish. Susan Onega notes that '[a]mong the many hypotheses entertained about the Ripper murders [...] was the conviction that the killer must be a foreigner [...]. The foreigners under suspicion were the Jews living in Old Jerusalem, the Jewish quarter of Limehouse [...] where Solomon Weil used to live' (1999, p. 139). In *City of Dreadful Delight*, Judith Walkowitz discusses a particular Jewish suspect, 'Leather Apron', named by the *Star*; 'a Jewish slipper-maker by trade', a 'Strange Character who Prowls about Whitechapel after midnight', inspiring 'universal fear' among women (2000, p. 203). On another level, the significance of the Golem and the subtext of Jewish persecution and sacrifice implicit in these novels suggest a narrative which traverses temporal and spatial boundaries. In Ackroyd's novel, the victim and the alleged perpetrator coalesce: Marx calls the Jew and the prostitute 'symbols of the city', telling the police that the 'Jew and the whore are the scapegoats in the desert of London' and that 'they must be ritually butchered to appease some terrible god' (Ackroyd, 1995, p. 92).

In *Dan Leno*, 'John' Cree outlines in his diary how he kills Solomon Weil. After washing the corpse, he takes out his knife and begins his work. He comments, '[t]he body is truly a *mappamundi* with its territories and continents, its rivers of fibre and its oceans of flesh', and proceeds to sever the scholar's penis which he places on an open book in which he sees the image of 'some mighty demon and, beside it, a short history of the golem' (Ackroyd, 1995, p. 86). He writes: 'I knew that such a thing was fashioned like a homunculus, from red clay; but now I read with interest how it preserved its life by feeding from the human soul' (Ackroyd, 1995, p. 86). Sinclair's Golem, too, is shaped from '[r]ed clay' by Frederick Treves into the 'Elephant Man' as he walks ritually 'seven times through the labyrinth' (2004, p. 98). Walkowitz observes that '[c]ommentators likened the Ripper story to a "dark labyrinth" where every corner revealed a new "depth of social blackness"; they also superimposed this labyrinthine image on the besieged city itself which, like the Golem, is represented as incoherent, fragmented, ungovernable' (2000, p. 197). Onega argues that, in *Dan Leno*, 'the Limehouse Golem may be described as the macrocosmic evil emanation of the whole area of Limehouse and a figment of the dream of sick Londoners' (Onega, 1999, p. 139). Yet, both Ackroyd's and Sinclair's novels suggest that it signifies much more than that. The 'red clay' of London, steeped in the blood of its victims, forms a labyrinthine *mappamundi*, a visceral version of the 'hand-drawn maps' of London found in Rodinsky's room, a symbol of the city which is personified in the Golem, who purportedly feeds from the human soul (Lichtenstein and Sinclair, 2000, p. 28). The Golem therefore functions both as a vertical labyrinth of the geological past, and a horizontal labyrinth of historical narratives of violence, activated by Ackroyd's and Sinclair's writing. However, it also represents the unmanageable 'truth' of such histories.

Ackroyd's novel presents characters which mirror both imagined and real Victorian personages including Dan Leno, Karl Marx, and George Gissing, while retrospectively 'doubling' the figure of David Rodinsky in the Jewish scholar, Solomon Weil. The present, in Sinclair's novel, is similarly composed of a labyrinthine series of distorted doublings, for example: between James Hinton and the Ripper suspect, William Gull; between Joblard and Gull; and between Frederick Treves and his ward, Joseph Merrick; and between the physical mapping of the city's past and present which prevents any conclusive solution of the Ripper murders. All inhabit the labyrinthine streets of an East End which both maps and erases the contemporary location. Yet, the figure of the Golem in their novels gestures towards a wider concern with the history of serial killing and mass murder. The novels stage a repetition of historical acts of violence which forms layers of significance. These acts function as 'events' which rupture time and, indeed, space. If, like the 'Late Watson', one builds one's own 'chain' of associations (Sinclair, 2004, p. 49), one might assert that the textual coupling of the prostitute and the Jew in Ackroyd's novel is suggestive and that the significance of the Ripper murders in Sinclair's text, which draws upon Stephen Knight's *Jack the Ripper: The Final Solution* (1976), points to Hitler's own 'final solution' and the brutal killings of the Jews in the Holocaust and its historical counterparts. Such 'events' play an important part in Rachel Lichtenstein's narrative in *Rodinsky's Room,* in which she associates the genesis of the Golem myth with periods of Jewish persecution. She writes that the 'fantastical tale' of the Golem developed in the middle of the seventeenth century, 'a dark time of massacres and pogroms for the Jews of Europe', and states: 'I don't believe there is such a thing as an accidental folk legend. These stories are not just fanciful fictions; rather, they are mirror images of the complex historical and cultural experience of a people' (Lichtenstein and Sinclair, 2000, p. 224).

Ackroyd's Jewish scholar recalls Sinclair's Rodinsky, while Sinclair's inclusion of the Golem in *White Chappell, Scarlet Tracings* necessarily resonates with his discussion of the myth in the later text, where Lichtenstein describes Rodinsky as a 'modern-day golem' (Lichtenstein and Sinclair, 2000, p. 225).[19] In her search for Rodinsky, Lichtenstein finds that his family came from a Hassidic community in the Ukraine, where a quarter of a million Jews were murdered during the pogroms of the 1880s, violent acts which prefigured the Holocaust (Lichtenstein and Sinclair, 2000, pp. 214–15). In Ackroyd's and Sinclair's labyrinthine novels, the violent 'events' which rupture time hint at the Holocaust to come, but the present distorts the past, and no solution or, indeed, absolution is possible. The 'truth' cannot be ascertained. In both texts the Golem functions as both 'truth' and 'lie', the 'truth' and 'myth' of Jewish history. According to tradition, the Golem comes to life when the word '*emeth*' (i.e. 'truth') is written on his forehead. Yet the Golem 'grows each day' and becomes unmanageable. The only way to stop it is to 'erase the first letter aleph from the word emeth on his forehead, so that there remains only the word *meth*, that is, dead' (quoted in Kieval, 1997, p. 4; original emphasis), 'original emphasis'. The Golem then, becomes 'myth' or a 'dead truth'. In its body of red clay it contains its own 'mappamundi', encompassing the 'world' time and 'world' history of the Jewish people. If the Golem functions as the 'truth' of Jewish history, it simultaneously erases even as it recalls the Holocaust and earlier histories of Jewish persecution. It represents both a challenge to historical 'truth' and narrative realism, embodying the potential for textual and historical disruption. Sinclair's narrator declares: '[u]nless we can exactly repeat the past, we will never make it repent; it will escape us. Nothing is exorcised.

It goes on for ever' (2004, p. 139). Yet some pasts are unrepeatable; some pasts must be simultaneously 'traced' and yet 'erased'. The neo-Victorian novel and, indeed, the metahistorical romance, express this dilemma: re-creations can never 'exactly repeat the past'; the literary past and its historical 'truth' therefore represents a 'lie', or 'dead truth' which remains a Golem-like spectre which haunts contemporary writing. Implicit in Ackroyd's and Sinclair's novels is the history of 'serial killers' who have escaped 'into the stream of time' (Sinclair, 2004, p. 117). They encompass not only the 'serial killers' of the Jewish Holocaust, but also the killers of serial history.

Notes

1. Peter Ackroyd's novel includes historical figures such as the music hall artist Dan Leno (George Wild Galvin, 1860–1904), the philosopher Karl Marx (1818–83), and the writer George Gissing (1857–1903). Among other Victorian figures, Iain Sinclair's features the physician Sir William Withey Gull (1816–90), surgeons James Hinton (1822–75) and Sir Frederick Treves (1853–1923), the latter famously known for his association with Joseph Merrick, 'The Elephant Man' (1862–90). Hinton's theories were deemed to have been influential on Gull, cited as a key suspect in Stephen Knight's 1976 book *Jack the Ripper: The Final Solution*. Sinclair draws upon Knight's work in his novel. In *From Hell*, a graphic novel written by Alan Moore and Eddie Campbell, it is again suggested that Gull was Jack the Ripper. Merrick has also been posited by some as a possible Ripper suspect. See the Jack the Ripper Casebook: http://www.casebook. org/ripper_media/book_reviews/non-fiction/cjmorley/131.html.
2. Jean-François Lyotard (1924–98). Lyotard argued that true historical events could not be articulated in existing genres of discourses and posed a challenge to literary expression.
3. The Ratcliffe Highway murders, which took place in December 1811, are discussed at length in three essays by Thomas De Quincey: 'On Murder Considered as One of the Fine Arts' (1827); 'Second Paper on Murder Considered as One of the Fine Arts' (1839); and 'Postscript [to On Murder Considered as One of the Fine Arts]' (1854). See De Quincey (2006).
4. In some versions the word is placed in the Golem's mouth rather than written on his forehead.
5. In *Recalling London: Literature and History in the Work of Peter Ackroyd and Iain Sinclair* (2007), Alex Murray reads both authors' works in relation to their political and cultural contexts, in particular the rise of Thatcherism and its historical legacy.
6. See Note 3 above.
7. Although these names are the most commonly known, there are thirteen other potential victims of Jack the Ripper spanning the years 1887–91.

8. A further connection between the killings can be made through social responses to the events. In the 'Postscript' to his essay 'On Murder Considered as One of the Fine Arts' (1854), Thomas De Quincey describes the public outcry at what he refers to as the Ratcliffe Highway murders (De Quincey, 2006, pp. 97–8). Similarly, in *City of Dreadful Delight* (1992), Judith Walkowitz remarks that the Ripper story became national news and provoked public 'hysteria'(Walkowitz, 2000, p. 191).
9. See Bond, 2005, esp. ch. 3.
10. In *Hawksmoor* (1985), Peter Ackroyd employs the mysticism associated with the area to develop a detective story which slips between the eighteenth and the twentieth centuries.
11. Murray refers to the 'lack of narrative direction' in *White Chappell, Scarlet Tracings* as 'anti-narrative' and suggests that this form of narrative 'is predicated on a rejection of a range of moral, social and cultural values that are at the heart of those models of narrative certainty that we associate with eighteenth and nineteenth-century canonical English literature' (2007, pp. 49; 53). Like anti-detective fiction, anti-narrative frustrates conventional expectations of traditional narrative trajectories.
12. The Piranesi 'labyrinths' refer to a series of prints by Giovanni Battista Piranesi (1720–78) entitled *Carceri d'invenzione* (Imaginary Prisons) begun in 1745 and first published in 1750.
13. The name 'Whitechapel' comes from a chapel called 'St Mary Matfellon' which reputedly had white walls.
14. Like the narrative in anti-detective fiction, the 'anti-narrative' in Sinclair's novel 'ruptures any attempt to give the narrative itself meaning', and 'also ruptures historical authority' (Murray, 2007, p. 57).
15. Metaphysical detective fiction shares anti-detective fiction's subversion of the structure of traditional detective fiction, and raises questions rather than offering solutions.
16. Elana Gomel notes that 'a steady stream' of ghostwritten texts emerged 'in the wake of the great spiritualist movement of the second half of the nineteenth century. Scientists, writers, musicians, saints, Indians, and pirates, not to mention Jesus and Buddha, vied in transmitting messages to the living through entranced mediums' (2007, p. 189).
17. 'On the Knocking at the Gate of Macbeth' was first published in the *London Magazine* in October 1823.
18. Religious persecution is also a subtext in *A Study in Scarlet*, in which the murders are traced back to the actions of a Mormon sect.
19. It is worth noting that Sinclair's work had earlier proved influential on Ackroyd. Sinclair's allusion to mystical forces associated with Hawksmoor churches in *Lud Heat* (first published in 1975) became a foundational feature of Ackroyd's *Hawksmoor* (1985).

Bibliography

Abraham, N. and Torok, M. (1986). *The Wolf Man's Magic Word: A Cryptonymy*. Trans. N. T. Rand. Minneapolis: University of Minnesota Press. (Original work published 1976)

Abraham, N. and Torok, M. (1994). *The Shell and the Kernel: Renewals of Psychoanalysis*. (Vol. 1). Ed. and trans. N. T. Rand. Chicago and London: University of Chicago Press.

Ackerman, D. (2000). *A Natural History of the Senses*. London: Phoenix. (Original work published 1987)

Ackroyd, P. (1985). *Hawksmoor*. London: Hamish Hamilton.

Ackroyd, P. (1994). *The House of Doctor Dee*. London: Penguin. (Original work published 1993)

Ackroyd, P. (1995). *Dan Leno and the Limehouse Golem*. London: Vintage. (Original work published 1994)

Ackroyd, P. (2001). *London: The Biography*. London: Vintage. (Original work published 2000)

Ackroyd, P. (2007). *Thames: Sacred River*. London: Chatto and Windus.

Allen, M. (2008). *Cleansing the City: Sanitary Geographies in Victorian London*. Athens: Ohio University Press.

Amenábar, A. (Director and Writer) (2001). *The Others* [Motion Picture]. United States: Dimension.

Arias Doblas, R. (2005). Talking with the Dead: Revisiting the Victorian Past and the Occult in Margaret Atwood's *Alias Grace* and Sarah Waters' *Affinity*. *Estudios Ingleses de la Universidad Complutense*, *13*, 85–105.

Armitt, L. and Gamble, S. (2006). The Haunted Geometries of Sarah Waters's *Affinity. Textual Practice*, *20* (1), 142–9.

Armstrong, I. (2008). *Victorian Glassworlds*. Oxford: Oxford University Press.

Arnim, E. von (1986). *Enchanted April*. London: Virago. (Original work published 1922)

Arnold, M. (1873). *Literature and Dogma*. London: Nelson.

Atwood, M. (1996). *Alias Grace*. London: Virago Press.

Bailin, M. (2002). The New Victorians. In C. Krueger (Ed.), *Functions of Victorian Culture at the Present Moment* (pp. 37–46). Athens: Ohio University Press.

Banhart, R. (Ed.). (2006). *Chambers Dictionary of Etymology*. NY: Chambers.

Barfield, S. (2007). Postface: Reflections on the Literary Thames: River, City and Chronotope. *Literary London: Interdisciplinary Studies in the Representation of London*, *5* (1). Retrieved 24 January 2008, from http://www.literarylondon. org/london-journal/march2007/barfield.html.

Barnes, J. (2005). *Arthur and George*. London: Jonathan Cape.

Barrett Browning, E. (1993). *Aurora Leigh*. Ed. C. Kaplan. London: Women's Press. (Original work published 1856)

Barsham, D. (1992). *The Trial of Woman: Feminism and the Occult Sciences in Victorian Literature and Society*. NY: New York University Press.

Baudrillard, J. (1983). *Simulations*. In A. Easthope and K. McGowan (Eds) *A Critical and Cultural Theory Reader* (pp. 218–20). Berkshire: Open University Press.

Bayard, L. (2005). *Mr Timothy*. London: John Murray.

Belsey, Catherine (2004). *Culture and the Real: Theorizing Cultural Criticism*. London: Routledge.

Bond, R. (2005). *Iain Sinclair*. Cambridge: Salt Publishing.

Bormann, D. C. (2005). *The Articulation of Science in the Neo-Victorian Novel. A Poetics (and Two Case Studies)*. Bern: Peter Lang.

Bown, N., Burdett, C. and Thurschwell, P. (Eds) (2004). *The Victorian Supernatural*. Cambridge: Cambridge University Press.

Brace, M. (4 July 2004). Good Girls, Bad Girls, Sex and Power. *Independent on Sunday*. Retrieved 4 February 2009, from http://www.independent.co.uk/arts-entertainment/books/features/valerie-martin-good-girls-bad-girls-sex-and-power-552147.html.

Braddon, M. E. (2007). *Lady Audley's Secret*. Ware: Wordsworth Editions. (Original work published 1862)

Brontë, C. (1985). *Jane Eyre*. Ed. Q. D. Leavis. London: Penguin. (Original work published 1847)

Bryk, M. (2004). The Maidservant in the Attic: Rewriting Stevenson's *Strange Case of Dr Jekyll and Mr Hyde* in Valerie Martin's *Mary Reilly*. *Women: A Cultural Review*, *15* (2), 204–16.

Burd, V. (Ed.) (1990). *Christmas Story: John Ruskin's Venetian Letters of 1876–77*. London: Associated University Presses.

Burkholder-Mosco, N. (2005). 'Wondrous Material to Play On': Children as Sites of Gothic Liminality in *The Turn of the Screw*, *The Innocents*, and *The Others*. *Studies in the Humanities*, *32* (2), 201–20.

Burr, C. (2004). *The Emperor of Scent. A Fine Story of Perfume and Obsession*. NY: Random House.

Buse, P. and Stott, A. (1999). Introduction: A Future for Haunting. In P. Buse and A. Stott (Eds), *Ghosts: Deconstruction, Psychoanalysis, History* (pp. 1–20). Basingstoke: Palgrave Macmillan.

Byatt, A. S. (1991). *Possession*. London: Vintage. (Original work published 1990)

Byatt, A. S. (1992). *Angels and Insects*. London: Chatto and Windus.

Byatt, A. S. (1994). *Angels and Insects*. London: Random House. (Original work published 1992)

Calvino, I. (2000). Il nome, il naso. In *Sotto il sole giaguaro*. Milano: Mondadori.

Carey, P. (2004). *Jack Maggs*. London: Faber and Faber.

Carlisle, J. (2004). *Commons Scents: Comparative Encounters in High Victorian Fiction*. Oxford: Oxford University Press.

Carlyle, T. (1843). *Past and Present*. London: Chapman and Hall.

Castle, T. (1993). *The Apparitional Lesbian: Female Homosexuality and Modern Culture*. NY: Columbia University Press.

Castricano, J. (2001). *Cryptomimesis: The Gothic and Jacques Derrida's Ghost Writing*. Montreal and Kingston: McGill-Queen's University Press.

Chapman, R. (1986). *The Sense of the Past in Victorian Literature*. London: Croom Helm.

Chase, M. and Shaw, C. (Eds) (1989). *The Imagined Past: History and Nostalgia*. Manchester: Manchester University Press.

Choi, T. Y. (2001). Writing the Victorian City: Discourses of Risk, Connection, and Inevitability. *Victorian Studies, 43* (4), 561–89.

Clark, C. (2005). *The Great Stink*. London: Viking.

Classen, C. and Howes, D. (Eds) (1994). *Aroma: A Cultural History of Smell*. London: Routledge.

Clausson, N. (2003). 'Culture and Corruption': Paterian Self-Development versus Gothic Degeneration in Oscar Wilde's *The Picture of Dorian Gray*. *Papers on Language and Literature, 39* (4), 339–64.

Clayton, J. (Director) (1961). *The Innocents*. United States: Twentieth-Century Fox.

Cohen, W. A. (2005). Introduction: Locating Filth. In W. A. Cohen and R. Johnson (Eds), *Filth: Dirt, Disgust, and Modern Life* (pp. vii–xxxvii). Minneapolis and London: University of Minnesota Press.

Coldplay. (2008). *Viva La Vida Or Death and All His Friends*. EMI.

Cokal, S. (29 September 2005) Review of *The Great Stink* by Clare Clark. *International Herald Tribune*, pp. 1–2.

Collins, W. (1982). *The Moonstone*. Ed. Anthea Trodd. Oxford: Oxford University Press. (Original work published 1868)

Collins, W. (2007). *The Woman in White*. London: Penguin Classics. (Original work published 1859–60)

Compton-Burnett, I. (1958). *A House and its Head*. Harmondsworth: Penguin. (Original work published 1935)

Corbin, A. (2005). *Storia sociale degli odori*. Milano: Mondadori.

Cox, M. (2006). *The Meaning of Night*. London: John Murray.

Cox, M. (2008). *The Glass of Time*. London: John Murray.

Craft, C. (1984). 'Kiss Me With Those Red Lips': Gender and Inversion in Bram Stoker's *Dracula*. *Representations, 8*, 107–33.

D'Aguiar, F. (1992). Sweet Thames. (s. l.)

Davidoff, L. (1979). Class and Gender in Victorian England: The Diaries of Arthur J. Munby and Hannah Cullwick. *Feminist Studies 5* (1), 87–134.

Davis, C. (2007). *Haunted Subjects: Deconstruction, Psychoanalysis and the Return of the Dead*. Basingstoke: Palgrave Macmillan.

Debray, R. (1995). *Contre Venise*. Paris: Éditions Gallimand.

Dennis, A. (2008). 'Ladies in Peril': Sarah Waters on Neo-Victorian Narrative Celebrations and Why She Stopped Writing about the Victorian Era. *Neo-Victorian Studies 1* (1), 41–52. Retrieved 6 October 2008, from www.neovictorianstudies.com.

De Quincey, T. (2006). *On Murder*. Ed. R. Morrison. Oxford: Oxford University Press.

Derrida, J. (1976). *Of Grammatology*. Trans. G. Spivak. Baltimore: Johns Hopkins University Press.

Derrida, J. (1986). Foreword: *Fors*: The Anglish Words of Nicolas Abraham and Maria Torok. Trans. B. Johnson. In N. Abraham and M. Torok, *The Wolf*

Man's Magic Word: A Crytonymy (pp. xi–xlviii). Trans. N. Rand. Minneapolis: University of Minnesota Press. (Original work published 1977)

Derrida, J. (1994). *Specters of Marx: The State of the Debt, the Work of Mourning, and the New International*. Trans. P. Kamuf. NY and London: Routledge.

Derrida, J. (1999). Marx and Sons. In M. Sprinker (Ed.), *Ghostly Demarcations: A Symposium on Jacques Derrida's Specters of Marx* (pp. 213–69). London and NY: Verso.

Dickens, C. (1988). *Little Dorrit*. Ed. Harvey Peter Sucksmith. Oxford: Oxford University Press. (Original work published 1855–7)

Dickens, C. (1971). *Our Mutual Friend*. Ed. S. Gill. Harmondsworth: Penguin. (Original work published 1865)

Dillon, S. (2007). *The Palimpsest: Literature, Criticism, Theory*. London: Continuum.

Dobraszczyk, P. (2005). Sewers: Wood Engraving and the Sulime: Picturing London's Main Drainage System in the *Illustrated London News, 1859–62*. *Victorian Periodicals Review, 38* (4), 349–78.

Doyle, A. C. (1999). *A Study in Scarlet*. Ed. Owen Dudley Edwards. Oxford: Oxford University Press. (Original work published 1887)

Elias, A. (2001). *Sublime Desire: History and Post-1960s Fiction*. Baltimore and London: The John Hopkins University Press.

Engen, T. (1982). *The Perceptions of Odors*. NY: Academic Press.

Faber, M. (2002). *The Crimson Petal and the White*. Edinburgh: Canongate.

Faber, M. (2003). Eccentricity and Authenticity: Fact into Fiction. *Victorians Institute Journal, 31*, 101–3.

Forster, E. M. (1908). *A Room with a View*. London: Arnold.

Foucault, M. (1990). *The History of Sexuality: An Introduction*. (Vol. 1, *An Introduction*). London: Penguin. (Original work published 1976)

Foucault, M. (1991). The Means of Correct Training. In P. Rabinow (Ed.), *The Foucault Reader* (pp. 188–205). London: Penguin. (Original work published 1975)

Foucault, M. (2002). *The Archaeology of Knowledge*. Trans. A. Sheridan. London and NY: Routledge. (Original work published 1969)

Fowles, J. (2004). *The French Lieutenant's Woman*. London: Vintage. (Original work published 1969)

Freedman, J. (Ed.) (1998). *The Cambridge Companion to Henry James*. Cambridge: Cambridge University Press.

Freud, S. (1955). The 'Uncanny'. In *The Standard Edition of the Complete Psychological Works of Sigmund Freud* (Vol. 17 (1917–19)). Ed. J. Strachey (pp. 218–52). London: The Hogarth Press. (Original work published 1919)

Freud, S. (2003). *The Uncanny*. Trans. D. McLintock. London: Penguin. (Original work published 1919)

Gardiner, J. (2004). Theme-park Victoriana. In M. Taylor and M. Wolff (Eds), *The Victorians since 1901* (pp. 167–80). Manchester: Manchester University Press.

Gardner, L. (22 May 1999). *The Lost Spirit of Spitalfields*. Retrieved 1 November 2008, from http://www.guardian.co.uk/books/1999/may/22/books.guardianreview9.

Gibson, J. and Wolfreys, J. (2000). *Peter Ackroyd: The Ludic and Labyrinthine Text*. London: Macmillan Press.

Gikandi, S. (2000). The Embarrassment of Victorianism: Colonial Subjects and the Lure of Englishness. In J. Kucich and D. F. Sadoff (Eds), *Victorian Afterlife: Postmodern Culture Rewrites the Nineteenth Century* (pp. 157–85). Minneapolis: University of Minnesota Press.

Gilbert, P. K. (2005). Medical Mapping: The Thames, the Body, and *Our Mutual Friend*. In W. A. Cohen and R. Johnson (Eds), *Filth: Dirt, Disgust, and Modern Life* (pp. 78–102). Minneapolis and London: University of Minnesota Press.

Goldman, M. and Saul, J. (2006). Talking with Ghosts: Haunting in Canadian Cultural Production. *University of Toronto Quarterly, 75*, 645–55.

Gomel, E. (2007). Spirits in the Material world: Spiritualism and Identity in the Fin de Siècle. *Victorian Literature and Culture, 35*, 189–213.

Green, S. (1991). Making a Marginal Text Central in the Undergraduate Literature Course: The Case of Hannah Cullwick's Diaries. *College Literature, 18* (3), [Electronic Version], 132–7 (n.p.).

Green-Lewis, J. (2000). At Home in the Nineteenth Century: Photography, Nostalgia and the Will to Authenticity. In J. Kucich and D. F. Sadoff (Eds), *Victorian Afterlife: Postmodern Culture Rewrites the Nineteenth Century* (pp. 29–49). Minneapolis: University of Minnesota Press.

Gunning, T. (1995). Phantom Images and Modern Manifestations: Spirit Photography, Magic Theater, Trick Films, and Photography's Uncanny. In P. Petro (Ed.), *Fugitive Images: From Photography to Video* (pp. 42–71). Bloomington and Indianapolis: Indiana University Press.

Gutleben, C. (2001). *Nostalgic Postmodernism: The Victorian Tradition and the Contemporary British Novel*. Amsterdam: Rodopi.

Haggard, H. R. (1905). *Ayesha: The Return of She*. London: Ward, Lock.

Haggard, H. R. (1923). *Wisdom's Daughter*. London: Hutchinson.

Haggard, H. R. (1998). *She*. Ed. D. Karlin. Oxford: Oxford University Press. (Original work published 1887)

Hall, R. (1992). *The Well of Loneliness*. London: Virago. (Original work published 1928)

Halliday, S. (2006). *The Great Stink of London: Sir Joseph Bazalgette and the Cleansing of the Victorian Metropolis*. Stroud: Sutton Publishing. (Original work published 1999)

Harris, J. (2006). *The Observations*. London: Faber and Faber.

Hartung, H. (2002). Walking and Writing the City: Visions of London in the Works of Peter Ackroyd and Iain Sinclair. In S. Onega and J. A. Stotesbury (Eds), *London in Literature: Visionary Mappings of the Metropolis* (pp. 141–63). Heidelberg: Universitätsverlag C. Winter.

Harwood, J. (2005). *The Ghost Writer*. London: Vintage. (Original work published 2004)

Harwood, J. (2008). *The Séance*. London: Jonathan Cape.

Hawtree, C. (9 September 2007). Go with the Flow. *The Independent on Sunday*, p. 31.

Helfield, R. (2006). Dead Women Do Tell Tales: Spiritualism, Browning, and the Dramatic Monologue. *Studies in Browning and His Circle, 27*, 7–25.

Heyns, M. (2005). *The Typewriter's Tale*. Johannesburg: Jonathan Ball.

Hiley, M. (1979). *Victorian Working Women: Portraits from Life*. London: Gordon Fraser.

Hogg, J. (2001). *The Private Memoirs and Confessions of a Justified Sinner*. Peterborough, Ontario: Broadview. (Original work published 1824)

Holquist, M. (1971). Whodunit and Other Questions: Metaphysical Detective Stories in Post-War Fiction. *New Literary History, 3* (1), *Modernism and Postmodernism: Inquiries, Reflections, and Speculations*, 135–56.

Hutcheon, Linda. (1988). *A Poetics of Postmodernism: History, Theory, Fiction*. London: Routledge.

Hutchison, H. (2006). *Seeing and Believing: Henry James and the Spiritual World*. Basingstoke: Palgrave Macmillan.

Huxley, A. (1994). *Brave New World*. London: Flamingo. (Original work published 1932)

James, H. (1902). *The Wings of the Dove*. Westminster: Constable.

James, H. (1908a). *The Turn of the Screw*. In P. G. Beidler (Ed.), *Henry James: The Turn of the Screw* (pp. 21–116). Boston: Bedford Books of St Martin's Press. (Original work published 1898)

James, H. (1908b). Preface to 1908 edition of *The Turn of the Screw*. In P. G. Beidler (Ed.), *Henry James: The Turn of the Screw* (pp. 117–24). Boston: Bedford Books of St Martin's Press.

Jameson, F. (1991). *Postmodernism or the Cultural Logic of Capitalism*. London: Verso.

Johnston, J. and Waters, C. (2008). Introduction: Victorian Turns, NeoVictorian Returns. In P. Gay, J. Johnston, and C. Waters (Eds), *Victorian Turns, NeoVictorian Returns: Essays on Fiction and Culture* (pp. 1–11). Newcastle-upon-Tyne: Cambridge Scholars Press.

Joyce, J. (1922). *Ulysses*. Paris: Shakespeare.

Joyce, S. (2002). The Victorians in the Rearview Mirror. In C. Krueger (Ed.), *Functions of Victorian Culture at the Present Moment* (pp. 3–17). Athens: Ohio University Press.

Kaplan, C. (2007). *Victoriana: Histories, Fictions, Criticism*. Edinburgh: Edinburgh University Press.

Kieval, H. (1997). Pursuing the Golem of Prague: Jewish Culture and the Invention of a Tradition. *Modern Judaism, 17* (1), 1–23.

Kincaid, J. (15 September 2002). The Nanny Diaries. *The New York Times*. Retrieved 20 September 2009, from http://query.nytimes.com/gst/fullpage.html.

Kneale, M. (2001a). Epilogue: The Real End. In *Sweet Thames* (pp. 313–17). London: Penguin. (Original work published 1992)

Kneale, M. (2001b). *Sweet Thames*. London: Penguin. (Original work published 1992)

Kohlke, M.-L. (2008). Introduction: Speculations in and on the Neo-Victorian Encounter. *Neo-Victorian Studies, 1* (1), 1–18. Retrieved 6 October 2008, from http://www.neovictorianstudies.com/.

Kristeva, J. (1993). Women's Time. In R. R. Warhol (Ed.), *Feminisms: An Anthology of Literary Theory and Criticism* (pp. 443–63). New Brunswick and NJ: Rutgers University Press. (Original work published 1979)

Krueger, C. (2002). Introduction. In C. Krueger (Ed.), *Functions of Victorian Culture at the Present Moment* (pp. xi–xx). Athens: Ohio University Press.

Kucich, J. and Sadoff, D. (2000). *Victorian Afterlife: Postmodern Culture Rewrites the Nineteenth Centuiry.* Minneapolis: University of Minnesota Press.

Lanser, S. (1992). *Fictions of Authority: Women Writers and Narrative Voice.* Ithaca and London: Cornell University Press.

Lee, V. (2006). *Hauntings and Other Fantastic Tales.* Eds Catherine Maxwell and Patricia Pulham. Ontario: Broadview Press.

Levine, G. (2006). *Darwin Loves You: Natural Selection and the Re-enchantment of the World.* Princeton: Princeton University Press.

Lichtenstein, R. and Sinclair, I. (2000). *Rodinsky's Room.* London: Granta Books. (Original work published 1999)

Linehan, K. (2003). Closer than a Wife: The Strange Case of Dr Jekyll's Significant Other. In W. B. (Ed.), *Robert Louis Stevenson Reconsidered: New Critical Perspectives* (pp. 85–100). London: McFarland and Company.

Literary London: Interdisciplinary Studies in the Representation of London (2007), *5* (1). Retrieved 20 January 2008, from http://www.literarylondon.org/london-journal/march2007/index.html.

Literary London:

Llewellyn, M. (2004). 'Queer? I should say it is criminal!': Sarah Waters' *Affinity. Journal of Gender Studies, 13* (3), 204–10.

Lloyd Smith, A. (1992). The Phantoms of *Drood* and *Rebecca*: The Uncanny Reencountered through Abraham and Torok's 'Cryptonymy', *Poetics Today, 13* (2), 285–308.

Lodge, D. (2004). *Author, Author: A Novel.* London: Secker and Warburg.

Lodge, D. (2006). The Year of Henry James; or, Timing is All: The Story of a Novel. In D. Lodge, *The Year of Henry James: The Story of a Novel* (pp. 1–103). London: Penguin.

Lovric, M. (2004). *The Floating Book: A Novel of Venice.* London: Regan Books.

Lowenthal, D. (1985). *The Past is a Foreign Country.* Cambridge: Cambridge University Press.

Lowenthal, D. (1989). Nostalgia tells it like it wasn't. In M. Chase and C. Shaw (Eds), *The Imagined Past: History and Nostalgia* (pp. 18–32). Manchester: Manchester University Press.

Lowenthal, D. (2005). *The Heritage Crusade and the Spoils of History.* Cambridge: Cambridge University Press.

Luckhurst, R. (2002). The Contemporary London Gothic and the Limits of the 'Spectral Turn'. *Textual Practice, 16* (3), 527–46.

Mann, T. (1998). *Der Tod in Venedig.* Berlin: Philipp Reclam jun. Verlag GmbH. (Original work published 1912)

Martin, V. (1990). *Mary Reilly.* London: Abacus.

Martin, V. (1999). *Italian Fever.* London: Phoenix.

Matus, J. (1993). Disclosure as 'Cover-up': The Disclosure of Madness in *Lady Audley's Secret. University of Toronto Quarterly, 62,* 334–56.

Maugham, W. S. (1946). *Then and Now.* London: Heinemann.

Mayhew, H. (1985). *London Labour and the London Poor: Selection.* Ed. V. Neuberg. London: Penguin. (Original work published 1861–2)

Mayhew, H. and Binny, J. (1968). *Criminal Prisons of London and Scenes of Prison Life.* London: Frank Cass. (Original work published 1862)

McClintock, A. (1995). *Imperial Leather: Race, Gender, and Sexuality in the Colonial Context.* London: Routledge.

Miller, W. (1997). *The Anatomy of Disgust.* Cambridge, MA: Harvard University Press.

Moore, A. and O'Neill, K. (2004). *The League of Extraordinary Gentlemen.* (Vol. 2). London: Titan Books Ltd.

Morris, P. (1993). *Literature and Feminism.* Oxford: Blackwell Publishers.

Mosaic: A Journal for the Interdisciplinary Study of Literature. (2001). *34* (4), 5–211.

Mosaic: A Journal for the Interdisciplinary Study of Literature (2002). *35* (1), 5–213.

Mosse, K. (2006). *Labyrinth.* London: Orion.

Murray, A. (2007). *Recalling London: Literature and History in the works of Peter Ackroyd and Iain Sinclair.* London: Continuum.

Nead, L. (2000). *Victorian Babylon: People, Streets and Images in Nineteenth-Century London.* New Haven and London: Yale University Press.

Niederhoff, B. (2000). How to Do Things with History: Researching Lives in Carol Shields' *Swann* and Margaret Atwood's *Alias Grace. Journal of Commonwealth Literature, 35* (2), 71–85.

Oates, J. C. (1994). Accursed Inhabitants of the House of Bly. *Haunted: Tales of the Grotesque* (pp. 254–83). New York: Dutton.

O'Gorman, F. (2007). Browning, Grief, and the Strangeness of Dramatic Poetry. *The Cambridge Quarterly, 36* (2), 155–73.

O'Gorman, F. (2005). Ruskin, Venice, and the Endurance of Authorship. *Nineteenth Century Studies, 19,* 83–97.

Onega, S. (1999). *Metafiction and Myth in the Novels of Peter Ackroyd.* Rochester, NY: Camden House.

Onega, S. (1993). An Obsessive Writer's Formula: Subtly Vivid, Enigmatically Engaging, Disturbingly Funny and Cruel. An Interview with Charles Palliser. *Atlantis, 15* (1–2), 269–83.

Oppenheim, J. (1988). *The Other World: Spiritualism and Psychical Research in England, 1850–1914.* Cambridge: Cambridge University Press.

Owen, A. (1989). *The Darkened Room: Women, Power and Spiritualism in Late-Victorian England.* London: Virago Press.

Palliser, C. (1989). *The Quincunx.* Edinburgh: Cannongate.

Palliser, C. (1999). *The Unburied.* London: Phoenix.

Pearl, M. (2004). *The Dante Club.* London: Vintage.

Pearsall, R. (1972). *The Table-Rappers: The Victorians and the Occult.* Stroud: Sutton.

Pike, D. L. (2005a). *Subterranean Cities: The World beneath Paris and London, 1800–1945.* Ithaca and London: Cornell University Press.

Pike, D. L. (2005b). Sewage Treatments: Vertical Space and Waste in Nineteenth-Century Paris and London. In W. A. Cohen and R. Johnson (Eds), *Filth: Dirt, Disgust, and Modern Life* (pp. 51–77). Minneapolis and London: University of Minnesota Press.

Poe, E. A. (2006). 'William Wilson'. In J. G. Kennedy (Ed.), *The Portable Edgar Allan Poe.* London: Penguin Classics.

Popola, Y. (2003). 'The Fool Sees with His Nose': Metaphoric Mappings in the Sense of Smell in Patrick Suskind's *Perfume. Language and Literature, 12* (2), 135–51.

Poster, J. (2002). *Courting Shadows.* London: Sceptre.

Price, D. (1999). *History Made, History Imagined: Contemporary Literature, Poiesis and the Past.* Chicago: The University of Illinois Press.

Pugin, A. W. N. (1836). *Contrasts.* London: n.p.

Quick, B. (2007). *Vivaldi's Virgins.* NY: HarperCollins.

Quill, S. (2000). *The Stones Revisited.* Aldershot: Ashgate.

Raskin, E. (1992). *Family Secrets and the Psychoanalysis of Narrative.* Princeton: Princeton University Press.

Reay, B. (2002). *Watching Hannah: Sex, Horror and Bodily De-Formation in Victorian England.* London : Reaktion Books.

Rhys, J. (1966). *Wide Sargasso Sea.* London: Penguin.

Ricoeur, P. (1988). *Tempo e racconto. Il tempo raccontato.* (Vol. 3). Milano: Jaca Book.

Rindisbacher, H. (1992). *The Smell of Books. A Cultural-Historical Study of Olfactory Perception in Literature.* Ann Arbor: The University of Michigan Press.

Rivière, W. (2004). *By the Grand Canal.* London: Hodder and Stoughton.

Roberts, A. (2004). Browning, the Dramatic Monologue and the Resuscitation of the Dead. In N. Bown, C. Burdett, and P. Thurschwell (Eds), *The Victorian Supernatural.* (pp. 109–27). Cambridge: Cambridge University Press.

Roberts, M. (1990). *In the Red Kitchen.* London: Vintage.

Robson, D. (2005). Drains and Draining. *The Telegraph Review.* Retrieved 3 March 2008, from http://www.telegraph.co.uk/culture/books/3638219/Drains-and-draining.html.

Rosenberg, J. (2005). *Elegy for an Age: The Presence of the Past in Victorian Literature.* London: Anthem Press.

Rowland, S. (2002). Women, Spiritualism and Depth Psychology in Michèle Roberts's Victorian Novel. In A. Jenkins and J. John (Eds), *Rereading Victorian Fiction* (pp. 201–14). Basingstoke and NY: Palgrave Macmillan.

Royle, N. (2003). *The Uncanny.* Manchester: Manchester University Press.

Ruskin, J. (1903–12). *Library Edition of the Complete Works of John Ruskin.* (39 vols). Eds E.T. Cook and A. Wedderburn. London: Allen.

Rust, M. (1994). In the Humble Service of Her Emancipation: Hannah Cullwick's Maid-of-All-Work Diaries. *Pacific Coast Philology, 29* (1), 95–108.

Sadoff, D. F. and Kucich, J. (2000). Introduction: Histories of the Present. In J. Kucich and D. F. Sadoff (Eds), *Victorian Afterlife: Postmodern Culture Rewrites the Nineteenth Century* (pp. ix–xxx). Minneapolis: University of Minnesota Press.

Schor, Hilary M. (2000). Sorting, Morphing, and Mourning: A. S. Byatt Ghostwrites Victorian Fiction. In J. Kucich and D. F. Sadoff (Eds), *Victorian Afterlife: Postmodern Culture Rewrites the Nineteenth Century* (pp. 234–51). Minneapolis: University of Minnesota Press.

Sedgwick, E. (1985). *Between Men: English Literature and Male Homosocial Desire*. NY: Columbia University Press.

Shakespeare, W. (1974). *The Riverside Shakespeare*. NY: Houghton Miffin.

Shiller, D. (1997). The Redemptive Past in the Neo-Victorian Novel. *Studies in the Novel, 29* (4), 538–60.

Showalter, E. (1987). *The Female Malady: Women, Madness and English Culture, 1830–1980*. London: Virago.

Showalter, E. (1995). *Sexual Anarchy: Gender and Culture at the Fin de Siècle*. London: Virago Press.

Shuttleworth, S. (1998). Natural History: The Retro-Victorian Novel. In E. S. Shaffer (Ed.), *The Third Culture: Literature and Science* (pp. 253–68). Berlin and NY: de Gruyter.

Sinclair, I. (1998). *Lud Heat and Suicide Bridge*. London: Granta Books. (Original work published 1975)

Sinclair, I. (2004). *White Chapell, Scarlet Tracings*. London: Vintage. (Original work published 1987)

Smith, C. (1999). Alfred Russel Wallace on Spiritualism, Man, and Evolution: An Analytical Essay. Retrieved 12 January 2008, from http://www.wku.edu/~smithch/essays/ARWPAMPH.htm#27.

Sommers, S. (Director and Writer) (1998). *The Mummy* [Motion Picture]. United States: Universal Pictures.

Spender, D. (1980). *Man Made Language*. London: Routledge and Kegan Paul.

Stanley, L. (1984). Introduction to L. Stanley (Ed.), *The Diaries of Hannah Cullwick: Victorian Maidservant* (pp.1–28). New Brunswick: Rutgers University Press.

Stevenson, R. (2003). *The Strange Case of Dr Jekyll and Mr Hyde and Other Tales of Terror*. London: Penguin. (Original work published 1886)

Stevenson, R. L. (1886). *The Strange Case of Dr. Jekyll and Mr. Hyde*. In E. Letley (Ed.), *Robert Louis Stevenson: Dr Jekyll and Mr Hyde, Weir of Hermiston* (pp.1–76). Oxford: Oxford University Press.

Stewart, G. (1995). Film's Victorian Retrofit. *Victorian Studies, 38* (2), 153–98.

Stotesbury, J. A. and Onega, S. (2002). Introduction: Visionary Mappings of the Metropolis. In S. Onega and J. A. Stotesbury (Eds), *London in Literature: Visionary Mappings of the Metropolis* (pp. 9–17). Heidelberg: Universitätsverlag C. Winter.

Strachey, L. (1918). *Eminent Victorians*. London: Chatto and Windus.

Sutherland, J. (15 September 2002). 'Making it': Review of *The Crimson Petal and the White*. *The Washington Post*. Retrieved 20 September 2008, from http://www.washingtonpost.com/ac2/wp-dyn?pagename=article&no de=&contentId=A12475-2002Sep13.

Sweet, M. (2001). *Inventing the Victorians.* London: Faber and Faber.

Swift, G. (2002). *Waterland.* London: Picador. (Original work published 1983)

Swindells, J. (1989). Liberating the Subject?: Autobiography and Women's History: A Reading of *The Diaries of Hannah Cullwick.* In Personal Narratives Group (Eds), *Interpreting Women's Lives: Feminist Theory and Personal Narratives* (pp. 24–38). Bloomington: Indiana University Press.

Tani, S. (1984). *The Doomed Detective: The Contribution of the Detective Novel to Postmodern American and Italian Fiction.* Edwardsville: Southern Illinois University Press.

Taylor, D. J. (2006). *Kept: A Victorian Mystery.* London: Chatto and Windus.

Tennant, E. (2002). *Felony: A Novel.* London: Jonathan Cape.

Tennyson, A. (1883). *The Works of Alfred Tennyson.* London: Kegan Paul; Trench and Co.

Tennyson, A. (1885). *Tiresias and Other Poems.* London: Macmillan.

Thackeray, W. (1983). *Vanity Fair: A Novel without a Hero.* Ed. J. Sutherland. Oxford: Oxford University Press. (Original work published 1853)

Thiher, A. (1990). Postmodern Fiction and History. In T. D'Haen and H. Bertens (Eds), *History and Post-War Writing* (pp. 9–31). Amsterdam: Rodopi.

Tóibín, C. (2004). *The Master.* London: Picador.

Toíbín, C. (2005). *The Master.* London: Picador.

Tremain, R. (2003). *The Colour.* London: Random House.

Tromp, M. (2006). *Altered States: Sex, Nation, Drugs, and Self-Transformation in Victorian Spiritualism.* Albany: State University of New York Press.

Trotter, D. (2000). *Cooking with Mud. The Idea of Mess in Nineteenth-Century Art and Fiction.* Oxford: Oxford University Press.

Vickers, S. (2000). *Miss Garnet's Angel.* London: HarperCollins.

Vroon, P. (1997). *Smell. The Great Seducer.* NY: Farrar, Straus and Giroux.

Veeder, W. (1988). *Children of the Night*: Stevenson and Patriarchy. In W. Veeder and G. Hirsch (Eds), *Dr. Jekyll and Mr. Hyde after One Hundred Years* (pp. 107–160). Chicago: University of Chicago Press.

Veeder, W. and Hirsch, G. (Eds). (1988). *Dr Jekyll and Mr Hyde after One Hundred Years.* Chicago: University of Chicago Press.

Waldrep, S. (1999). *The Seventies: The Edge of Glitter in Popular Culture.* London and NY: Routledge.

Walkowitz, J. (2000). *City of Dreadful Delight: Narratives of Sexual Danger in Late-Victorian London.* London: Virago Press. (Original work published 1992)

Waters, S. (1999). *Affinity.* London: Virago.

Waters, S. (2000). *Affinity.* London: Virago. (Original work published 1999)

Waters, S. (2003). *Fingersmith.* London: Virago. (Original work published 2002)

Watson, L. (2001). *Jacobson's Organ and the Remarkable Nature of Smell.* Harmondsworth: Penguin.

White, R. (2004). Visions and Re-visions: Women and Time in Michèle Roberts's *In the Red Kitchen. Women: A Cultural Review, 15* (2), 180–91.

Whyte, C. (2000). *The Cloud Machinery.* London: Orion.

Wilde, O. (2007). *The Picture of Dorian Gray.* London: Penguin Classics. (Original work published 1890–1)

Wilson, A. N. (2005). *A Jealous Ghost.* London: Hutchinson.

Winter, A. (1998). *Mesmerized: Powers of Mind in Victorian Britain.* Chicago and London: University of Chicago Press.

Winterson, J. (1987). *The Passion.* New York: Grove Press.

Wolfreys, J. (2002). Undoing London or, Urban Haunts: The Fracturing of Representation in the 1990s. In P. K. Gilbert (Ed.), *Imagined Londons* (pp. 193–217). Albany: State University of New York Press.

Wolfreys, J. (2002). *Victorian Hauntings: Spectrality, Gothic, the Uncanny and Literature.* Basingstoke: Palgrave Macmillan.

Wolfreys, J. (2004). *Writing London.* (Vol. 2, *Materiality, Memory, Spectrality*). Basingstoke: Palgrave Macmillan.

Wolfreys, J. (2007). *Writing London.* (Vol. 3, *Inventions of the City*). Basingstoke: Palgrave Macmillan.

Žižeck, S. (1991). *Looking Awry: An Introduction to Jacques Lacan through Popular Culture.* Cambridge, MA: MIT Press.

Žižek, S. (1994). The Spectre of Ideology. In S. Žižek (Ed.), *Mapping Ideology* (pp. 1–33). London and New York: Verso Books.

Index